An Overland Odyssey Kathmandu-Paris-Kathmandu in 1970

(that influenced the course of life afterwards)

An Alchemist like stories of a young Nepali

Shyam Mohan Shrestha

Contents

Summary

An Overland Odyssey: Kathmandu-Paris-Kathmandu in 1970 by Shyam Mohan Shrestha is an adventurous and romantic travel memoir set during the Hippie era of the 1970s. The book narrates the journey of a young Nepalese man who embarks on a bold exploration across continents, offering readers a glimpse into the life and experiences of youth during that time. The story begins with Shyam's desire to travel to France, driven by his youthful dreams of adventure. At the age of 22, he leaves Kathmandu and embarks on a life-changing journey that takes him through various countries, including Afghanistan, Turkey, and France. Along the way, Shyam encounters a series of fascinating events, such as being tricked by an older German man in Kabul and navigating an emotional relationship with a mother and daughter in Istanbul. These anecdotes illustrate the challenges and adventures he faced, all set against the vibrant backdrop of the Hippie trail. The book is filled with rich personal reflections, recounting Shyam's encounters with diverse people, the lessons he learned, and the personal growth he experienced. Through hundreds of photographs and vivid descriptions, the author brings the 1970s alive for readers, offering an authentic and nostalgic view of that era. Shyam's travel experiences shape his character, teaching him resilience, adaptability, and a deeper understanding of the world and himself. In addition to the travel narrative, the book reflects on Shyam's life journey over seven decades, encompassing moments of success, failure, love, and personal growth. He highlights his perseverance, determination, and gratitude for the opportunities he received, including the honor of receiving a prestigious medal from the French government in 2019. The memoir captures the essence of youthful ambition, adventure, and self-discovery, while also offering wisdom on life's complexities. It is a tale of embracing challenges, chasing dreams, and reflecting on the rich tapestry of experiences that make up a fulfilling life.

NOTICE:

No part of this Book may be reproduced, distributed or transmitted in any form or by any means including photocopying, recording, or other electronic or mechanical methods, without the prior written, prior permission of the author, except in the case of brief quotations embodied in review and certain other non-commercial uses permitted by copyright law,

ISBN; 978-9937-0-8201-3 (First one in Nepal)

Copyright @ Shyam Mohan Shrestha 2020

Translation copyright @ Shyam Mohan Shrestha 2024

FOREWORD,

Spanning seven decades, my life journey has been a whirlwind of diverse experiences and activities—comprising good luck and bad, wisdom and folly, simplicity and vanity, kindness and cruelty, deep love, and passing infatuation—all stemming from a crybaby with a tender heart. While I embody patience and understanding, I can assume the role of a revenge seeker when faced with what I perceive as mistreatment or injustice. Nevertheless, I've also acquired the wisdom to know when to forgive and let go.

Reflecting from my current standpoint and experiences, I find myself without regrets in my life. Although no life is without missteps, mine has been a mix of many good and bad decisions, leaving me with a deep and enduring sense of contentment at the end of the day.

In my journey on this Earth, I've observed people, knowingly or unknowingly, doing both good and bad deeds. This seemingly dates back to the dawn of human existence and has continued throughout our evolution. This understanding has deepened as I've gone through life. Within me also lies vulnerabilities, instances where I might have inadvertently caused hurt. This tendency might arise from the innate human aspiration to view oneself as morally pure and just.

During my life, I've encountered a diverse range of friends and well-wishers, each contributing their unique presence to my journey. I've grappled with a couple of negative traits—weakness and occasional poor judgment. However, these imperfections are all part of my life experience.

My professional and business endeavors have offered immense opportunities, allowing me to accumulate wealth. However, indulging myself in the world's intricacies—traveling around and enjoying life—has also played a deterrent factor.

Inspirations for Writing the Book

I still remember that time of energetic youthfulness when, despite being an adolescent incapable of deeply understanding any situation, I kept dreaming of traveling to France. As is typical, young hearts secretly weave futures, constructing imaginary towers of desires and achievements. They move ahead energetically in their life and along their career path. I was no exception to this ideal.

In my youth, a deep desire to travel to France constantly burned within me. Regardless of ticket costs, expenses, or future job prospects, I embarked on planning the trip. My determination remained strong. Consequently, a boy named Shyam Shrestha, hailing from the alleys of Tyoda Tole in Kathmandu, found himself in Paris at the age of 22. Later, within four years of working with the French people, he changed himself in the French way of life. This dream culminated in an unexpected honor—one of the most prestigious medals from the French government in the later part of his life in 2019.

This journey imparted invaluable life lessons, shaping me into a resilient individual who returned to Nepal, undaunted by unforeseen challenges and delights along the way.

Moreover, I've learned that adapting to circumstances and persevering attracts opportunities. While I remain atheistic regarding visual depictions of gods, I hold reverence for the Almighty and am consistently grateful. This could be labeled superstition, but my experiences confirm that despite our earnest efforts, God can introduce unexpected obstacles or remarkably rescue us from despair. Overall, contentment derives from a higher power that has blessed me abundantly in this life. In my next life, if there is such a thing, I will work harder.

While writing this book and reflecting on my journey, I've realized how much it has shaped my character and reinforced key traits that have helped me along the way. One important trait is my unwavering determination, which has played a pivotal role. Looking back at my career, I see these qualities as essential for success. Achieving a goal starts with summoning courage and commitment. Once these are in place, the next step is to move forward fearlessly. Along this path, it's crucial to maintain discipline, patience, and civility. Staying in this zone is demanding and challenging. With this mindset, facing tough situations and enduring hardships didn't catch me by surprise. I've often heard that persistently pursuing ambitions is crucial, and my experiences confirm its truth.

This journey as a young man significantly shaped my life's course, a story I always aimed to share. So, after returning from a seven-month journey to Paris and other European countries in 1970 (equivalent to 2027 BS in Nepal), I was resolute about penning a travelog-style book. However, the demands of job hunting, a busy schedule scouting for new trade and industry prospects, swept me into the whirlwind of life. This reality postponed my writing dream. It's almost surreal that after fifty years, I've finally turned this aspiration into reality!

While my trip to France and other countries might not stand out today, this book aims to show that in the past, one could explore Europe using buses and trains across borders. Decades ago, Nepal had a population of around twelve to thirteen million, and only a handful of young Nepalese embarked on such journeys. This expedition brought a mix of experiences, both bitter and sweet, which I believe readers will find engaging. My numerous passports, pocket diaries, office logs, and vivid memories have motivated me to write this memoir.

Within this book, I've chosen to share only true incidents. Given the span of fifty years, readers might have doubts, but feel free to ask questions within legal bounds. Certain parts I've shared might raise questions, but they're real episodes from my life. I've included them to bring lightness and humor to the book, never intending to be vulgar. I hope readers understand this intent, and I apologize for any differing viewpoints.

I once read that keeping photos keeps you feeling young, regardless of age. I agree when I look at my old pictures. This might be why I've added more images than necessary to this memoir. It's a chance for me to capture and share history, the love, and affection from family and friends. A quick flip through the book can conjure the history of the last seven decades in readers' and friends' minds.

In conclusion, this journey to France marked a pivotal stage in my life. Returning to Nepal, feeling the soil and joy, set me on life's path. Amid new circumstances, I searched for my path, leading me through nearly fifty years of ups and downs. Looking back, I've encountered both successes and failures. The Almighty guided me toward a promising career early on. Instead of wealth, I exchanged successes for a chance to explore the world and make global friendships. I also invested in my children's higher education in renowned international schools.

As time went on, regular trips to Paris as an Air France staff member became routine. The city's charm and French culture drew me in. Financial limits kept me from fully immersing myself, but my dream of experiencing fancy restaurants and making luxury purchases remained. Owning an apartment in Paris, driving, indulging in desires, and dining out felt out of reach on a modest Nepali income. But time turned that dream into reality, and I'm grateful for it.

The words of my Air France boss, Mr. Rieffel, linger in my mind: "Success or failure hinges on two things—effort and the whims of luck."

My Gratitude

I would like to thank my wife, Kathy Shrestha, who kept me regularly inspired; my son, Robert Ryan Shrestha, who helped immensely with the design of the book; and my daughters, Cecile Ann Shrestha and Angela Shrestha, as well as my life companion, Lakpa Diki Lama.

Kathleen and Robert are the ones who helped bring this book to life by working hard day and night to make the final corrections needed to shape it into a completed version.

My younger daughter, Angela, worked hard from Paris, to compose and retype the correct expressions. My brother-in-law, Sushil Ram Mathema, has been instrumental in giving me the right advice to enhance the quality of the subjects in the story. My friend of half a century, Bala Bahadur Kunwar, provided constructive advice on various fronts for the final book.

A huge thank you to my brother, Mohan Krishna Shrestha (Ambassador to France), who provided me with inspiration and advice in bringing this book to life. I also want to thank my very close friends: Dr. Dileep Kumar Adhikary, Dr. Kashi Raj Pandey, Devendra Pratap Shah, Ramsharan Pokharel, Preeti Karki, Krishna Acharya, Sunil Poudel, and Bhumishwor Poudel. Raju KC, who read the book letter by letter in the process of surveying and editing both Nepali and English Version deserves a thousand or more thanks.

Likewise, thanks also go to Mr. Binod Thapa, who helped me take the first step in beginning this book, and Mr. Sudarshan Lamichhane, who typed and designed this book.

PART I:

AN ADVENTURE JOURNEY: KATHMANDU-PARIS-KATHMANDU

1.1 THE ROAD TO MARSEILLE

The Beginning of My Travel

In the 1970s, nestled along the eastern edges of Bhugol Park, there stood a modern restaurant known as "Indira."in Kathmandu. This charming restaurant was located just above the first floor of a bustling variety store. Its doors welcomed well-to-do families, businessmen, traders, aristocrats, and even inquisitive foreigners. A crossroads of society, it became a favored destination for me, and I was often accompanied by a mixture of friends, both male and female.

Through the expansive windows of "Indira," I could see the mysterious peeks of the Jamacho and Nagarjun hills. My exploration as a young boy had acquainted me with the southern geography, including the area of Bhimphedi. Yet, the mysteries of the valley's eastern and western domains remained.

In my imagination, France, a distant land I had heard of, graced the western side of Nepal, which was aligned in my mind with the presence of the Jamacho hills. My thoughts continued with an enduring curiosity: What panoramas lay beyond those gentle hills? How many sunsets would I experience on a westward jaunt to France, and what landscapes would present the ever-changing lands of that journey? These visions were continually in my mind.

Thus, with every visit to "Indira," my determined dream, along with my wishes for overland travel west, blended with the restaurant's ambiance. Amid my tasty meals, my mind embarked on a journey of its own—land travel through totally new territory that would trace for me the lands and cultures of the yet unexplored journey to France. What was beyond the well-known hills of Jamacho? During my evening meal, I followed my dream, which led me to the distant explorations of France. My anticipation and imagination were overflowing.

At the time, I had already been working at Casino Nepal for over a year and had been enjoying a very good income and a full life. However, my desire to travel to France grew stronger with each passing day. I was talking to various friends about quitting my job and traveling to France.

I received many forms of advice from my friends when they became aware of my imminent visit to France. My Bhutanese casino boss used to tease me laughingly, "Alright then, Mohen, French girls will say, 'Oh la la, Mohen,' and will come to befriend you." "Oh, la la" was my first chance to learn a colloquial French term. I was surprised to hear this phrase as well.

The owner of the casino was Lenny Dorji, with whom I had a very good relationship. However, my relationship with the Bhutanese manager had started to sour. It seemed like the Bhutanese manager did not like my progress, so I was slowly losing interest. This provided me with the encouragement and the right timing to quit my job and leave for France. At last, on the 15th of March 1970, I resigned from my casino job.

Preparation For The Travel/Journey

After I made my decision to go to France, I prepared my passport and applied for a visa at the French Embassy in Nepal. I was worried that I would not get the visa as I had already resigned from my casino job. If I did not receive the visa, I would be stuck in limbo. Fortunately, the French Embassy awarded me a three-month visa. It was not as difficult as it is today to get a French visa.

Although I had received the French visa in Nepal, I had to apply for visas for other countries along the way. The economic situation of Nepal at that time was good. Ten Nepali rupees were equivalent to one dollar. Two Nepali rupees were equal to one French franc. I had heard that in those days, the per capita income of South Korea and Nepal was almost equal. Due to the strength of our currency, other countries did not have trust issues with Nepal. Accordingly, it wasn't difficult for a Nepali to get a foreign visa.

In those days, I lived in a rented room apart from my family house in Tyouda Tol, on Pako Street, which converged into New Road. An American girl named Linda, who was of Indian origin, had opened a store on Pako Street named "Ma's Fountain of Youth." She sold the latest fashion garments as well as other artistic products. She was also interested in travel and had valuable experience and knowledge to share.

She taught me how to travel safely, what precautions to take, and what kind of goods to carry for my upcoming trip. Linda also told me that every major city had youth hostels and that staying in these hostels would save me a good amount of money. She also suggested that I become a member of the International Youth Hostel Association. Since the nearest youth hostel was in Delhi, she suggested that I apply for membership when I reached India. She also gave me a rucksack and a sleeping bag that she had used so that I could carry my load comfortably.

Kathmandu To Patna

I had a deep desire in my heart to visit France by traveling overland from Kathmandu. Remembering, however, the troubles that I had experienced in 1969 while traveling by road from Kathmandu to Patna and then on to Delhi, I decided not to go through that again. To ensure that the initial journey would not be troublesome, I decided to fly from Kathmandu to Patna and then travel from Patna to Delhi by train.

I left my home for France on the twenty-third of March 1970. I was just twenty-two years and eight months old. My parents, some family members, and some friends came to the airport to say goodbye. We took some farewell pictures, concealing the heaviness in our hearts. In the small Kathmandu airport, there was a delay in my flight for some reason. At around six in the evening, my plane slowly ascended into the sky, and darkness gradually descended onto the earth. I had not been worried before arriving at the airport and boarding the flight. The more the plane ascended into the sky, the better my heart began to feel.

I thought, "Oh! I'm on such a long journey. What's going to happen? What circumstances must I face?" These thoughts started going through my mind. Although I wasn't frightened, I felt that I was plunging into darkness. Once the light was switched on and spread throughout the cabin, the airplane light also spread into my heart. Outside the window, it was total darkness. There were no passengers in the airplane that I knew. I headed into this journey with courage, curiosity, and excitement. The level of fear was very low, but still, my heart did experience some panic. The plane continued to fly, and these thoughts continued to play in my mind. After a forty-five-minute flight, the plane landed at Patna Airport.

From Patna Airport, an Indian Airlines bus carried passengers to its office in the city. As I remember, Patna wasn't as crowded as it is today but there were far fewer people in 1970. I didn't know about any places to visit, so I headed straight to Patna Railway Station on a rickshaw. After reaching the station, I began inquiring about the ticket counter. As soon as I mentioned Delhi, I was showered with advice and proposals. Some suggested that I head toward Allahabad and catch another train from there, while others suggested that I go to Lucknow. There was also a train coming from Kolkata at eleven p.m. which would head directly to Delhi, so the people around me suggested boarding that train. Speaking to and answering these people's questions without becoming involved was annoying. My eardrums were filled with jibber-jabber, and I didn't know what a berth was! At last, after getting rid of this horde of men, I went straight to the ticket counter, and the ticket seller sold me a ticket for the eleven-p.m. train headed toward Delhi. I bought the ticket and had completely forgotten about the purchase of a berth.

Patna To Delhi

Since I had to travel the entire night, I went to a restaurant and bought some snacks. My heart was beating fast, and I was carrying a twelve-kilogram bag. How was I to board the train? It was a third-class ticket. From a previous experience, I knew that the third-class cabin would be heavily crowded and difficult to enter. I had seen this in movies and knew firsthand how crowded and difficult it would be to board a third-class compartment of the train.

My heart was racing. Soon, a large train with a loud and deafening whistle arrived. Breathing heavily, I stormed past the crowd and boarded the carriage that was right ahead of me. Since the train was coming from Kolkata and a crowd had already entered, there was not a single seat remaining. While I was watching the crowd get aboard the train, a group of twenty girls also boarded the same carriage. Later, I found out that they were all students. They sat on the floor just like me. After the train started moving, I was relieved when I thought that I would finally reach Delhi. Slowly, with a little "hi" and "hello," I started to chat with the students.

Among the Indian students, there was also an American student. During the conversation, I learned that they were all students from Lady Shree Ram College in Delhi. They had been on an educational tour and were returning home. Slowly, the girls started falling asleep, leaning on each other's backs. On the southern side of the carriage were three Indian men who had seats on a wooden bench. They were enjoying themselves with loud conversation and laughter. They showed no signs of slowing down or sleeping.

The American girl's name was Georgette, and she was a little chubby. Since her other friends were asleep, she passed some girls and came to sit with me. We were conversing continually. Later, I found out that she was the daughter of a staff member working in the American Commission Office in India. She was an interesting and smiley person. Our conversation continued, and I then introduced myself. I explained to Georgette my plan to visit France while traveling overland through different countries. Visiting France would last for a few months, and then I would apply for a US visa in France. She became even more impressed with me. Our conversation turned out to be deep, cordial, and soulful. The physical intimacy was also building. We weren't aware of what other people were talking about in front of us, behind us, or beside us!

One time, in the middle of the night, one or two friends looked at us, raised their heads, smiled faintly, and then went back to sleep. A few Indian men seated a little further back by the window were looking at us and talking about us in Hindi. I felt bad and was also annoyed hearing their conversation. I mentioned to Georgette, "These people are teasing us, so we should converse with less volume." We continued in lower voices. Later, I noticed that they were still looking at us and teasing us. I felt even angrier. I said to Georgette, "Why are these men teasing us? Even though they are old fellows, we haven't talked about them. Why are they disturbing us?"

Suddenly, one man loudly shouted, "Who is old, who is young, and who knows? We can also exhibit our youth if we get a chance!" I felt a feeling of aggression in his words. We did not respond to them, and I slowly told Georgette that these people seemed to be angry, and we should remain quiet for a while. We didn't raise our heads and look at them again.

In the meantime, during our conversation, the train was stopping at a few stations, which I knew as Allahabad and Lucknow. We didn't take any notice of these stops and were awake all night, chatting in a low voice until we reached Delhi in the early morning. Her friends had already woken up and had managed to arrange their belongings even before the train had stopped. Some of her friends were smiling. Meanwhile, Georgette gave me her contact number in Delhi and said that I could call her if there was any chance of a reunion. I couldn't understand the reason, but people were getting down on the right side of the train instead of the platform. We were among them too. Her friends moved ahead and waved me goodbye. She stood with me for a while, and then we hugged each other tightly and bid one another farewell.

I knew a hotel in Delhi from my previous year's trip. I went to the same hotel, which was not far from the station near the center of Delhi, on Connaught Place. I rested the entire day in the hotel. It had been an interesting train journey because I had spent the entire night in conversation with Georgette. I wasn't in any physical condition to move even a foot further after arriving at the hotel. The next day, I found a youth hostel and went to stay there. Upon reaching the hostel, I got an International Youth Hostel membership card for a dollar. It was fun staying there. It was crowded with youth from different countries like Japan, Hong Kong, France, and Thailand. People from other European countries and North America had come from their home countries for travel purposes. I also met some people who had visited Nepal and India. I searched the hostel for someone who was going to visit France; I thought that if I could find a friend to travel with during my trip, I could reach France easily. During my search, I couldn't find anybody who was traveling to France overland. Even though there was no one going to France, I did find that there were some people traveling to other European countries. After a few days in Delhi, I remembered Georgette and thought about calling her. But because of my busy schedule and mental state, I did not call.

Delhi To Kabul, To reach France by road, I had to first cross Pakistan and then enter Afghanistan. I went to the Pakistan Embassy in Delhi to get my travel visa. The following day, I went to the Afghan Embassy, which was also in Delhi. I felt a sense of frustration looking around the Afghan Embassy. There were many people gathered, and the seating arrangement was poor. There were only a few chairs, which were already occupied. In the middle of the room, there was a large table with people filling out their visa forms as they stood around the edge of the table.

I was also filling out my visa form and saw two elderly foreigners. One of them, around the age of fifty, approached me and started a conversation by asking me where I was from. I told them of my plan to visit France and that I was from Nepal. During the conversation, I found out that one of them was American and the other was German.

The German had a gold crown tooth, which wasn't very pleasing to look at. Still, they were friendly and continued to talk to me. The German asked, "How will you reach Afghanistan?" I told them that I would reach Afghanistan via Pakistan by train. The elderly German said, "Hey, should you be taking such a long train journey at such a young age? Many Pakistanis are evil, and they will give you many troubles. Moreover, if you take the train and then the bus, it will take you at least five days to reach Afghanistan. We are leaving on a plane, and you can join us."

I was confused while listening to them. I responded, "Taking a plane is probably more expensive than a train, isn't it?" The German said that they were traveling on a plane and that it would only cost twenty dollars. I answered, "The train and bus journey will only cost me around ten dollars, so why should I spend so much money?" The German then offered to pay the extra ten dollars if I traveled with them. I believed what they said and was convinced that traveling by plane was a better option than taking the train. I went to Afghanistan's Ariana Airlines office at Connaught Place to buy a ticket for the next day's flight. I then found out that the elderly American was traveling to Afghanistan a few days later. This left me with a strange feeling.

The following day, on March twenty-ninth, 1970, I reached the airport on time. The German took my ticket and passport and went through the check-in process for me. Sitting in the queue along with him, I completed the immigration and customs check myself. I wanted to show him that I was a capable and independent young man.

Our airplane was a jet made in Caravelle, France. I wanted to be in the window seat, and the German man stayed in the adjacent seat. After takeoff, the central city of Delhi and the surrounding settlements came into view. As far as I can recall, the population of Delhi was about three million. There was not a single skyscraper. It was a daytime flight; from the window, agricultural land could be seen for many miles in the northern parts of India. Reaching Pakistan from India, you could see the same kind of topography. When entering Afghanistan, you could only see dry, barren mountains. I thought that we were flying above the Khyber Pass and would soon land in Kabul. I was totally engaged in watching the scenery outside the window. The old man kept asking me a variety of questions. Time and again, I paid no attention to what he asked. Two or three times, he mentioned that I was very good-looking and that I must have many girlfriends. I didn't have any interest in what he was asking, and I unwillingly replied that I had one or two. He also told me about himself. He had been to Australia to earn money and was returning home through India. He explained how hard he had physically worked in Australia.

"It's too hot in the field during summer. Snakes and scorpions are littered all over, so many precautions must be taken. If you aren't careful, the snakes and the scorpions will jump up and bite you like this!" he explained while touching my neck with his hand. I was disgusted by being touched like this, and I shoved his hand to remove it from my neck. I was dumbfounded for a moment and scolded him in my mind, wondering what kind of an old chap he was. He told me about all the hard work he had done for two years in Australia just to earn money. He also took out two bundles of one-hundred-dollar bills from his coat pocket and showed them to me. I watched silently and did not respond.

He asked me the purpose of my visit to France. He also asked me which city I was visiting, who I knew there, and what job I would be doing. I gave him honest and straightforward answers. I would first go to Marseilles, then Paris, and after a few months, to America where I had a friend. If I got a job and a visa extension, I would stay there. He then proposed to find me a job if I went to Germany instead of America. I wasn't very interested in his offer. My aim was to go to America from

France, so I didn't pay any attention to what the old man had to say. We kept on having this type of conversation on the plane.

Two hours later, we landed at Kabul Airport in Afghanistan's capital. The old man knew all about Afghanistan as he had been through the country before. He had helped me in getting my ticket, and because Kabul was a new place to me, I followed him. We hired a taxi and went to a hotel in Kabul that he was familiar with. We booked a double bedroom. I kept quiet even though the hotel wasn't very appealing. After putting our luggage in the hotel, we went out to take a stroll. Afghanistan was the second foreign country I was visiting after India.

Ten years earlier, when I was a student in Bhimphedi, while living with my grandparents, there was a teacher named Rich from the American Peace Corps. He was working in our school when I was in the fourth grade. Rich had taken one of my friends, Rambahadur Lama, for a visit to India and Afghanistan in 1959. After he returned, Rambahadur showed us several photographs of the places he had visited. He described the sites of his journey in detail. Based on this, I had a great interest in visiting Afghanistan.

Eleven years later, I finally arrived in this country. I was excited and curious to visit the city and know the physical surroundings. Our hotel was centrally located in the city of Kabul. It was full of shops and restaurants; I felt the vibes of an old Delhi market. The restaurants looked like the ones in Delhi, but the difference was in the chapattis. The Afghani chapattis that were hanging in the dhabas (restaurants) were as long and as big as an elephant's ear. The scene made me wonder. Firstly, how can one eat such a huge chapati? How many people would it take to finish this one? Can one person in this country finish this whole chapati? These kinds of questions were playing in my mind. I thought that I would never want to eat this kind of chapati even if I had to. The smell of kebab and other kinds of meat was spreading onto the streets. Instead of that chapati, I ate dal bhat (rice and lentil) and after roaming the streets until the evening, we returned to the hotel.

We had booked a twin bedroom. The two beds were placed on either side of the wall. The door didn't lock properly; the wood frames were misplaced and decaying, and there were holes. Despite that, we lay down on the beds because of exhaustion. The old guy started rambling gibberish and scolding me.

"You do not try to listen or understand me!" he rambled.

When in Delhi, my American friend had told me, "Even though this guy looks innocent, he is quite smart and won't listen to you. There is no way that you can take control of this guy!"

Upon hearing that, I replied to him, "When did I not listen to you? You are similar in age to my father, so I respect what you say. What are you complaining about?"

After that, he was still murmuring something, and I asked him in an annoyed voice what he wanted. Suddenly he asked me to come and sleep in his bed. Upon hearing this, I felt like I was falling down a waterfall. I felt the fire of anger bursting from my eyes. I felt a little insecure inside my heart too. It was around eleven pm. There was still some noise coming from the market area. You could hear the chanting of Allah in some nearby houses and in faraway mosques. The market outside was still open, so I was not afraid of the situation.

Then I said to him, "I am not coming. If you are not happy about that, I will find another place to sleep." The old chap was a bit quieter, although still murmuring. After some time, he was asleep. I stayed quietly without sleeping for the entire night. I was going to leave the hotel very early the next morning.

At around six in the morning, I quietly packed my belongings and left the hotel without waking him. Then the questions in my mind began to arise: Where should I go from here? Which hotel should I stay in? Without deciding my destination, I immediately started walking to the right of the hotel to be as far away from him as possible.

After a twenty-minute walk, the road took a left turn, and I did the same. The street was wide, there were new houses, and it looked a bit more modern too. I kept walking along and finally found a moderately priced hotel.

After entering my room, I lay down flat on the bed and began to think, *So that is why the strange old man proposed to pay the extra ten dollars for my plane ticket and had me travel with him.*

As I had been awake all night and was exhausted, I was also hungry. I had a heavy breakfast and went back to my room to rest.

After six hours of sleep, I woke up around four p.m. and went out. I was feeling independent, like a bird recently released from its cage.

The city of Kabul is at an elevation of around six thousand feet and lies to the northwest of Nepal. Therefore, it was quite cold outside. After exiting the hotel, I walked to the right again. The city looked cleaner and more civilized. There were some good hotels too.

At that time, there were plans for a large development project in Afghanistan with significant help from Russia. In the supermarkets, you could see many 'Made in Russia' products. Even the toilet paper sold was made in Russia.

Kabul was in a valley just like Kathmandu. There were surrounding hills, and some were very near to the city. Even though it was the end of March, the top to the middle sections of the hills were covered in snow. Most Afghans on the street were seen wearing their traditional attires. Most women wore burqas, while men wore turbans on their heads with long shirts and loose trousers. The men were good-looking and, in another way, frightening, with tall, broad shoulders and sunken eyes. I was afraid to look straight at them.

The young women on the streets were dressed in western fashion. The students wore shirts, skirts, and blazers. It looked like Afghanistan was entering a new age.

That day, I just roamed around the hotel and kept regularly peeking up at the snow-covered mountains from the street. I spent the evening with mixed feelings of happiness and some fear. I slept that night wondering how and where to get a bus ticket to Iran.

Kabul To Herat

The next day, after doing some research, I went to the bus company's office to buy a ticket to Herat, the Afghan city on the border with Iran. I met a lot of other European travelers who were also taking the land route. There was also a large crowd of Afghan people. The bus company informed me that it took two days to reach Herat, with one night spent in the city of Kandahar. I was also informed that the entire distance to Herat was one thousand kilometers.

While buying the ticket, I got to talking with a foreign guy named Daniel who was a little older than me. He was traveling to Herat as well. Daniel was Belgian and was returning to his country after having visited Nepal. After buying the ticket, I accompanied him to the center of the city. I felt much more secure being with him. That evening, we went to a restaurant. During dinner, I told him about my incidents with the German guy. He was quite surprised and said, "Don't worry, from now on you must be extremely cautious with strangers." After dinner, we went back to our respective hotels, agreeing to meet at the bus station the next day.

The next day, we boarded the bus at 6:30 in the morning. It was packed with passengers. Seventy percent of them were Afghans, while the remainder were foreigners. Once the journey began, my heart was filled with excitement and joy. The conversation with Daniel resumed. After a twenty-five-minute drive from Kabul, the highway to Kandahar began. It was a very smooth, two-lane tarmac road. White lines were drawn in the middle to divide it into two halves. Nepal didn't have any road that compared with this one. I was very impressed. I was told it was built by the Russians, but later I heard it was the Americans.

The one thing that I found unpleasant on the bus was the smell of the thick clothes worn by the Afghans. I struggled with this for a while but later stopped noticing because I had grown used to it. After exiting Kabul, I felt that we were traveling through a wide gorge. There were similarly sized small rocky hills on both sides. They looked to be continuous for miles and miles. Greenery on those hills was rarely sighted. From my window, I kept looking towards the end of the highway wondering what lay ahead. Nothing except the open plains could be seen.

I talked briefly with Daniel; he told me about the places he had visited in Nepal. He was asleep most of the time. Repeatedly, I would watch towards the end of the gorge, calculating how much time it would take to reach a certain hill that I had previously chosen.

It was a game I played in my mind. Continuing with this game, the bus eventually reached a hotel restaurant outside the city of Ghazni at around twelve noon. The bus driver informed us that this was the place for lunch and that it would be a one-hour stop. He told us to be back on the bus quickly after the meal. We followed his instructions without fail. After one hour, the bus was back to speed again.

The gorges continued; the bus continued to move through the middle of the rocky hills. We stopped once again for tea at around six pm. We had reached a hotel on the highway near the city of Kandahar. The driver informed us that this was where we would have dinner and stay for the night. Although the rest stop wasn't a good place, we had no other options. The bus was leaving at six thirty the next day, so there was no possibility of entering the city and finding another hotel.

After dinner, Daniel and I went for a stroll around the area. We had an early dinner and went to sleep. There were no sleeping rooms in the hotel. There was a large hall where ten beds were set upside by side on the floor. Daniel and I took a bed each. There were only foreigners in the main room, and I wondered where the Afghan travelers slept.

Although bedding was available, it lacked a warm blanket. I slept with all my clothes on. I realized that I needed to wake up early the next day; otherwise, it would be impossible for me to get to the restroom in time. I was awake by five am and finished my toilette early. I also woke up Daniel and then joined him for a cup of tea. I had not seen any other passengers after getting up and was really surprised to see that everyone had already gathered by the bus for departure.

The journey to Herat began after everyone was on board the bus. The highway from Kandahar to Herat was as smooth as the previous day, and we reached there by evening. The distance was around five hundred kilometers. Once the bus started moving, Daniel and I talked for a while. He told me then that he was staying in Herat for a few days. I was going to be alone again!

Daniel fell asleep again, and I started marking the last hills on the gorge, guessing how much time it would take for the bus to reach there. I kept checking whether my guesses were correct. This helped to pass the time. Hours and hours of driving sometimes overwhelmed me, but there was no other way for me to deal with the long journey. I tried to sleep but couldn't. When I opened my eyes, it was the same hill! I wondered when I would reach France. Hopelessness, at times, began to grow in me.

At around one pm, the bus stopped in front of a restaurant near a small city. We were informed that this was the location for lunch. We got off the bus with hungry bellies and exhausted bodies. Instead of the elephant ear-sized chapati, I ate something different. Forty-five minutes later, all the travelers were ready to go. Our journey resumed for another four hours, we stopped for another tea break and reached Herat that evening. The driver stopped in front of another hotel with which he had contacts.

Herat was the second largest city in Afghanistan. It was situated along an ancient trade and travel route between Asia and central Eastern Europe. Since it was nighttime, there was no chance of roaming around, and I was exhausted by the long all-day travel. I had dinner and slept in the same hotel. I had no real interest in looking around the city of Herat.

I began to inquire about how to cross the Iranian border and learned that I had to head to the border town of Eslam Qala. There was a jeep service to reach this border town. Fortunately, Daniel came along with me to bid farewell. Unfortunately, the German guy had also reached the same station! He came to me and started shouting that I should return his ten dollars. I was speechless! As Daniel had known the complete background of my experience with the German, he said to the old guy, "Which money are you talking about? Shyam came on a plane because you offered him the money; otherwise, he would have taken the bus and train. He wouldn't have spent so much of his own money!"

Just as Daniel said this, the old man yelled with a ferocious shout, "Hey mister! This is between me and Shyam. You have no right to interfere in this matter. I will solve this problem between us!"

Seeing the potential for an unpleasant situation, I immediately said to him, "I will return your money. I have a traveler's check, and I will give you that." After that, he agreed and stopped shouting.

I then signed the traveler's cheque and handed it to him. He returned it, demanding I write my passport number on the check. I wrote my number and returned it to him. He hastily grabbed the check from my hand and went running away.

My mental state was disturbed because of his behavior.

During those days, if you traveled by train, ten dollars would be enough to reach Afghanistan from Delhi. A dollar was much more valuable in those days. One dollar would be enough for food and accommodation at an average hotel. I had to spend twenty dollars because I traveled with him. The money that I could have spent on hotels was now gone! More than this, the shouting from the old man had taken away my peace of mind.

Herat To Iran Border

From Herat, I traveled by jeep to the Iranian border town of Eslam Qala. Once I reached there, I crossed the border on a rickshaw. The road was dusty and in very bad condition. There was a check post and other government offices as soon as you crossed the border. I had obtained my Iranian visa in Delhi, so I entered Iran without an issue.

I then took a local jeep and went to the city of Mashhad on the eastern side of Iran. I searched for a small hotel and checked in there. There was no chance of visiting the city as it was already late, so I only looked around the hotel neighborhood. Mashhad looked well managed compared to Kabul. The roads looked clean, and there were fewer people too.

Mashhad is a large city and is also considered a religious city. It had a mosque called Imam Reza which looked quite large and attractive. The round roof was painted in golden color. I traveled throughout the city, but the main attraction for me was Imam Reza. It could be seen from everywhere.

Mashhad To Tehran

There was a direct train service from Mashhad to Tehran. Once I learned this, I went to the train station and booked my ticket. The train was leaving in two hours. I wasn't sure if food was available on the train, so

I bought some snacks at the station. I had only experienced the Indian railway system; I was surprised to see the Iranian train. It had different classes and was well-managed. The first-class cabin had seats covered in red velvet upholstery. The seat I chose was clean and had a wide cabin that could accommodate ten people.

I had boarded the train early; later, the Iranian travelers rushed on board only ten minutes before departure. The male passengers were well dressed, both suited and booted. The girls and women were also well decorated with various gold ornaments. I wondered about this very different country of Iran and how much of a Western influence it had. It made me a bit self-conscious of where I was coming from.

After five hours of travel, I reached Tehran.

Upon reaching the train station, I looked up the youth hostels address and headed in that direction. The hostel was inside a gully in the central part of Tehran. I was amazed upon reaching the place. There was a gathering of youth from various countries, and the hostel provided dinner as well. It was busy with a continuous flow of people in and out. I had a chance to see the city of Tehran while arriving on the train.

Tehran was the largest city in Iran, and its citizens looked well-off. I found it to be a modern city, and I immediately fell in love with it. I was also interested in learning about its long history.

Iran had three capital cities in its long history. The current capital was established in the year 1795. People had migrated and settled here from all parts of the country. There were important and historically significant palaces, mosques, and churches. The ruler of the country, Mohammad Reza Pahlavi, had plans to uplift the city to the level of European cities' development, and I already saw how much this development had progressed.

I saw a television for the first time in Tehran; the antennas were placed on the roof of every house. That evening, I enjoyed visiting all the wonderful places in the main area and then went back to my hostel to sleep. I felt a little chill while visiting the city, which had been the coldest so far on my journey.

The next day, I searched for and went to the Turkish Embassy to get my visa. After that, I walked around on foot wherever I wished to go. I had the chance to look at some historical sites from the outside. Then, I used the map to find my way back to the hostel. I was quite tired by the time I reached the hostel. I ordered some food, talked to some other travelers there, and listened to their stories. There were young people from various countries, including Indians. When I heard them speak English with their accent, it suddenly made me remember my home, and I felt homesick and lost.

I inquired with some people on how to reach Turkey from Iran and listened to where they were traveling. During the conversation, I found out that there was a direct bus from Tehran to Istanbul, the capital city of Turkey. The journey took four nights and five days of travel.

While at the restaurant, I began to have body aches with a little fever. I was compelled to go to bed early even though there was an atmosphere of fun. I spent the night suffering from a disrupted sleep pattern. In the morning, I felt much better than the previous night. After breakfast, I went out to visit the city once again.

Tehran is also a very old city. The famous Golestan Palace was made into a royal palace after it was upgraded in the nineteenth century. There were also many large modern hotels. I enjoyed traveling around the city on foot. During the day when I was visiting the city, I felt fine. After I reached the hotel, I started having body aches and fever just like the previous day. That evening, I took a rest after having a light dinner. The fever was still there when I woke up in the morning. My body felt heavy.

I began to wonder how I would reach France with such an unfit body. I thought that it might be better to return to Nepal. I had already come so far that I didn't dare go back. However, feeling so ill, I then planned to take a plane from Tehran to Delhi. I felt that reaching Kathmandu wouldn't be very difficult from there.

With great difficulty, I left the hotel and went to the TWA office at the Intercontinental Hotel to inquire about the price of a ticket from Tehran to Kathmandu. The lady staff member told me in a very sweet tone that it would cost one hundred and sixty-two dollars. She wrote it on a piece of paper and handed it to me.

I thought that the cost was huge. I wondered what would happen if I spent so much money to get back to Nepal and then became well as soon as I returned. Also, the thought of not being able to reach my dream destination of France started playing in my mind. I couldn't immediately decide what to do. Therefore, without getting the ticket, I returned to the hostel and took a rest.

In the evening, I went to the restaurant to eat something, wondering what to eat. I wasn't very fond of chapati and had heard back in Nepal that one shouldn't consume rice and meat during a fever. I could find no food that appealed to my appetite in the restaurant. I was in a state of confusion. An American guy seated before me had ordered a plate full of rice, in the middle of which was a fantastic smelling sheesh kebab in light red and yellowish colors, flavored with lots of spices. My eyes were fixed on his dinner. Seeing this, the American asked, "Would you like to have a taste of this?"

I answered, "I really would, but I have a little fever, and in my country, we are advised to avoid meat or rice in such condition"

"Hey, who said that?" he asked. "Have a full plate of this hot meal and go to sleep; you will be alright tomorrow." Then I couldn't resist myself. Without much thought, I ordered kebab and rice just as the American had. The restaurant owner brought a plate of rice with shish kebab placed in the middle. I ate until my stomach felt tight. This turned out to be the best food I had eaten since the journey began.

Without much fuss, I went to my room to get some much-needed deep sleep. When I woke up during the night after fulfilling half of my sleeping quota, I was sweating heavily. I was afraid because I had consumed rice and meat during my fever. What's going to happen now? With this fear, I fell asleep again. Surprisingly, when I woke up the next morning, my body was fresh and strong with no pain. The fever was gone. The meal of rice and meat apparently worked to heal my body.

I then realized that I didn't have to go back home and drown in confusion concerning my future. Returning to Nepal, I didn't know if I would get my job back after I had quit. Would I get the same position? Would I be pushed back to the beginning of my struggling life again? The memories of these bittersweet experiences flashed before my eyes. I then remembered my childhood.

1.1.1 Flashback Memories

My Birth And Growing Up

I was born in Tyauda Tole, Kathmandu, on the twenty-seventh of Shrawan 2004 BS, the eleventh of August, nineteen forty-seven. My mother's name is Shakuntala Shrestha and my father's name is the late Chandra Bahadur Shrestha.

We are a total of nine siblings with six brothers and three sisters. I have a sister older than me, and I am the eldest of the sons. Among my brothers, the third brother, Mohan Krishna Shrestha, served the government in a diplomatic job for thirty years, ultimately being appointed as an ambassador to France. The remaining brothers have been involved in professions best suited for them. Whenever my father talked to me about life, he constantly reminded me of one thing: business is boundless; this is what you must be involved in.

Even though my father did not have a high school education, he had a wealth of knowledge concerning the Second World War in Europe. He kept reminding me of the incidents related to this world war in European history. The names of countries such as France, Germany, Italy, and Britain were always being referred to. It was then that I first heard the name of the country, France.

It was probably due to his work pressure and family responsibilities that my father had issues with high blood pressure. He suffered a stroke and remained at the Arya Ghat, the site of Hindu funeral rituals, for eleven days. Dr. Sundarmani Dixit, who was at Arya Ghat to treat him, had said it was a surprise that he had remained alive for so long. My family and I still had hope in our hearts that he would somehow recover.

Unfortunately, on the twelfth day of his time at Arya Ghat, around two o'clock in the morning, the Ghate Baidhya, a traditional doctor working by the ghat, informed us that it was time to take our father to Brahmanal on the bank of the Bagmati River. This is where the holy water offered from Pashupatinath flows into the Bagmati River. The dead bodies are cleansed before being taken to the funeral pyre. We did as was suggested. Watching over our father's dead body, a deafening cry burst out from my entire family. Our hearts were torn apart, and our cries spread throughout the silent, pitch-black horizon. Even though my heart was already torn, the pain continued into the night. My father ultimately left us, and with all my emotions, I then cried out loud!

Even though my father was a general employee of the Nepali government, as well as a grassroots citizen, he can be considered a successful civil servant of his country. He was awarded by the state three medals for his loyalty, efficiency, and dedication. On the social and family front, he was a very popular person among his friends and neighbors. He had been a very good father, husband, and relative. Unfortunately, he passed away at the age of fifty-six.

My Education

I wasn't very interested in formal education from my early childhood due to various reasons which I couldn't understand myself. I left home early as if I were headed to school but spent most of the day in the city. Once the school hours were over, I returned home. One day, my mother sent my uncle to spy on me, and my ingenuity in skipping school was over! After the school incident, my mother decided to send me to Bhimphedi for schooling.

At ten years of age, I was sent there to stay with my grandparents. My grandfather was especially kind and showed me great affection; he really liked me. My grandmother was more affectionate toward my second younger brother. This tendency of sharing less respect for me continued through life both from my grandmother and my brother.

Before leaving for Bhimphedi, my childhood days were spent in a simple Newari family culture. I was never regular at school. My friends were the kids from the community and my cousins. In terms of sports, we played with marbles, rolled bicycle wheels, and sometimes visited

Tundikhel to play football. My sports experience was limited within these boundaries.

Once in Bhimphedi, I became more involved in everything. I returned to an ordinary student's life in the company of my friends, teachers, parents, wise men, and other seniors. Even though I was in a junior grade, I was interested in hanging out with the seniors. These older friends were inspired by communist ideology.

A foreign policy expert, Hiranyalal Shrestha, had come up with the idea of 'Young Communists'. Our job was to spread propaganda. In those days, seniors and other elders like Dhanlal Shrestha, Nhuchchhe Lal, and Keshab Das Shrestha assumed the leadership from the students' side to conduct cultural and literary programs. They did this along with drama and other extracurricular activities. Dhan Lal Shrestha was also a teacher. I wanted to be as close to him as possible to gain extra knowledge.

One time, the student leaders were looking for someone to fulfill the role of a child actor in the play, "Kohi Kina Barbad Hos," which translates to "Why Should one Be Ruined?" It was written by Govinda Bahadur Malla. I was present and said, "I can give this a try." The older students then taught me the lines, as well as the tone of voice used by the main child actor in the play. I auditioned for the part later. I followed their advice, and as soon as they heard my voice and observed my acting, the directors told me that I was fit for the character.

Every evening after that, my friends trained me for the play. The play was staged successfully on the designated day. I was able to win people's hearts with my successful portrayal. The most important point for me was that through this play experience, I was able to develop confidence and courage while in front of a crowd, which was useful for me during my business career.

Durbar High School

After five years in Bhimphedi, I returned to Kathmandu for my high school education. My close friends were also in Kathmandu for the same purpose. We were admitted to different high schools in the city. I entered Durbar High School and was able to bypass three grades, entering the senior class.

Upon returning to Kathmandu, I once again became interested in roaming the streets around my school. By the time I reached grade ten, I did not have much enthusiasm for school. Every day, I used to sit on the last bench by the door and would run away as soon as attendance was taken. On occasion, I had to sit in front, where the hardworking students would sit. One of the names I remember is Kumed Kumar Kafle, who is now a famous medical doctor that I haven't seen since nineteen sixty-three.

That year, the first hurdle of my life appeared. All my friends passed the exam for entrance to the School Leaving Certificate; I was the only one who failed! I was so upset and hurt that I went to see the headmaster and then the subject teacher. I was weeping and pleading for mercy. Sindhu Nath Pyakurel was adamant in his position; all my attempts at pleading were unsuccessful. Once I understood that there was no chance of passing and I accepted the fact that I had lost another academic year, I did pass my SLC. My friends were now studying in different colleges. I was the only one to pass the final exam of Intermediate Arts. Looking back, I had never been a diligent or laborious student for my entire life. I studied a little before the examinations and always passed.

Even though I was admitted to the Patan Campus to study for my Bachelor of Arts, I couldn't manage my time properly. I had to board the bus by seven in the evening for my job at the casino. My duty started at eight and often continued from three to five am. Sometimes it lasted until ten o'clock in the morning. I couldn't attend my college classes because of this. Many times, I went to campus at six am, lacking strength and energy. I couldn't give proper time and attention to my studies. After getting my job with Air France, I retook the examination in nineteen seventy-two and completed my Bachelor of Arts degree.

French Youths At New Road

From the year 1960 tourists began arriving in Nepal via the land route. Air travel was very expensive, yet every day there was an increasing number of foreign youths arriving in the streets of Kathmandu.

One day in the autumn of 1965, I met with a group of four French youngsters in New Road. Although I didn't know the French language,

I chatted with them using the little English I knew. We roamed around the whole day together. I was studying at Durbar High School at that time. Since my childhood, I had been very curious to know about the culture and history of other countries. And through our regular meetings and conversations I was able to gain a little knowledge about France.

I learned a few French words from them. I was also able to observe the way in which they behaved with other people. I became more acquainted with their habits and behaviors. This made my curiosity of France continue to grow, and kept thinking about how amazing it would be to one day visit.

During my time with the young French men, they told me that they were heading to Nagarkot and invited me along on the trip. I had only heard about Nagarkot. I was very interested in the visit, so I immediately accepted their invitation with happiness. There was no proper transport facility to visit Nagarkot from Kathmandu. As far as I can remember, we boarded a lorry truck from Kathmandu and reached Bhaktapur early in the morning. From there, we walked the entire day uphill to Nagarkot.

I got a bad headache in the evening after reaching Nagarkot. I had never experienced a headache so painful before. It was likely due to spending the whole day walking under the sun at a rising altitude. I endured the headache for some time without mentioning it to my new friends. After a while, it became too unbearable and was becoming more intense. I then informed them of my headache. They gave me medicine, and after half an hour, I was fine. It was pleasantly shocking; I kept on wondering how such a miraculous medicine could exist in the world.

The next day, we went for a walk. They chatted with each other in French and used English when speaking with me. While roaming around with them for two days, I learned to say a few French words such as "Bonjour", "Merci", and "D'accord."

During that time, I thought about how amazing it would be if I were able to speak French and converse with them in their native language. Since I had spent so much time with these French tourists, learning their ways and listening to their language, I was determined to learn French at any cost.

Upon returning to Kathmandu, my new French friends stayed for a few more days and then returned to France. My friendship with one of them, Jean Michel Binoist, grew to be special and we started exchanging letters. He turned out to be a wonderful person; one day while opening the envelope of one of his letters, I found a ten-dollar bill. My eyes sparkled. I became very happy from within. After this surprise I replied and thanked him from the bottom of my heart. One surprising fact is that letters from France arrived in Kathmandu within two or three days. Michel regularly sent me money in this way for one or two months. The money posted arrived safely in my hands every time. This illustrates how safe and reliable the postal service was. Moreover, these letters were aerograms, I do not know if this possibility exists today.

My contact and letter exchange with Michel continued to grow. In his letters, he often explained that I could visit France if I wanted to. At that point I decided that I would go to France and joined The Campus of International Languages which operated during the evening at Durbar High School Complex. I started to learn French. This was in the year nineteen sixty-seven (BS 2024). I kept learning French from then onwards with strong determination and concentration.

In March,1968, Casino Nepal opened at The Soaltee Hotel in Tahachal. Even though my income at Casino Nepal was very handsome my attention was only focused on how to go to France. I will go into further details about securing a job at the casino shortly. I was also having conversations with Michel concerning my goal of visiting France. At the same time, a very close friend of mine from Kathmandu, Bhagatlal Gorkhali, was to go to the United States in nineteen sixty-nine on an immigration visa. We walked around on New Road discussing our futures and we became very close. During one such conversation he told me, "What great things will you be doing here? Come to the US". Due to this I kept having the feeling that I wanted to quit my job, leave for France and from there go to the US. I would find work and earn a good amount of money. Along with that, another friend of mine from Bhimphedi, Ram Bahadur Lama, was already in the US. The topic of me quitting the job to leave for France created a big stir among my friends and relatives.

"Why do you want to quit a job which pays as good as a foreign job?" was the question from one group.

While some others advised me in this way, "What's so special about this job? You don't know when you will be fired, going abroad instead is obviously right." This situation caused a huge dilemma. Along with this I had promised to loan more than half of the money I had saved to my friends. However, I had decided to go to France at any cost with an intense desire in my heart. I had already saved around a thousand dollars for my trip. The loan I had given to my friends was with the hope and belief that I would get it back after reaching France. When my French trip was confirmed, I asked my French contact about the cost of the trip, and he informed me that two hundred dollars would suffice. I also planned to buy Nepali handicrafts to sell in France which would help with my expenses there.

My Job In 'Casino Nepal'

After completing my three-month French Language lessons at the school of international languages in 1967, I joined the Bachelor of Arts at Patan Campus. Along with that I was also admitted to the evening classes at the Bishwa Bhasa Paathsala, (College of international Languages), at Durbar High School to learn French. With the purpose of having my own source of income in the upcoming days, I started searching for possibilities and moved ahead accordingly. I began to look for any kind of vacancy posted in Gorkhapatra and The Rising Nepal. I saw an advertisement announcing a vacancy for the position of a 'croupier' in the newly opened casino at Soaltee Hotel. I had no idea what a croupier was and what responsibilities they had. When I checked the dictionary, I found that 'croupier' was someone who dealt games in the gambling houses. I was more concerned about getting a job rather than the type of job itself. As soon as I read about it, I applied for the position of 'croupier' at Soaltee Hotel Casino at the end of nineteen sixty-seven.

It was two weeks after I had the interview; I was on my way to visit my friend Mahen from Bhimphedi where he lived in his rented room in one of the gullies of Chikamughal. While walking along the same road

I met another interviewee for the casino job. He was my college mate from Patan Campus who was also taking the same road, he asked, "What are you here for? Weren't you called?" I asked him what he was talking about. He then said," Training begins tomorrow, do you know!"

I was in shock hearing this and thought I had failed the interview. I went immediately to the Soaltee Hotel with my friend Mahen. One of the English interviewers I had seen before, was standing right in front of reception. Going near him, I saw that he had a bandage applied on his hand, where blood could be seen, his face had a wound with patches of stained blood. I carefully approached him and greeted him with concern. He asked me what the matter was.

"I have heard that there is a training session starting tomorrow, I wasn't called. I wish to join the training as well."

He then said, "All right, you come tomorrow, I will manage it, I am the one who is training all of you."

He turned out to be the chief operator of the casino, who conducted the technical aspect of the training. His name was Mr. Al Mattock. Back then, the main investor in Casino Nepal was the brother of the queen of Bhutan, Lenny Dorje.

After two months of training which I was successful with, the casino was formally inaugurated in the month of March, nineteen sixty-eight. (B.S 2025). The decorations, the sound of western music, the family bar, the foreign faces, and the glittering lights made me feel like I was entering a totally new world. It was a lucky time for me because my table was on the first right after the entrance. The very first game played by the very first customer, who was the Director of USAID in Nepal, sat at my table and played the game of Blackjack. Every time he lost a hand, he would gently say, "son of a gun!" This was a new expression in English for me.

Many customers who played at my table told me that they always believed that I would never cheat them even though they had lost their money. I was also compassionate with my customers. Some old merchants from Indrachowk, who were always drunk, sometimes bowed down to my hand and said, "You are a very genuine person and like a saint, arrest all the robbers in this casino!". One year after the casino started operation, I was the person with the highest income and salary. My overtime income and tips far exceeded my salary. Due to my high income the Bhutanese manager later lowered the rate. For example, the rate of overtime was twenty rupees per hour. Later overtime was reduced to rupees ten per hour. For one year, I enjoyed my work and still remember many fond stories from that time.

King Mahendra's second younger brother, Prince Himalaya Bir Bikram Shah, along with his wife Princess Princep, used to visit the casino and sit at my table. As soon as they lost a few times, the Princess would shout, "How is it that this kid devours the money all the time?"

One day, the Prince ordered a drink and later paid the bill with a hundred rupee note, leaving it as a tip on the table. Seeing this, the Princess took the hundred rupee note, put it in her purse, and took out a ten rupee note to pay the tip instead! I pretended not to see and was shocked by the behavior of some rich people.

Among the croupiers, there was a very clever and active Anglo-Indian guy named Paul. Like me, he oversaw a Blackjack table. He also hosted a card game called Flush and received a huge amount of money in tips every evening. One night, Paul disappeared and didn't show up for his duty. There was a big buzz as to why Paul had vanished. Later, we came to know he was arrested at the airport while trying to smuggle out illegal diamonds and pearls.

Customers had already gathered around the Flush table. Paul's absence meant that his table needed another croupier. John Emmery approached me and asked me to cover his table. I was scared because, on the one hand, this was a table where the elites like Dorje played, and on the other hand, I had little knowledge of the Flush game. John insisted that I cover it!

Now it was my job to run a big game and earn money. My income was very good. Money often fell from my pockets because it was cramped with so many bills. My monthly salary was eight hundred rupees. But the tips alone amounted to one or two thousand rupees each day. Sometimes the players picked up the money that fell out of my pockets and handed it to me.

Even amidst these interesting circumstances I resigned from the job on the 15th of March 1970, to pursue my dream of visiting France.

1.1.2 Trip continuation

Tehran To Ankara

After the flashbacks and my dreams of childhood leading into my young life, I woke up to the reality of my trip in Tehran. Forgetting all the bitter, sweet, fun, and fond memories, I now had the energy to move ahead, and this gave me encouragement. Since I had already received the Turkish visa a few days earlier, I decided to continue my journey toward France. There was a bus service from Tehran to Istanbul, so I left my hotel to go to the bus company and buy my ticket.

I had already gathered enough information to know that it took four nights and five days to reach Istanbul from Tehran. The bus fare was twenty dollars. After getting the ticket, I went back to the hotel, visiting some places of interest on the way back. The bus was leaving at six a.m. the next day. Therefore, I woke up early in the morning and headed to the bus station.

It was a very modern bus. For someone accustomed to the Sajha bus in Kathmandu, I was surprised to see the in-house toilet; the seats were as thick as mattresses and decorated with a red velvet cloth—they looked comfortable. The bus left the station according to schedule. There were mostly foreigners and a few Iranian and Turkish passengers.

About an hour after departure, the bus reached the outskirts of Tehran. There was a mountainous region towards the north of the city; you could see a little snow on top of the mountains. The highway was constructed through the middle of dry mountains and deserts. Since Istanbul was to the west of Tehran, I suspected that we were heading in the same direction. The bus was building up more speed by then. The roads were excellent, and there were many buses traveling in both directions. I was feeling happy and curious at the same time.

My determination to see the world was growing even stronger, and I did not have to return to Nepal halfway through my trip.

After traveling for four hours, the bus stopped at a tea house in the middle of the highway. We were advised to have tea or coffee quickly and return because the bus was stopping for only twenty minutes.

I watched as the bus passed through a continuous desert terrain with a few hillocks here and there. Suddenly, I pictured and imagined Marco Polo and his co-travelers galloping on horses at high speeds, taking the same route I was taking. I imagined them with their swords, guns, and other weapons, well-dressed and fluttering their flags. They must have been very brave as they traveled this route. I constantly wondered how much time it must have taken them to reach China. This journey wasn't as breathtaking as Afghanistan. Deserts seemed monotonous in comparison to the beauty of rocks. The bus kept running and moving along.

At around one in the afternoon, we stopped in front of a highway restaurant in the city of Soltaniyeh. The stop there was for forty-five minutes. We spread out at different tables and prepared to get our meals.

The atmosphere was lively because of the presence of young European travelers. As we had to travel together for four nights and five days, there was a happy atmosphere and a willingness to get to know one another. There was a feeling of closeness. We asked each other about the origin and destination of our journeys. From these conversations, I found that most of them were returning to their countries in Europe after visiting places like India, Afghanistan, and Thailand. After forty-five minutes, we boarded the bus and moved ahead along the desert highway.

Hours passed as we woke up and then went to sleep again. We finally reached Tabriz in the evening, the second largest city in Iran. We stopped in front of a hotel that the driver knew. The driver said, "Here you must get your dinner, go to sleep, and wake up early tomorrow. The bus isn't going to wait if anyone is delayed." After that, we all quickly ate our dinner and went to sleep without much conversation.

The next day I woke up at five a.m., finished my routine tasks, and was ready to get on board before everyone else. We boarded the bus after having a simple breakfast of tea and bread. The bus left two minutes past five a.m., just as the driver had previously informed us.

On the way, two or three hours after the journey began, the passengers began to speak excitedly. We knew that a huge mountain was about to come into view. The name of the mountain was Mount Ararat. It had the same shape as Mt. Fuji in Japan. The passengers got out of their seats to take pictures. I wanted to take pictures too and felt bad for not having a camera. Mount Ararat lies on the eastern edge of Turkey, which is connected to the western border of Iran.

The more the bus moved toward the Turkish border, the more beautiful the snow-capped mountains became. The somewhat bland views of the Iranian landscape became a distant memory. The bus stopped briefly near the Turkish-Iranian border. We had our noon meal and then crossed the border. The trade exchange between Iran and Turkey was prosperous and busy. Large trucks and buses were constantly crossing from both sides of the border.

In a few hours, our bus started climbing up into a hilly region. No plain land was visible. The bus began to slow down because of the slope of the hill and the full load of passengers. I watched curiously through the window; outside, it was all mountains covered with dry grass. The bus continued uphill. We traveled through one pass, then another, always moving uphill. Climbing in this way, the bus reached the city of Erzurum in the evening. We stopped at a hotel where the bus driver had his contacts.

We had reached such a high elevation that we could see the clouds below us. It was quite romantic to travel above the clouds. I was so delighted to see the snow, the clouds and the mountains all at the same time. It was a new experience for me. These places were so beautiful that it made me feel as though I was in some other world. Some of the mountains were so high that they couldn't be crossed within a few hours'drive. We also saw the Fort of Erzurum.

Erzurum was the largest city on the eastern side of Turkey. I felt cold upon reaching this city situated at an altitude of two thousand meters. We didn't leave the hotel for this reason and went to bed early after having dinner.

We were departing at six a.m. I woke up early, completed my daily chores, and got ready by a quarter before six. I had also told my fellow passengers to wake up before six a.m. After boarding the bus at the scheduled time, we headed toward another Turkish city called Sivas. The geography was similar. The bus was driving through the mountains, but there was no greenery; only a few patches of grass could be seen. The mountains were covered in fog, and visibility was low.

As we headed out of Erzurum, the bus slowly descended through the mountains. The fog was still prevalent in the morning, but as we traveled down, some of the mountain tops slowly became visible. At one point, the fog cleared away, and you could see clearly into the distance.

The bus ride continued, taking us along the winding roads. We took small breaks for tea, and the bus finally stopped for lunch at one o'clock in a little town. During the forty-five-minute break, after having our meal, we again headed toward Sivas. With more uphill and downhills along the way, the bus finally arrived at Sivas.

Since it was still bright outside, people went for a tour around the city. I also went out to visit the local market and saw a variety of clothes, food items, and fake jewelry. Since I had no interest in buying anything from the market, I returned to the hotel and took a rest.

The bus driver had already informed us of an early six a.m. departure the following morning. Since leaving Tehran, I always woke up at five and called my fellow passengers at five-thirty, letting them know it was time for departure. During that evening's dinner in Sivas, some folks were complaining about having difficulty waking up so early in the morning. At the same time, somebody said, "Don't worry, we have Shyam here, **Mr. Alarm**!" Everybody laughed upon hearing this, and I continued to be called Mister Alarm all the way to Istanbul.

We passed through dry mountains and small villages after leaving Sivas. We stopped at one of the villages for a twenty-minute tea break at around ten a.m. During these tea and lunch breaks, some of the travelers looked at me and asked excitedly where I was from. Learning that I was from Nepal always surprised and excited people. It seemed my fellow passengers thought Nepal was a very backward and small country. It was a shock for them that a person from such a country had ventured on such a courageous journey. Most of them were friendly and affectionate toward me.

The bus continued moving toward its destination. The scenery outside was monotonous, with no diversity. The geographical region was situated on the Anatolia Plateau. The bus then stopped for a lunch break at a place called Yozgat. After a forty-five-minute lunch break, the journey resumed once again.

I was curious about the city of Ankara, the capital of Turkey. I was very interested to see the city because I had heard about it for a long time. We arrived in Ankara before dusk. The bus driver took us directly to the main bus station.

I saw something a little surprising there. Our bus was parked on a small hillock. Just below it was a vast area where hundreds of other buses were parked in a queue. Buses were coming and going from there too. I had never seen such a large congregation of buses at one time. The bus driver pointed out a hotel for us from a distance. We went to the same hotel and stayed there.

In the evening, we went out to visit nearby places for a couple of hours. In the market, some of the Turkish people looked like Afghans. I was surprised and said to myself, "Where have I arrived?" I went to bed after dinner. The responsibility of waking up everybody the following morning was once again handed to Mr. Alarm!

Ankara To Istanbul

We left Ankara for Istanbul at the scheduled time the next morning. The driver asked everybody to hurry up, as Istanbul was around four hundred and sixty kilometers from Ankara. He requested that we have our tea and lunch faster than before because of the time it took to reach Istanbul with the heavy traffic there.

The road from Ankara to Istanbul was of a higher standard in comparison to the previous ones we had experienced between other cities. It was wider too. The bus picked up speed after leaving Ankara. It was a beautiful time as we watched the scenery along the side of the road. At around twelve noon, we arrived near the city of Duzce. The bus stopped by a hotel near the highway for lunch. During the lunch break, excitement, curiosity, and anticipation were visible on people's faces. We were finally reaching our destination after a continuous journey of four days.

I was more concerned about where I would stay and with whom I would stay. I found out that the three Americans were staying in Istanbul too, so I decided to go with them. I felt relieved and planned to follow them. I will find a room in the hotel where they decided to stay.

At around five p.m. the following day, it began to feel like we were about to arrive in Istanbul. Our bus was riding high on a mountaintop above the city. As we neared Istanbul, we could see two seas connected by a small channel of water. I later came to know that the channel was known as the Marmara Bosphorus Strait, which separated the continent of Europe from the continent of Asia. You could also see a bridge above this channel which connected these two gigantic pieces of land.

Istanbul was the largest city in Turkey and the center of history, culture, and economy. Even though Ankara was the capital city, Istanbul was the largest and most important city in terms of international trade and business.

In this way, I was entering the land of Europe, leaving behind the land of Asia. The nearer we reached Istanbul, the more we could see the innumerable houses, mosques, and bridges on all sides. My curiosity swelled even more. I had to find a hotel, so I asked one of the Americans, "Where are you guys staying in Istanbul?"

One of the guys said, "We are staying on the European side of Istanbul in a hotel near the bus terminal, which is near the Blue Mosque." I asked them whether the hotel was expensive. They said that they had stayed there earlier, and it wasn't too expensive. "Then I will come with you too," I said. They agreed.

We arrived at the bus station in the evening. All the passengers vanished in a few minutes. I don't know where they went, but I followed the Americans. We reached the hotel on foot; it was on the main street. There was a big garden in front of us, and behind us was the grand Blue Mosque.

I got a single room for around one dollar. From the hotel room window, I could see vehicles on the street, a beautiful garden on the other side, the grand Blue Mosque behind it, and the sea towards the left. I was spellbound by the scenery in front of me.

That evening, I left the hotel alone and headed towards the left, which went downhill and ultimately reached Galata Bridge. There were many stalls selling different types of fish dishes and a variety of restaurants. I ate at a restaurant there and then returned to the hotel to sleep.

I woke up early in the morning. There were many places to see and explore in Istanbul. However, I was concentrating on heading to Europe, so I focused more on getting visas for different European countries and gathering information on transportation modes such as the railway. I bought a map of Istanbul from the hotel and increased my knowledge of the city's geographical details. Using the map and asking the hotel staff, I also gathered information about the location of the Yugoslavian and Italian embassies. I felt relieved after that.

For a while, I forgot the tickling in my stomach to immediately reach Europe. I knew that European countries were expensive, whereas I was getting a good hotel for a dollar in Istanbul; the food was equally affordable. Since it was an enjoyable environment, I thought I could spend a few days just having fun.

The next day, after finding its location and route on the map, I reached the Yugoslav Embassy. I applied for the visa there and then returned on foot. I decided to visit the Blue Mosque I had seen the previous day. I took another route using the map and headed towards the mosque. On the way, I reached a confusing junction where the road headed both right and left. I was deeply concentrating on my map. At the same time, a middle-aged woman and her twenty-year-old daughter were apparently watching me in my confusion.

Upon seeing them, I asked the way to the Blue Mosque. It was my guess that they were mother and daughter. The mother immediately started saying something in Turkish. Obviously, I couldn't understand any of it, so I said, "English, English."

The mother said, "No."

I said, "OK, OK." She held my hand immediately and spoke in her language. I thought she had offered to take me to the mosque. I agreed by shaking my head. The girl said nothing. On the way, I took a chance to look at the daughter. She had a lean attractive figure, fair skin tone, almost green eyes, a height like mine, 5'4" and was wearing a flower-patterned frock. I found her beautiful. Her mother was a little chubbier and was wearing a long skirt. Her hair was covered with a scarf, and she was a cheerful-looking woman. We continued our conversation along the way even though we couldn't understand one another's language.

We reached the Blue Mosque in fifteen minutes.

They were talking, and I couldn't understand anything they were saying. They didn't leave me; all three of us went inside and visited the mosque. After leaving the mosque, I bought some ice cream and gave some to them as well. We then went to a nearby park and sat for a while. As we sat there, I understood from their expressions that they wanted to know which country I had come from. I replied, "Nepal." They asked if I had said Japan. I repeated, "Nepal," once again. The woman understood "Japan," so I kept quiet after that. I thought they may have never heard of Nepal. Convincing them of my country of origin was going to be fruitless, so I just nodded my head and said yes to them.

It was nearly evening by then. We spent three hours communicating with various hand gestures. It was a fun time for me. During our time together, my eyes were sometimes fixed on the fair, long legs of the daughter. I felt like she was noticing me too. Eventually, I told them that I had to return to my hotel. They nodded yes and inquired where I had to go. I pointed to a hotel that I saw. The mother nodded as if she understood and said something. I then realized that they wanted to escort me to my hotel. I nodded my head in agreement.

They came inside the hotel with me and directly went to the reception to talk to the staff in their own language. The receptionist, a lady, spoke to me and said, "These days, Emel has a school vacation. They want to take you on a city tour tomorrow if you are free. They will arrive at ten a.m."

I said, "It's alright, but I must go to get the visa for Yugoslavia tomorrow morning at ten a.m. It is a little early, so maybe they could come around eleven." The mother and daughter left after hearing this. I went to my room and thought about them with a delightful feeling. It was such a pleasant surprise. The daughter looked at me a few times but then pretended not to. I couldn't make any concrete assumptions about them. What kind of people are they? What do they want from me? I didn't go anywhere that evening as I kept thinking about my good fortune and went to bed after having only some light snacks from the hotel.

The next day, I went to the Yugoslav Embassy to get my visa and passport. I had returned to the hotel by ten-thirty a.m. and waited for the mother and daughter. It was eleven a.m., but they weren't there. They hadn't even arrived by a quarter past eleven. Then, at around eleven-thirty, I saw them on the other side of the street, crossing and coming toward my hotel. I became elated in my heart after they had finally arrived. I went to the main gate of the hotel to receive them. We greeted each other by shaking our heads, and then we left within a few moments.

I proposed a visit to the city center by pointing to the map. They understood me, and we slowly walked in that direction. I had nothing to say to them since they didn't understand any English. I had many things

I wanted to ask and know about them, but language was the barrier again. They were continuously talking in their own language. Sometimes they talked between themselves and at times with me.

After touring for two hours, we went inside a restaurant and had lunch. After leaving the restaurant, we strolled around and arrived in front of a cinema hall. They asked me if I wanted to go to the cinema. I nodded yes because I didn't want to be separated from them. All three of us went inside the cinema. The daughter sat in the middle, with me on one side and the mother on the other side. Even though I couldn't understand the language, I was not bored because the movie was a comedy. I laughed along with them even though I didn't fully understand. I enjoyed spending time with them more than the movie itself.

After coming out of the cinema, I understood from the mother's gestures that she wanted to invite me to her house for dinner. I was happy about this and thought they wanted me to go with them. But I had no idea how far their home was. How would I return from there? What time would the dinner end? What time will it be by the time I return to the hotel? I was alone and had heard that Turkey could be a dangerous place.

I had heard rumors about the dangers in Turkey and the knives bandits used to rob people. I was constantly aware of this fact. Politely, I told them, "No thank you. See you tomorrow." I pointed to the clock at twelve o'clock and proposed to meet the next day. They looked a little downcast but nodded their heads in agreement. I walked back to the hotel from there, while they went back to their home.

Lying on my hotel room bed, I reflected on what a surprise these two days had turned out to be. What was my purpose? Where was my destination? The closeness I had experienced with the mother and daughter was comforting, but I was also worried that my plans to go to France would be affected by these new circumstances. I came to a decision: I could not waste my time here in Istanbul. I must leave the city soon and head towards France. I decided to get a train to Belgrade, leaving in two days' time, and then went to sleep.

After a shower and breakfast in the morning, I took a local bus and reached the train station. It was larger and cleaner than the railway stations in India. I inquired about different trains leaving for Belgrade and their departure schedules. A train to the Yugoslav capital was leaving the evening of the next day. I bought a ticket according to this plan and returned to my hotel.

Then I decided to spend the rest of my free time with the mother and daughter duo and board the train the next evening. It was already around 11 a.m. by then, and I took a little rest in my bed. I came down at twelve noon, and both arrived shortly after that. We greeted each other by bowing our heads cheerfully. I felt good in this environment. I pointed to the map and proposed a visit to Topkapi Palace Museum and the Grand Bazaar. They replied yes with a gentle smile.

We followed the directions on the map. They knew the way very well, and we reached there with a gradual walk. The museum had been a former palace and an administrative building for past rulers.

The palace had been constructed five centuries earlier during the Ottoman rule in Turkey. The main palace was fortified with a large, tall wall made of stones. We found out that we had to pay an entry fee to enter the museum. We decided that it would be good enough to visit the palace from the outside. After that, we roamed around the outside and then bought some ice cream. I gestured to them to rest as I was a little tired. We rested on a green lawn for about an hour. The mother spoke in Turkish. I didn't understand anything but kept smiling.

Then I pointed to the map again and proposed visiting the Grand Bazaar. They agreed with a smile. It didn't look very far on the map, so we decided to walk there. On our way, we stopped at a coffee shop and had some coffee. The Turkish coffee was quite thick, bitter, and small-sized. No matter how much sugar you added to it, it still tasted bitter. It was also a small rest spot for us on the way. After taking a break of twenty minutes, we continued our way to the Grand Bazaar.

I was very surprised upon reaching there. It really was a grand market. There were tunnels and shops everywhere, brightened by many lights. This market was also established during the reign of the Ottomans. There were a variety of fake jewelry stores, as well as many gold and silver jewelers. The shops were laden with garments, leather bags, and shoes.

I wished to buy them something from there but couldn't for many reasons. They seemed to have no such expectations from me either. The shops and gullies seemed infinite. After looking around for two hours, I wanted to go back to the hotel and rest. However, I then understood that the mother wanted to invite me for a meal at their home again. I showed no interest in this. Then we slowly moved towards the hotel. The street was a little quiet. In a more secluded area of the street, the mother took out both her hands and clenched her fists. Then she took out the index fingers on each hand and rubbed them against each other, showing it to me and her daughter.

I understood a little, but I couldn't make out the whole meaning. I gathered that the rubbing of the two fingers together meant she wanted her daughter and me to have a friendship. I nodded my head with a smile. We went ahead and entered a restaurant to have dinner. Upon entering, I realized that only the mother was there with me. Looking outside, I saw that Emel was standing on the footpath outside the restaurant. I went outside and invited her in. She stayed there without any response, and then she came into the restaurant.

After having some food, I asked them to go to the hotel with me, and they came along. After reaching the hotel, I asked the receptionist about what the mother meant by rubbing her fingers together. They talked to each other for a while, and the receptionist finally said, "The mother wants her daughter to get married to you."

I was speechless. I couldn't give an answer for a while. Then I said, "I am not going to my country right now. I am going to France and then the US. I have no idea when I will return, so getting married now is impossible." The receptionist translated what I had said for the mother. Then the mother again said something, and the receptionist translated for me, "You can take her with you wherever you are going after you get married."

I was stunned but slowly convinced them, "This is not possible. I am returning through Istanbul again. We can meet again and discuss. I am leaving for Belgrade tomorrow, and it is my last day in Istanbul. I have a train at eight p.m. tomorrow evening, and I am free during the day. We can go for another tour if you wish; you can come at ten a.m." After saying this, the receptionist translated. They made a grim face upon hearing this and left nodding their heads.

The next morning, I took a shower and had some breakfast, then left the hotel to visit another monument shown on the map. It was a morning walk, and upon returning, I got a little confused about the route. It was already half past ten by the time I arrived back at the hotel. I didn't see the mother and daughter. There was a fat old man at the reception. I asked him if the two women had been there. It turned out that the man couldn't speak a word of English. He raised both his hands, threw them behind his head, and yelled "Yok." I didn't understand anything. I tried to explain what I meant, but he yelled "Yok" again, becoming a little angry.

I was desperate, but I sat on a nearby chair. Slowly and fearfully, I approached the old man again and asked if there had been a call at the reception with a message for me, specifically asking if there was any phone call for room number five. Suddenly, the old man angrily screamed "Yok" again. I felt a little embarrassed and went back to my seat.

In the meantime, the mother and daughter duo magically arrived at around eleven a.m. Seeing them made me very happy and relieved. I had them sit in the lobby for a while. I thought they understood eleven a.m. from what I had said the previous day.

I had already decided to visit the Taksim region across the Galata Bridge. I showed them the map and signaled for them to accompany me. They agreed by shaking their heads, and we gradually walked toward our destination. We reached there in about two hours. I was surprised again. It was like a modern city. We had been in the Fatih area, which was a little chaotic. In Taksim, there were wide roads, large houses, and shops, and it looked comparatively very modern.

There was a large hotel with fifteen stories, the Intercontinental, on the right-hand side of the road. We went inside and ordered a cup of coffee for each of us. I assumed that they had probably never been to such a hotel.

We took a break there for a while. After leaving the hotel, we continued roaming here and there. I then remembered that I had to return to the hotel by six in the evening. Keeping this in mind, we slowly walked back to the hotel. By then, the English-speaking receptionist was back at her desk. I felt a little better, thinking that now I could make the mother and daughter understand my situation.

I asked the receptionist to tell them that my train was leaving at eight p.m. and that I must reach the station by seven. They should now return to their house. The mother and daughter proposed to escort me to the station. I felt uncomfortable. This would deepen our relationship and also waste two hours of their time. The better option would be to send them home and go to the station by myself. I told the receptionist that I would write them letters from France if I was given their address. They did give me their address.

It was an emotional farewell, even though that was not what we wanted. I went back to my room and lay on my bed. I had observed a lot of hopelessness on Emel's face. However, the situation was now beyond my control.

Istanbul To Belgrade

I went to the train station at around seven o'clock that evening. I bought some snacks before boarding the train because I had heard that the train traveled all night long. It departed at the scheduled time. I kept thinking deeply about the mother and daughter. I may never come back to Istanbul again; even if I do, I don't know when it will be. I don't know if I will ever meet them again. These thoughts kept pulling at my heart.

The train was comfortable. My eyes slowly started shutting because of the exhaustion from the long walk during the day. I fell into a deep sleep. The next day, I heard the brakes stopping the train. The speed gradually declined, and I woke up. When I looked out of the window, the land was covered in fog. We had arrived in Sofia, the capital of Bulgaria. Many passengers got out. I went along with them to a nearby coffee stall. After having a coffee, I returned to the train. I had no idea how long we had stopped. The train left on time after boarding some passengers.

As it was morning, the scenery outside was clearly visible. There was beautiful greenery everywhere, with fields and some small hills. I was very excited about the fact that I was going to reach France in a few days' time. The mother and daughter of Istanbul flashed into my mind time and again. I wondered what they had been doing during my travel time. It was in my best interest to go ahead with my journey and reach my destination without becoming confused and stuck. Keeping this in mind, I tried to forget about them.

Hearing other passengers' chatter, I realized that we had entered Yugoslavia. It was quite sunny outside. From the train, you could see villages and cities along the way.

I was confused for a while after leaving the train; I had no idea what to do or where to go. I then saw some hotels and restaurants in front of the station. I went to one of the restaurants and had a meal. I talked to the waiter for a while. When he asked where I was from, I told him that I was coming from Nepal. He was really surprised that I had arrived from such a faraway place. After the meal, I paid for the food and gave the waiter a handsome tip, which made him happy.

I requested that he keep watch over my bag for a few hours. I wanted to have a little tour of the city. I also asked him how long the restaurant would remain open. He said that he would be there until the evening and that watching my bag was no problem. He kept my bag in a corner inside the restaurant. My body felt much better since I didn't have to carry a heavy bag. I went wherever my feet took me.

Belgrade was the capital of Yugoslavia and its largest city. The city was the center for culture, education, economics, and science of the entire country.

The name "Belgrade" literally means "white city." This city looked much different than Istanbul. There were large buildings that looked like palaces. The roads were wide, beautiful, and lined with trees. It was also very clean. In those days, Yugoslavia was a communist country, although the lifestyle, food, and culture seemed to be heavily inspired by Western democratic countries. The boys grew long hair and wore bell-bottom pants. The girls walked in provocative outfits.

I had received a postcard of a beautiful street in Belgrade from someone when I was still living in Nepal. I had carried that picture with me. As soon as I reached Belgrade, I showed the picture of the street to the locals and inquired about where the street was. I finally reached there; it was even more beautiful than the picture itself. I felt as though I had fulfilled one of my wishes in life.

I gradually returned to the station and the restaurant; it was getting a bit dark. First, I went to the restaurant to pick up my bag and then headed to the train station. When I inquired at the station, I found out that the train to Italy was only departing the following evening. I began to think about accommodation for the night. I also considered sleeping on one of the benches in the station. However, there were no benches, only a few chairs. It was not suitable for sleep, and there were a lot of people. I became really exhausted as I stood there continuously for hours.

There were some steel pipes installed on the floor near the walls. These were apparently radiator pipes used to keep the station warm. I sat there for a while but got tired just after ten minutes, thinking that it was impossible to sit on a three-inch-long pipe all night! As time passed, it got colder and colder in the station. Then I remembered the sleeping bag Linda had given me in Nepal and decided to sleep on the floor.

I opened my rucksack and took out the sleeping bag, which was inside a cover and tied with a cotton rope. As soon as I opened the knot to take out the bag, I nearly fainted from the foul smell. I threw it down immediately. I assumed that Linda had never washed or dry cleaned the sleeping bag after buying and using it. I slowly picked up the bag with my two fingers and threw it in a concrete garbage bin, breathing heavily afterward. I thought to myself, how can anyone give such smelly and overused things!

After the plan to spend the night in a sleeping bag in the train station failed, I had no option but to find a hotel. There were many well-lit hotels in front of the station, but I thought they would be expensive. "How do I find a cheap hotel?" I wondered. I didn't know where or how to find youth hostels. While I was considering all of this near the station gate, a Yugoslavian lady suddenly said hello to me and approached with a question. I shook my head to greet her.

She asked, "Oh, you need a hotel?"

I said, "Yes."

Then she said, "I can give you a room in my house and breakfast in the morning, and I will charge you three dollars."

I thought about my physical state and, as it was so late, I immediately agreed and went with her. Her house wasn't very far. We arrived there after a five-minute walk from the station. Her apartment was on the second floor. After reaching there, she showed me to my room and immediately asked for the money. I paid her accordingly.

I was curious about the room. Surprisingly, it was something I had never witnessed before. The blanket was light, thick, and pure white, and the mattress was almost two feet thick. I immediately jumped onto the bed and went to sleep, exhausted. When I went under the blanket, it felt like a pile of cotton. I was so surprised by how comfortable it was.

I felt half-drowned in bed. The bedsheet was pure white and warm. Seeing this, I thought the kings and aristocrats probably slept in this type of bed. I fell asleep in no time. After waking up the next day, I realized that I had found a comfortable facility for just three dollars. The host lady pointed me to the bathroom, and after getting a proper shower, I sat at the breakfast table.

She had decorated the table with three types of bread, cheese, butter, jam, boiled eggs, honey, black coffee, hot milk, and fruit, with cups and plates of different sizes. Seeing this, my heart became elated, and I felt like God had been my savior from the previous night. I had a heavy breakfast and, after taking a rest for a while, headed for the train station. I bought a ticket for the city of Milan in Italy. The train was departing in the evening, so I had to spend the day in Belgrade. I left my bag in the station locker, which allowed me to explore the city with ease.

Then I left to see the city. I learned that this city played an important role during the reign of the Romans. It was situated almost at the center of Europe and therefore had a lot of historical palaces and buildings.

I also visited Saint Mary's Church, which was beautiful and grand. I arrived at a riverbank where the Danube and Sava Rivers meet. Later, I used my map to navigate back to the station.

While looking around the city center in the area where I had lunch, I found a cinema hall. Since I had a lot of time, I decided to go inside to watch a movie to pass the time, even though I didn't understand the language. The movie hadn't started yet. The environment inside was shocking. There were a lot of girls and boys with long hair wearing T-shirts and jeans. Most of them were smoking and making a lot of noise. The rowdy audience made me wonder what kind of a communist country this was. I had always assumed that people from a communist country would be peaceful and disciplined. Seeing this, I thought that communism was in decay here. I left the hall after an hour and felt refreshed.

Belgrade To Milan, Italy

I boarded the train to the city of Milan, Italy, at around seven in the evening. It was better than all the trains I had previously been on. Inside, there was a separate cabin to get tea and other food items. The train provided this facility for travelers to enjoy their meals along with wine and beer during the journey. I thought it was amazing, although I slept that night without eating anything. I wasn't particularly hungry since I had already eaten in Belgrade.

I was the only one in my compartment. The seat was a sofa type, as long as a bed. It was fine for sleeping. The cushion was thick and covered with a leatherette material. Later, I realized that I didn't have any drinking water and was very thirsty. I went to the toilet, where there was a water tap. There was a notice that said, "Non potable (Non drinkable)." I drank a good amount without hesitation and slept through the night without an issue. I did not have diarrhea or any pain when I woke up in the morning.

As it started getting bright enough the next morning, the movement of passengers began inside the train. They were going to the toilet to wash their faces and brush their teeth.

Back in Nepal some of my friends had given me a suggestion to manage my expenses in foreign countries. I could carry some Nepali handicraft items and then sell them for a profit. Europeans liked our handicraft items and for this reason, I had carried some souvenirs from Kathmandu. I was also wearing a silver ring on my middle finger which had the carving of Lord Buddha's statue on it.

Inside the train, there was a family with three boys and one girl. They were boisterously moving to and from. I was standing in the hallway, watching through the window, and I noticed them smiling and looking at me. After a while, they approached me and asked where I had come from. When I told them that I was from Nepal, we exchanged a few words about why and where our journeys were taking us.

One girl's eyes fell on my ring, which made her exclaim with joyous surprise. She asked if she could try it on. After trying it on, she excitedly said, "I will show this to my parents and be right back." Leaving her brother and sister, she rushed back to her cabin. Around five minutes later, she returned with her parents.

Her father then asked me, "Can you sell this ring? My daughter is quite fond of it." With a little hesitation, I said I could sell it for ten dollars. They whispered among themselves in Italian. From their facial expressions, I guessed that the father felt ten dollars was too expensive. I was right, as the girl returned the ring to me with a sad face. Feeling bad, I said I could give the ring for five dollars. The father immediately agreed to this, and the girl jumped for joy. I had only paid two dollars for the ring in Nepal.

The Italians then moved back to their compartments. I was seated near the window, enjoying the scenery of Italian fields, grasslands, greenery, and small villages along the way.

This was my first sale in all of Europe. After this experience, I only sold one or two other rings in France because I wasn't comfortable being a seller of Nepali goods. Since then, I have given most of the handicrafts and jewelry to my friends as souvenirs. This made my backpack even lighter.

Near the end of our journey, some local Italians appeared outside the train selling a variety of goods, just like in India. There were expensive items like Rolex and Omega watches, as well as gold ornaments. They promised to sell these items at very cheap prices. They harassed the passengers by saying, "This is your only chance to buy it. I can give you a Rolex watch for one hundred dollars and a gold chain for fifty dollars!" The same type of people would return with gold pens and gold chains, persistently urging us to buy.

I found it to be a strange scenario in a European country. We passengers faced this situation all along the way. I finally realized that we were about to reach the city of Milan. I was so excited to see Milan and, at the same time, concerned about how and where to find a youth hostel.

The train reached Milan train station in about an hour. It was the second largest city in Italy, both industrial and modern. Like Paris, it was also considered a worldwide center of men's and women's fashion. I disembarked slowly once the train had stopped, looking to the right, left, up, and down. I looked at the ceiling of the station and was in awe. Dharahara, the Bhimsen tower of Kathmandu, is about 230 feet tall. I slowly walked on to leave the station. I had the address of a youth hostel but had no idea how to get there.

I got a map from the information center at the station and headed towards the main gate. I was shocked to see the gate and stairs. The gate was about two stories high. The staircase was made of marble and was twenty feet wide. I looked back at the exit with amazement. The large statues adorning the wall looked equally attractive. Later, I wrote letters to a few of my friends in Nepal about how impressed I was by the gate and staircase.

It was quite sunny outside. I was confused upon leaving the station and looked at the map to find my route to the hostel. Seeing a foreigner in confusion, an Italian girl came near me and asked if I needed any help. Her name was Maria, and she knew a bit of English. I told her everything about me and then asked her for directions to the youth hostel. Listening to me, she said, "You must go there by metro. When it arrives, I will take you there."

I had no idea where she was headed but was nonetheless relieved when she offered to guide me. I had no idea what a metro was! We had to go down the stairs and then underground. She bought tickets for both of us and then said, "The metro is about to arrive. OK! Let's get to the platform fast." I was carrying my rucksack. The metro was apparently just a smaller train. It stopped right at the platform. All the doors opened at once. There was a huge crowd inside. Maria urged me to get onboard fast as soon as some passengers exited. I entered along with others. The doors shut automatically. Within moments, there was an alarm bell ringing. Everybody started looking around. It was the bag on my back that was stuck in the door!

"Oh! Bag! Bag!" Maria shouted. I tried to pull my rucksack in, but there was no chance. Suddenly, there was another alarm sound at the door, and it opened again. Maria pulled both me and the bag inside. I felt a little embarrassed, but Maria said, "It's nothing, don't worry." (Surprisingly, two and a half months after that incident when I had arrived in Paris and was heading to my destination on the metro, the same incident happened again).

While the metro was running underground, Maria said to me, "My home is nearby. We can go there. I will introduce you to my mother and sister and offer you food. After that, I will take you to your hostel. I will also take you for a visit to the city." I was really delighted to hear this and immediately agreed. We stopped four stops later, left the metro, and headed towards her home.

I met her mother, who was a genuine lady and welcomed me with an open heart. They were really impressed that I had traveled so far from Nepal. They knew about Nepal because of the famous Sagarmatha (Mt. Everest). We sat down for lunch. Her mother poured a glass of water and a glass of red wine for me. Then she gave me a salad on a small plate, which had diced tomatoes at the base, diced cheese in the middle, and diced tomatoes on top. Some oil was poured on top with salt, pepper, and herbs. This type of meal was very new to me. There was bread alongside it too. Everyone else started eating, and later I joined in, using a fork and knife. I found the meal extremely delicious. It was my first experience with common European food.

After the salad was finished, the mother removed the plate and replaced it with a larger one. She put a good portion of meat mixed with pasta on my plate. It was my first introduction to Italian cuisine. I couldn't ask what animal the meat was from, but the food gave me great satisfaction. From the sips of wine, I slowly became intoxicated. The environment seemed more entertaining and deeply satisfying. Maria had recently returned from a vacation to Palermo. She was all brown, and some skin had peeled off from the tip of her nose.

She gave me a photograph of her area, which I still have to this day. After our meal, we left her house, and with her help, I reached the youth hostel. After registering my name, I left my bag in the hostel, and we headed out to visit the center of the city. We went to a cathedral named Duomo. After leaving the metro, I realized that you had to look vertically upward to see the top of the cathedral. I was mesmerized by this grand structure. Maria invited me to visit the inside of the cathedral as well. I was even more impressed with the inside. The ceiling was as high as you could see, and the walls were decorated with a variety of colorful glass. This was the first large church I had seen in Europe. Later during my travels through Europe, I saw other grand cathedrals in France, Spain, and Germany.

Maria and I spent a long time inside Duomo, which was very cold. This cathedral was centrally located in the city of Milan. It is said that it took six hundred years to build this monument. Maria then informed me that we were going to visit Galleria Vittorio Emanuele II, and I agreed. I was even more delighted because moments like these felt so romantic. I thought to myself, I wish I could stay and be with her until my time in Milan is over.

We were slowly and casually walking along the streets. When we crossed the road, she held my arm tightly to keep me safe. Sometimes I felt like she was expressing a mother's protective care for her child. Other times, I felt the effect of a growing love towards her and the protective feeling of a lover.

We arrived at Galleria after an hour's walk. Looking up, I was amazed; Galleria was another miracle for me. It was divided into three halls and was huge. The tall roofs were made of colorful stained and painted glass. You had to strain your neck at such an extreme angle that if you were wearing a hat, it would probably fall off. Inside, there were a variety of shops, restaurants, and cafes. There were expensive clothing stores, shoe stores, and purse stores. Numerous luxury perfume stores and other high-end boutiques offered expensive goods. Large mirrors adorned the space, reflecting our faces at every turn. We explored all the stores, enjoying ourselves. Later, we visited a coffee shop and enjoyed a nice coffee break.

Maria had just finished high school and was preparing to go to university. We had become very close within a day. As evening approached, I was feeling exhausted. I told her I needed to return to my hostel. She said, "You will get lost in the metro because you have to change lines. I will escort you to your hostel."

We arrived at the hostel, where many young people were moving in and out. The environment was engaging and fun. Maria stayed for a while and then gave me a gentle hug with a smile. She said, "I must work tomorrow morning. I will come to meet you at twelve noon. Then we can go to my house, have a meal, and go out for another visit in the city of Milan."

The next day, as promised, she came to my hostel. We went to her home, had a meal, and then went out for a visit. I got to see many new places, and we spent the entire day having a lot of fun.

Earlier that morning I had decided to go on to Marseille that same evening. I wanted to visit my friend, Jean Michell. My destination was France, so nothing could prevent me from heading in that direction. When I informed Maria of my plan, she said, "Really" and seemed slightly upset, yet remained civilized and loving.

After I informed Maria of my plan, we headed towards Galleria on the metro. We continued to visit many places, including parks. We returned to the hostel to get my bag and then headed to the station. There was some time left before departure, so we had a meal at the station. The time we spent together made me very fond of her, and I felt it deep in my heart.

Maria and I exchanged addresses and contacts and promised to remain in touch. We then expressed our deep affection for one another. I boarded the train fifteen minutes early, with great agony in my heart. Maria and I continued to regularly exchange letters. Ten years later, she came to Nepal with her husband and met with me. By then, I was also married.

Milan, Italy To Marseilles, France

The train departed on time, and after an hour, we were out of the city of Milan. It was dark both inside the cabin and outside the train. Feeling sleepy, I quickly fell asleep. After a few hours, I heard the train stopping. Looking outside, I saw a huge city located on a seacoast, known as Genoa. After a short halt, the train departed once again towards France. I had already noticed the Mediterranean Sea on the left side. On the right side, there were uniform-like stone cliffs all along the way. They looked like they were carved out with a knife. I fell asleep again.

The train stopped again at dusk. We were at the border town between Italy and France, called Ventimiglia. The French police came onboard and began to ask for everyone's passport. I gave my passport to the officer like everybody else, and my French visa was stamped with the date, April eighteenth, 1970. I saw rocky mountains with beautiful houses built below; I found out later that most of these houses were vacation homes for rich tourists from Switzerland, Italy, and other countries in Europe. Many celebrities and wealthy citizens of Europe had built houses on these mountains and visited them to spend their holidays.

Once we entered French territory, the seacoast was known as the Riviera. Each house had its own swimming pool. People visited this coastal area during the summer for swimming and developing their suntan. These houses were called summer homes. They looked beautiful and comfortable. Beautiful gardens had been constructed inside the compounds. I felt that I was in a completely new world. The hills were full of greenery with black and white rocks. The Riviera was breathtaking and heavenly even all those years ago.

Once I was employed with Air France, I went back to the Riviera numerous times, especially to Nice, Cannes, Monte Carlo, and Saint Raphael.

The train I was traveling on was moving slowly. Later, I discovered that there were many small stations nearby due to the proximity of people's settlements. The train stopped and started for many miles. At around ten in the morning, the train arrived at St. Charles station in Marseille. The train was just above sea level, on a raised platform. When I went outside, I saw that there were many stone stairs going down, leading to the main street. If you kept going south from there, you would end up at the sea. On the opposite side, while going down the stairs, you would see the streets heading right and left.

I called my friend Jean Michel from the telephone booth at the train station. He was quite shocked to receive my call. I never had the chance to call or write to him since I had departed from Nepal because I was constantly shifting places. Jean Michel had no idea when or if I would arrive from Nepal!

He explained to me over the phone, "I live ten kilometers away from the train station. You must catch a bus to reach here. It's easy though; there will be no issue." He gave me detailed directions, including the bus number and where to get off. The area in which he lived was called Parc Calliste, Hôpital Nord. According to him, I had to go down the stairs and take the broad road towards the southern port. The street was wide and full of houses that looked like ancient castles. The ground floors of these houses were full of large shops and restaurants. The street was called La Canebière, which was like Durbar Marg of Kathmandu, Champs-Élysées of Paris, and Fifth Avenue of New York.

I walked slowly down the stairs, looking up, down, left, and right. I went to a café to have a cup of coffee. There were two or three tables outside on the sidewalk, which was interesting to me; inside, it was an elaborate space filled with people. They were mainly young boys and girls. More surprisingly, when I looked closer, many of these youngsters appeared to be Chinese, Japanese, African, and Arabian. There were French people too. I was curious to know which country this variety of people had come from and why they were staying in France. I was delighted by the overall atmosphere of the place.

I ordered a coffee and stayed there for a while. These youngsters were at the café just talking to one another. I later learned more about the café culture of ordering a beverage while enjoying conversation. After I had my coffee, I stayed for a while longer, listening to the people speaking in French. It sounded like the chirping of birds in an interesting rhythm. This first experience of seeing French people in their native country was very exciting. It was what I had been dreaming of.

The port city of Marseille is the second largest city in France. This was the entry point for cargo arriving from the Middle East, Africa, and other countries via the sea route. It had a two thousand four hundred fifty-year legacy, having been established by the Greeks. One of my friends told me that this city was first inhabited as a fishing village.

I also found out that Marseille had more criminal activities than other cities in France. When leaving the station, I headed towards the bus terminal, moving my head in all directions as a precaution. As Jean had said, there was a bus terminal at the end of the road towards the right. I boarded the correct bus bound for Parc Calliste, Hôpital Nord.

After a few minutes, the bus arrived on the highway. We sometimes passed between hills and sometimes by the seacoast. The sun outside was shining brightly, the blue water of the ocean was on the left, and the greenery of the mountains was on the right, which made me feel as though I was traveling through paradise.

After an hour's ride, the bus reached Hôpital Nord and parked in the underground. I called Jean Michel from there, and he said he would arrive in ten minutes. He arrived on time, just as he had promised, and for a while, we were both speechless and a little emotional. It had been nearly five years since we had last met in Nepal. He looked sturdier than before. Jean Michel carried my bag, and we started walking uphill.

On the way, he looked at me and said, "My friend Shyam, you have such black hair; French girls will be crazy for you, be careful!" I laughed upon hearing this but also became a little excited. We continued to chat as we walked along the street. We finally reached his eighteen-story apartment building. His wife Lilianee and his daughter Eleanor, who wasn't even a year old, were waiting for us as we reached the apartment. We had climbed up to the tenth floor!

Looking out the window, I saw many buildings like Jean Michel's; it was called a residential area. I spent the rest of the day talking with Jean Michel while staying inside the house. I went to bed after dinner with a glass of red wine.

The next day we sat at the breakfast table, and I was surprised. I had never seen the kind of bread that was on the table. In Nepal, I had seen naan and other small breads, but in France, the bread was nearly a meter long. It was round and roasted in the oven, with a hard crust outside and a dark yellowish color. Even though the outer layer was hard and reddish from the burn, the inside was soft. They called it a baguette. This bread is apparently exported to many other countries around the world. I have heard that one or two jumbo jets full of baguettes take off from France bound for New York every morning.

Along with the baguette, there was black coffee in a large ceramic bowl. There was jam and butter too. You could add hot milk to the coffee if you wanted, but most French people preferred black coffee. There were also two or three types of cheese. I had my first French breakfast, which was unique and delicious. Nowadays, this baguette bread is prepared in many bakeries, even in Nepal. However, due to the difference in flour quality, the taste of the baguette in Nepal is unlike that in France.

I arrived just before the weekend. On weekends, French people have fun by going to the sea for swimming, sunbathing, enjoying a picnic, or visiting a restaurant. Jean Michel took me along with his family to the beach. We went to a coastal city called La Ciotat, nearly forty kilometers from where they lived. As the beach was quite crowded, we had to drive further away to park.

Everywhere we saw men in their swim trunks and women wearing bikinis while lying on the sandy beach. Their eyes were closed and facing the sun, with oil rubbed on their faces and bodies. Some women wore swimsuit bottoms but were baring their breasts. Many people were swimming by the beach while some had ventured even further into the sea. Coming from a landlocked country, this was one of my first experiences by the sea. This was a totally different world for me.

People left their vehicles on the street and walked to the beach. People of all classes visited this beach. In the meantime, my friend Jean Michel signaled me with his eyes to look towards a guy and said, "See there, the guy is swiveling (showing off) his car keys while coming here because it is the keys to a 'Porsche.'"

Once we had reserved our place on the beach, Jean Michel started swimming. He went into the depths. I had always seen him in clothes, and I was surprised as he undressed. His body was like that of a bodybuilder. After he returned from the water, Lilianee went swimming. Once she returned, we sat for a picnic lunch. We had baguette, butter, cheese, ham, pizza, yogurt, juice, and wine while sitting on a towel.

I wasn't very good at swimming, so there was no question of swimming for me. The waves from the sea crashed into the white stones on the coast just near us and then flowed back into the ocean as clean and pure water. It was a breathtaking experience for me, surrounded by beautiful scenery.

I enjoyed soaking my feet in the cold water and shaking them up and down. The salty lunch earlier and the scorching sun on my forehead made me thirsty. So, I thought, "Instead of going back to look for water, I'd rather try the clean water right here in front of me from the sea; this will quench my thirst." It looked crystal clear. I gathered the seawater with my two hands and gulped it down. Shockingly, I couldn't decide whether to swallow it or spit it out. It was like a brine solution. It was so salty that my eyes were rolling. I had already swallowed half and spit out the rest. I was making a gagging sound to get the salt content out of my mouth, while at the same time shouting for Jean Michel to bring me a bottle of water.

He and his wife laughed hysterically, pressing their bellies upon knowing my state of confusion. Jean Michel brought me a bottle of pure water. I gargled once, and then he asked me, "Didn't you know that the Mediterranean Sea water is salty?"

I replied, "I have never heard of such a thing!" Later, Jean Michel and his wife would tease me by asking if I wanted to drink Mediterranean water whenever I said I was thirsty!

We returned home that evening. That same night, they had invited three friends over for dinner. Lilianee took a brief rest and then started preparing dinner. Jean Michel helped his wife as much as he could. They informed me of their friends' arrival later in the evening and suggested that I rest for a while in my room.

First Dinner In France

At around eight o'clock in the evening, a French girl named Katie, who was a little short, and another French couple arrived at Jean's place. The couple had brought wine, and Katie had brought dessert. After the introductions were over, we began with wine, whisky, and some snacks. The conversation, as well as the jokes, continued. The women joked about the men, and the men joked about the women. Almost everyone understood English. The environment heated up even more as more wine was shared.

During the conversation, I was told that Jean Michel and his wife belonged to the faith of Jehovah's Witnesses. They explained the beliefs concerning their faith, and I kept listening. By chance, I saw a book under the table that explained their faith. I took it out and turned to the first page. With a glance, I suddenly wanted to burst out in laughter because it said, "Jehovah's Witnesses is not a superstitious faith." I compared this with some Hindu beliefs that proclaimed that the earth rests on the shoulder of a giant elephant. I kept quiet, put the book back, and had a good internal laugh.

They asked me about the religious situation in Nepal. I said, "In Nepal and India, we are mostly Hindus, although on a personal level, I am not immersed in any faith system. I do celebrate the culture and festivities of the Hindu and Buddhist communities. I do not visit temples and other religious sites."

Wine and conversation went hand in hand. The jokes resumed. Jean Michel asked me, "How do you make a rooster sound in your country?" I answered with the sound that was used and recognized in the Newari community, which sounded like 'kukulyang Ku!' Hearing this, the French guys laughed so hard and then asked me to repeat the sound.

In fact, I had never imagined that there were different ways of producing the sound of a rooster other than the one we used in the Newari community. For this reason, I asked them, "How do you do it in your culture then?" Jean Michel explained that they used 'Kukuru Ku,' making the sound himself. Hearing that, I also laughed hard.

The jokes continued, mainly centered around men and women. Jean Michel then made a joke and asked me, "Hey Shyam, do you know one thing?"

I asked, "What?"

Then he said, "Pregnant women can't even see themselves peeing." After hearing this, everyone, including the women, laughed quite hard.

It was then dinner time, and we continued in a similar way, having fun and drinking wine. I was really enjoying these moments. I had never experienced spending such a long time at dinner. After that, it was decided that we would drink a digestive called Cognac. It was an even harder drink. While drinking the Cognac, Katie came over and sat down on the floor just below the sofa, positioning herself between my legs; the conversation continued.

At midnight, the French couple decided to leave. Since Katie stayed in the city, Jean offered to take her home in his car. As he was getting ready, his wife said, "You must drive all the way back alone, so we will go with you as well." Deciding that this was a good idea, we all got into the vehicle and headed towards the city. Lilianee sat with her baby on her lap in the front of the vehicle. Katie and I were seated in the back.

The car started rolling down the highway. The couple in front talked for a while. Katie was really drunk, and I was having a hard time keeping my eyes open. The car was piercing through the silence and darkness of the highway, and it was pitch black outside. After a while, the couple stopped talking. Within a few moments, Katie came close to me. The car continued its way, and she started touching my body. I was confused about what to do and what not to do.

I was very intrigued but was at the same time nervous as my friends were in the front seats. Katie did not take notice or did not care about the couple in front. I was really scared, because I had just arrived at Jean's the previous day, and I had no clue as to how long I would be staying there. I did not want to do something inappropriate right at the beginning of my stay. I felt that this could spell trouble for me.

Katie didn't seem to care, but I motioned towards my friends in the front seat, which made her stop. After that, she remained a bit quieter. Sometime later, we arrived at her house. She got out of the car a little wobbly. We all got out and kissed each other's cheeks according to French tradition. We bid farewell, and she then went to her place.

We didn't have much conversation while returning to their home, and I fell into a deep sleep. The next morning, as I was waking up, the incidents of the previous night flashed before my eyes. I was concerned that my friends would complain. Jean Michel and Lilianee said nothing much, and I was very relieved. We had lunch in the house that day. Along with other food items, Lilianee had also cooked rice. She knew that we consumed a lot of rice in Nepal. Surprisingly, the rice she cooked was so good, I had never tasted such delicious rice in my life.

That remains true until today; I have never had such delicious rice anywhere. It was like pulao in Nepal, with long grains of rice that were separated from each other. On top of the rice, there was a little bit of butter or oil which was slightly salty in taste. I ate it all without leaving a single grain of rice on the plate. I immediately asked for the recipe. She said, "You must fry the rice first in oil or butter, sprinkle some salt, then pour the right amount of water and cook it using a rice cooker."

I tried the recipe, but my family hasn't been able to produce the same taste even though I have shared the instructions with them. Fifty-two years later, when Jean Michel came to visit me in Nepal, he told me that I had dropped a grain of rice on the floor. I picked it up gently with my finger and placed it on the side of my plate.

After the meal, we went out again to see the center of Marseille. From the city center, the car started going uphill, and after a while, we reached a hilltop where a huge basilica named Notre Dame De La Garde was located. The construction of this place began in the twelfth century. It was made in honor of the Virgin Mary. I felt that this place was no less beautiful than heaven itself. A cold breeze was gently blowing in from the southwest. You could see the deep blue ocean as far as your eyes could reach, while the city of Marseille lay to the northwest.

Towards the west was the port of Marseille, with small boats lined up by the port side. A little further out at sea, you could also see large ships and boats. This was the best spot to view the entire city of Marseille and the Mediterranean Sea facing west. We enjoyed this view for a while and took some photos. Then Jean Michel proposed that we visit La Canebière Street, which was like New Road in Kathmandu. I had been there during my first day in France but hadn't spent a significant amount of time, only stopping for a coffee.

We arrived at La Canebière, parked our vehicle, and started exploring.

I mentioned to Jean that the street looked beautiful, to which he replied, "My friend, there are about ten streets like this in Paris." This statement still resonates in my ears today. Once I heard this, I was excited to go to Paris and see those streets. After visiting a church at the edge of La Canebière, we returned home. In the evening, we received a phone call from Katie saying that her parents had invited us all for dinner.

The following day, Jean Michel went to work. At first, I didn't know what his occupation was, but during our conversation, I discovered that he was involved in house construction, specializing in wall masonry and roofing. It made sense given his sturdy physique. Before leaving for work, Jean advised me, "You can have lunch at home and then explore the area. Just make sure you have the proper address with you in case you get lost and need to find your way back." After lunch, I ventured out alone. Heading downhill, I reached a bustling market area that connected to the road leading to Marseille. I recalled walking along this same road for three kilometers when I first arrived at Jean's place. The street was lined with a variety of shops, cafes, small hotels, a post office, salons, and dry cleaners. I was thrilled to have found my way there and continued exploring as I walked further downhill.

On my way, I came across a group of young men using large drilling machines to construct the road. Further along, I saw another group of young men digging the foundation for a new house, dressed in their construction attire. I was impressed to see these long-haired youths, who appeared to be college students, working so diligently. I thought to myself that their physically demanding jobs likely contributed to their sturdy, well-built bodies.

As evening approached, I realized I had ventured quite far into the market area. The street seemed endless, stretching for kilometers. After walking for several kilometers, I slowly turned back to head home, the dusk settling in. Along the way, I was surprised to see the same young men who had been working earlier, now relaxing in cafes, smoking, and enjoying beer, after cleaning up and changing into their casual attire. They were lively and cheerful, a stark contrast to their earlier laborious tasks.

It was also surprising for me to see girls working at the petrol station. I admired the diligence and hard work of the young people here. In Nepal, digging roads might be considered a low-status job, but here in France, it seemed different. At that moment, I made an emotionally driven resolution that once I returned to Nepal, I would gladly take on the job of road digging. I would embrace the work with happiness and without hesitation, aiming to develop a sturdy body like those of the young French workers. I even wrote to a few friends in Nepal, expressing my newfound admiration for this line of work.

After Jean returned from work in the evening, we followed the address provided by Katie and arrived at her parents' house around eight-thirty pm. The location was a bit outside the main city. Katie's parents were retired officers, and she had a fifteen-year-old brother who lived with them. Katie herself had her own apartment in Marseille.

I learned that in Western tradition, once young people mature and reach a certain age, they often leave their parental home to live independently. They choose a place closer to their workplace, allowing them to maintain their independence while still staying connected with their family. It was a contrast to the familial structure I was accustomed to in Nepal, where multigenerational households were more common.

We had some drinks before dinner and were having a great time. The father lit a cigarette and started smoking. I was shocked when, after smoking a few puffs, he passed the cigarette to his 15-year-old son. I was surprised by this aspect of the society they lived in. The son smoked without any hesitation. At that time, I also smoked. I enjoyed having a cigarette with whisky. My way of smoking was a little lighter; I only inhaled one fourth of the smoke. This was because I nearly fainted from nausea when I first began learning how to smoke.

There is also a story behind how I learned to smoke. It took place while I was working at the Soaltee Casino in Nepal. Gautam Das Shrestha of Toyota Company had given me a beautiful steel gas lighter. Although I didn't smoke myself, most of my workplace colleagues did. On one occasion, a friend named Malla said to me, "Hey Mohan! Are you only going to light another person's cigarette? If you buy your own packet of 555 Cigarettes and light it with your lighter, you will look so fancy and elegant." His suggestion interested me. The next day, I did as he told me. I found it to be fun. Slowly I got habituated to smoking. It was only fifteen years later that I was able to quit the habit.

Drinks lasted for an hour and a half, and Katie was playing a particularly gracious host to me. We enjoyed an excellent dinner with a wide variety of dishes while the wine flowed like a river. As we had a long way back to drive home, we left after drinking Cognac, the digestive drink of French tradition after a big meal.

Jean took me for a visit every two or three days: sometimes we went to the forest, and other times to cities on the seaside, like Cassis and Toulon.

On the second Saturday after arriving in Marseille, we planned to visit a hill in the coastal area. We went to pick up Katie from her apartment, then headed towards our destination. Jean Michel, Liliane, and their baby were seated in the front while Katie and I were in the back, and we enjoyed the opportunity to go on a trip together.

The hillside we visited was a huge, vertical rock cliff by the seaside. To reach the cliff top, you had to climb another hill by its side. We parked our car at the lot which was at the bottom of the hill. It would take about twenty-five minutes to reach the top. I carried Eleanor at first, having no idea how heavy a one-year-old child could be. In five minutes, I was huffing and puffing. Seeing this, Michel, Lillian, Katie, and I all took turns to carry the child, finally reaching the hilltop.

There was a strong, cold breeze as we reached the top. The clothes I had worn weren't suitable for the weather conditions. The view of the sea from there was my first experience of seeing it from such a high elevation. You could clearly see the deep blue Mediterranean Sea stretched out toward the horizon from this cliff, which was five hundred meters above sea level.

Even though the scenery was beautiful, I was becoming worried about my next destination. In the coming days, how would my relationship with Katie develop? How long would Jean and Lillian keep me as their house guest? Despite my concerns, the stunning surroundings made me feel like I had been transported to a world I had never known.

From the same place, you could also see other coastal cities toward the east. There were green forests and other hills towards the north which reminded me of hills in Nepal. Other French families had also come for a picnic, just like us. Their presence added to my joy and sense of celebration.

During all this, Katie took every opportunity to make physical contact with me. Despite the fun we were having, the chilly wind was a problem. My main priority was to get down the hill to escape the cold and warm up. We finally came down after spending one and a half hours having a picnic lunch.

We then headed to a very famous sea beach in an area called Promenade des Anglaises.

The hotels and restaurants along the streets of Promenade des Anglaises were filled with customers. Across the street and to the south, there was a wide sandy beach that stretched out a long way. The people there spent their time swimming in the sea and lying down on the beach to get a suntan. This was an important and favorite way to spend their holidays.

We walked around and then headed to a café, spending hours talking and having coffee. I listened for the most part. During this time, Katie gave me her home phone number. She told me to call her the following week, and we would arrange to go out for lunch. I agreed and was desperate to meet with her alone.

In the evening, Jean Michel sometimes made dinner at home, and at other times took me to restaurants. I felt uncomfortable when the bill came. I couldn't pay even if I wanted to as I had very little money. The memory of lending money to my friends in Nepal was often in my thoughts. If I hadn't done so, I could have been happily paying my bills and at least showing some gratitude for their hospitality.

I didn't really have anything to do during the day. I would go to visit Marseilles by bus and then return in the evening. Later, Jean gave me a small Solex motorcycle and said, "This motorcycle gives a mileage of forty kilometers per liter. You can use this and visit any place you want."

Around two days after the picnic, I went to meet Katie at La Canbièrre Street during lunchtime. Her office was nearby. She came on foot, and we had lunch in a restaurant. Afterwards, she proposed a coffee at her place. I agreed. In fact, she had taken a day off from her office that day. Then I informed her that I had to get my Solex, which was parked in another place. She was surprised to hear this and asked, "How did you make such a long journey on the highway?"

I said, "It was easy. I took it slow." We went to her apartment on the Solex and spent some time talking intimately with one another. I had a feeling that she was a little different and was more distant from the person I had met earlier.

Because it would be very tough to ride the Solex on a busy highway, I left and returned to Jean Michel's before the traffic got heavy.

Just as I feared, the highway to Hospital Nord was quite busy because people were returning to their homes in the suburbs from their workplaces in the city. The road to Hospital Nord was the main highway that led to Paris from Marseilles.

There were no lamp posts on the road after I left the main city, and the highway was quite dark, only lights from the vehicles shone on the black pitch road. I slowly and safely rode my way back on the Solex. My friends were a little worried but were happy to see me. I said, "It was a little difficult and I got delayed because of the traffic." They didn't show much response. We sat down for dinner, and all three of us were quiet that night.

The Dinner I Never Had Before

One evening that week, Michel said that he would take me to a French restaurant for dinner and ordered the food himself. It was steak, and there were some rice and green vegetables on the side. The meat was thick and was served with wine sauce, which made the whole dish flavorful. I really enjoyed the meal.

After dinner, Michel asked me, "Do you know what meat you just ate?"

I said, "This must be beef."

He said, "No, this is horse meat!"

I was really enjoying the meat earlier but hearing what it was made me want to vomit. I kept my stomach in check with great difficulty. It was like sea waves crashing in my stomach. I felt a little better after I had coffee and dessert later.

Then we slowly headed home. We had drunk enough wine. At that time, it wasn't prohibited to drive under the minimum influence of alcohol. Still, people remained aware of their condition. Michel took us home safely.

That week, I used the Solex daily and visited many different places. Sometimes I met Katie for lunch. Jean Michel spoke with me in English. Lillian didn't know English, so I spoke with her only in French. It was the same with Katie, for she knew very little English.

In other places like cafes, restaurants, and shops that only used French to communicate, I became comfortable with the French language within two weeks. My confidence in using the language grew. I was slowly able to use the French words and create sentences that I had learned earlier in Nepal.

One Saturday, Jean Michel had prepared a plan to visit an important historic city called Avignon, which was on the northern side of Marseilles. On the way to Avignon, there was an airport. For the first time ever, they were landing a Boeing 747 as part of a test flight at eleven am in the morning. I had only heard about a Jumbo Jet but had never seen one.

In Nepal, I had heard that there was a new Boeing 747 aircraft that could accommodate five hundred passengers. I was very excited to see how the aircraft looked. We left our home in time. Arriving near the airport, we could see that the airplane was circling the sky, and we had the opportunity to see it landing.

That airplane looked two times larger than the largest aircraft I had ever seen. It was a delightful moment for me. I was in awe that such a large aircraft could fly in the sky.

After that, we headed north towards the city of Avignon and reached there at one pm. This city was situated on the banks of the Rhone River. There was a palace fort in dilapidated condition which was called the Pope's Palace. From the fourteenth century to the eighteenth century, the Catholic priests and Bishops had a dominant role in ruling the state, the religion, and the administration of the land which was centered in Avignon.

We went inside to see the palace fort which was constructed entirely of stones. I was overwhelmed to see a historical site that was hundreds of years old. I had only seen such monuments in movies and postcards. After that, we went to the center of the city, had lunch, and returned home. The journey of one hundred kilometers, along with walking all day, had made Jean Michel tired. We reached home safely in the evening. I felt like it was a fruitful day.

The next day, I went to Marseilles again. I called Katie but couldn't reach her. Therefore, I decided to go to another city called Cassis, which was near Marseilles. To go there, I had to take the coastal road of Promenade des Anglais where I had been before and then travelling twenty-five kilometers further. I went ahead along the coast, then from Avenue du Prado headed North.

The highway known as the Auto Route started from this point. I was racing ahead on my tiny Solex. Suddenly, I heard two police motorcycle sirens behind me. The cars and motorcycles of the traffic police always sounded deafening when using their sirens; since I had arrived in France, it was not something new for me.

I didn't pay much attention to the sirens because I had not run any red lights or made any other mistakes. The police suddenly drove in front of me, stopped me, and directly shouted 'Papiers Papiers (Papers Papers)' and pointed their hands towards me. I had no documents related to the motorcycle. Luckily, I had my passport, and I showed it to them. They conversed with each other, saying that I was a foreigner.

I pretended not to understand and looked at their faces while appearing clueless. Then the policeman said, "This is AutoRoute expressway, No Solex, No Solex!"

I understood and nodded my head and then said, "Pardon (sorry)" to them. They said, "OK, OK!" Then I returned home on the same motorcycle. Jean Michel was at home because it was Sunday. After I told them my story and described the incident, Jean and Michel laughed hard and said that the officers were correct. Solex was not permitted on the highway.

During the following days, I started using the long road to go to the marketplace and Marseilles. The next day, Jean Michel went back to his work, and I went to Marseilles. After parking my Solex, I went and explored new places. There was a plan to meet Katie at a café in the evening. I went there at the proper time.

Katie brought a French guy with her. She introduced him to me as her friend Jack. I greeted him with a smile. He responded with a smile. We ordered coffee. I was feeling a little uncomfortable, but to keep the environment positive, I pretended to be OK.

When Katie had gone to the toilet, Jack, who could speak English, said, "Siam, don't worry, I have two or three girlfriends, you can keep Katie for yourself."

I was awestruck to hear that so suddenly. On one hand, I wondered how this topic came up, and on the other hand, I had no immediate response to give. I kept quiet and exhibited a faint smile. I also began to understand what must have been happening in Katie's mind. She had returned by this time, and they had a little chat. Then Jack asked me why I had come to France, what places I had planned to visit, and how long I had planned to stay.

I had no answers for Jack and Katie. I hadn't revealed any of my plans to Katie. I had to say something, so I said I planned to go to the United States after staying for two or three more weeks in France. I saw Katie's facial expression change. We stayed there for a while and drank coffee. As I was not feeling very comfortable, I told them I had to be on my way and went to another café on Levieu Port. I drank a cup of coffee by myself.

I had already become friends with a waiter and waitress named Patrick and Lilie. After chatting with them for a while, I felt better about the awkward meeting with Katie and Jack.

After returning home to Jean Michel's, I felt empty and barren in my heart. This feeling continued for a few more days while living at Michel's house. Once again, Jean and Lillian took me on a tour to a city called Aix-En-Provence northeast of Marseille. It was also known as a small city of students. The main activity there revolved around trade, students, and tourists.

Aix-En-Provence was also called University City, and although it was small, it was beautiful. I really liked this city. Later, when I said that I had stayed in Marseilles for two months, all the French people asked me whether I had gone to Aix-En-Provence. I felt a deep satisfaction in replying "yes".

In the following days, I went to Marseilles on my own. Levieu Port is the innermost port of the city which connects to the main business street La Canbièrre. The seaside here is full of restaurants, hotels, and tourists.

I had already become friends with a waitress named Lilie. She was studying to become a doctor. During their student years, many of the young people worked part-time in restaurants and coffee shops.

There wasn't a very good salary, but they earned much more money through tipping.

I had experienced the importance of tipping when I was working in the casino in Nepal. I had developed a habit of tipping even when my financial situation didn't allow for this. This made it easy for me to get help and make friends anywhere I went.

My relationship with Lilie was developing well. I was affectionate with her, and she often came to have coffee with me in other cafes. Sometimes she took me home and hosted me with generosity. Despite having a good friend, I was feeling uneasy in view of my future in Marseille.

I was concerned about the days ahead and the lack of money. My mood kept swinging. Lilie understood this and thus one day she asked me if I wanted to work. By then, I was already thinking about how to leave Marseille and travel to Paris, eventually reaching America. Therefore, I declined her offer for work at a restaurant and let her know that I had to travel to Paris. I continued to meet Lilie occasionally. Patrick also used to offer me free coffee as he liked me as a traveler from Nepal.

I continued to pass my days staying with Jean Michel. One Saturday, Jean Michel and Lillian took me to a hilly area far from Marseille. We had lunch at their friend's house. These friends seemed to be living their lives as farmers even though it was a hilly region.

At eleven in the morning, we sat down at a wooden table in their garden which had a tablecloth, four types of wine along with some water. We started drinking and eating our appetizers. I was surprised to see so many varieties of food. Every small slice of cheese was unbelievably delicious. The cucumbers were sliced into very small pieces and placed one after another. It was like the salad I had in Milan, Italy.

There were also boiled eggs from which the yolk was powdered and sprinkled on top; all surprisingly tasty. There are cucumbers and there are eggs in Nepal as well. Why don't the Nepali people know how to combine these items which makes it taste so delicious? There were also sliced tomatoes prepared in a salad with Italian cheese and seven different varieties of sausage similarly sliced into small pieces. There was also a variety of cheese.

All this food was a bit overwhelming, and I was not sure what to eat first. Hours were spent eating; they kept on adding more wine to our glasses. Only at one pm did the main course, called Boeuf Bourguignon, arrive. No words can adequately praise this food for me. I kept on saying to myself how tasty the meat was. It was like a thick chicken or mutton curry but was faintly sweet and I really enjoyed it.

Sitting at the table, eating delicious food, and drinking wine all day, I was unable to move by the time dessert was brought around five pm. I was now able to understand the popular belief that French meals were grand. Later, I had four more similar meals with other French families.

A few days later, I heard Jean Michel and Lillian whispering in their room. They were wondering how much longer I was going to stay with them and where I would travel next. From the beginning, I had already told Jean Michel that I was going to travel to the United States next.

I was supposed to write a letter to my friend Bhagat Gorkhali who was in the U.S., but I had forgotten to do so, and I now felt the urgency to write to him. I immediately prepared a letter, sent an express letter from the post office. I informed him that I had arrived in France and mentioned that I would be ready to leave in the following two weeks for the United States.

I also asked him to write an "Invitation Letter" needed in the visa process. I then requested that he send some money if possible. On the same day, I informed Jean Michel that I had written to my friend Bhagat and informed him that departure from France would be arranged in one or two weeks.

Jean Michel passed this information on to his wife, and the evening was well spent. I had many concerns going through my mind at bedtime: What if I didn't receive a reply from the US? I didn't have enough money to get back to Nepal. How long will I stay here? The opportunities here are not promising. It was also quite shameful for me to stay on with Jean Michel like this. I also felt that Jean Michel and Lillian must have had some conversation about the confused state of my travel plans and destinations.

More days passed this way. My pocket money slowly started decreasing. I expected a reply to my letter every day, but it never came. Keeping my economic situation in mind, I distanced myself from meeting Katie. The memory of meeting her friend Jack, and listening to what he had to say, while trying to understand the meaning, kept bothering me from time to time.

1.1.3 Looming Crisis

Various Steps To Overcome

I realized I must look for other possibilities. Suddenly, I remembered the manager of a casino in France. He had come to visit Casino Nepal when I was working there in Kathmandu. I met with him, and we became friends. Upon hearing the description of Les Bains from him, I explained that I planned to visit France and would like to meet him there. He was very friendly, and I was hopeful in turn. In my mind, I had the feeling that he could find me a job if he wanted to. I had carried his visiting card with me while leaving Nepal. I wrote him a letter.

To convince Jean Michel that I was looking for other alternatives, as well as America, I showed him the letter I had written. I asked for his suggestions. He said that it was alright but had deleted the part where I had requested a reply. Jean Michel explained to me that it was a French tradition to never ask for a reply because that person will reply only if he or she wants to; you cannot pressure them to do so.

I sent the letter to the manager in just the way Jean had approved it and hoped for some kind of reply. Even though I didn't ask for a reply, the manager sent a letter back to me which said, "I understand that you have arrived in France, and I am happy to hear that. There is no possibility for me to find you a job even if I wanted to. I hope that your journey ahead will be successful and enjoyable." Reading it saddened my heart once more.

In desperation, I wrote another letter to my friend in America and urgently appealed to him by writing, 'I am in a heap of trouble. I must get out of Marseille very soon. Therefore, please help me.' I received no reply.

Early one morning, I had another idea: I will sell my Seiko wristwatch. This will bring me enough money for simple food, drinks, and bus fare for a few more days. I also wrote to my friends in Nepal to immediately repay the six hundred dollars that I had loaned them; this would be enough for me to go back to Nepal and make another round trip from Nepal to France.

After that, I went to my regular café in Marseille. My watch was very beautiful and in a golden color which looked like real gold. The design was quite modern as well. I was sitting at a small table having coffee, and there was a large table by the side where a group of young boys and girls were enjoying their coffee. Some of them paid attention to me, and I greeted them with a 'hello' and a smile. I also noticed that some of them already had their eyes on my watch.

One of them came to my table and started inquiring about me. He was shocked to hear that I had come all the way from Nepal, and he mentioned it to his group of friends as well. During our conversation, he looked at my watch and in French said that he liked it and asked me if I wanted to sell it. I showed a little hesitation but said that I could do so if he really wanted to buy it.

By this time, everyone's attention was concentrated on the watch. Either sex could wear it. My boss at the casino, Al Mattocks, had bought it for me from Bangkok for twenty-five dollars. When the guy asked me the price, I calculated wrong and asked for two hundred francs. He hesitated for a while. At the same time, his friends said they would buy it if he didn't. Then he said that he was buying it and gave me cash. After a while, all of them left.

When I sat down and calculated properly, I discovered that it had only cost me one hundred twenty-five Francs because at that time one dollar was equal to five Francs. I had made a good profit on my cost price. Coffee cost only one Franc at the time. When I left the café looking at my empty wrist, I was sad.

When I shared the watch story with Jean Michel, he was unsure of his reaction. Two days earlier he had assumed that I had spent all my money. When leaving the house, he had given me a ten Franc note and said to me, 'Shyam my friend, take this, if you don't even have ten francs in your pocket, they will call you a vagabond.' I took the ten Franc note without saying anything.

I stayed with Jean and Lillian for four more days. It was time for me to leave, for I had stayed with them for over a month. I then decided to go to a youth hostel. I also remembered that my boss from the casino in Nepal, Al Mattock, was in England. He had finished the job in Nepal and had returned to London. Luckily, I had his London phone number. I called him and upon hearing that I had already reached France, he laughed hard and said, 'Good Boy.' Then he laughed again. I shared with him the entire story of my journey since I had left Nepal. He said 'alright' and told me to go to the post office the next day where he would send me some money. Just as he promised, I was sent two hundred Francs the very next day. I was so relieved and ready for the upcoming days.

I found a youth hostel. It was in the coastal area called Promenade des Anglaises which I knew very well. I told Jean Michel that I was leaving their home to stay in the hostel. A youth hostel in the French language is called Auberge De La Jeunesse. I left some of my stuff with him and went to stay in the hostel.

I had fun when I reached there. It was just like any other youth hostel in other cities filled with young boys and girls; you could always hear some kind of music and happy chatter in the evening. There was always some sort of dance program happening as well. It was easy to spend time there.

On the second morning of my stay there, I walked a long way along the coastline and then sat down at a restaurant for lunch. I was hungry and decided to order the famous delicacy of the city, which I had already experienced called Bouillabaisse. It was prepared with different types of fish combined and at the same time soup was added. I hadn't become accustomed to the taste, but I thought it would be alright to eat even though there was limited opportunity for me to eat fish in Nepal.

When I returned to the hostel in the evening, I met with a Moroccan guy. We introduced ourselves and started to chat. I felt relieved to share my story with him concerning my troubled state which I had been in for quite a while. He was older than me and looked very handsome.

I felt strange when he said that it had been a week since he arrived at Marseille; he had come straight to the hostel from the port and never left the place once. I said, 'So you have not been to the city center of Marseille?'

He then replied, 'Oh! I won't go there. There are a lot of thugs and hooligans in the city of Marseille. I will return home after spending a week right here by the coast.' I was quite surprised to hear this. Though he was a mature man with a strong body, he was scared to visit the central parts of Marseille.

I then remembered an old Nepali proverb: Even though the elephant is large, it cannot be eaten.

A German Girl At The Beach, A Lifetime Memory

The next day, I went to the beach area which can be reached by crossing the broad street of Promenade Des Anglaises. Many young people, couples, and families had gathered there from France and other European countries. They were swimming and sunbathing, spending hours on the sandy beach. They only wore bikinis; they used sunblock and lay flat or face down with their towels as bed sheets.

I was enjoying the sand with my bare feet when a girl called me by signaling to me. When I was near her, she requested that I apply oil onto her body. She was only wearing a bikini bottom and no top. She was very beautiful, standing at around five feet eight inches. I had only seen such a beautiful girl in English magazines. In fact, there were miles upon miles where you could see hundreds of half-naked women. It was like this every day on that beach.

When seeing her and then hearing her request, I was surprised and confused. It was an unexpected situation. She then requested this again, and I said 'OK!'."

I slowly rubbed oil all over her body. Fifteen minutes had already passed since I had begun rubbing. She didn't say anything; she continued to lay comfortably on the sand with her eyes closed. I also decided to continue rubbing as long as she didn't say anything. My head started spinning with an intense desire.

I stopped the oil rubbing and it was only then that she started to talk a little. She asked me which country I had come from and was really surprised when I said Nepal. She said, 'You are a brave traveler to have come from such a faraway country.' She also mentioned that she had come from Germany for a few weeks of vacation.

Coincidentally, she was staying in the same hostel that I was staying in. I thought that I would like to invite her for dinner in the evening if she was free. I said nothing, however, because of the importance of every single penny I had at the time.

I had already spent an hour in the blazing sun. My body and my mind were going haywire. I couldn't stay there for any more time. I mentioned to her that we could meet again in the hostel since we stayed in the same one and then left immediately. There was an auto photo kiosk on the other side of the road; I clicked a photo there. When I looked at the photograph of myself, I was shocked at how dark I had become.

I wanted to search for the German girl that evening in the hostel. I was sitting in the garden but couldn't muster up the courage to find her. After a while, I saw her with her five German friends leaving the hostel. They looked like they were going out for dinner and then to a dance party later.

I had no intention of being involved in these activities. I just kept looking at them cluelessly.

When I saw her the next day with her group of friends at breakfast, we exchanged greetings. She then asked me where I had been last evening. I said that I was in the hostel itself. Her group was leaving Marseilles the same day. We said goodbye to each other. She had given me an experience I had never expected in life. After this incident, she remained in my thoughts for many days!

After staying in the hostel for a week, Michel called me back to his home again. One day, Jean Michel invited me to his workplace and showed me what his job consisted of. At dinner time, he asked if I liked this kind of work. 'If you do like it, then I can teach you. There is no lack of jobs. I can also ask my boss if he needs more workers. You can earn some money as well.' Unfortunately, I couldn't work as hard as was needed, as well as cope with the bricks and cement.

I also have acrophobia so while working three or four floors above the ground would be an impossible task. I couldn't even stand high above the ground for a while. Along with all this, I was suffering from mental stress. I met Katie one or two more times for coffee. These meetings didn't lead to any improvement in our relationship. Consequently, our meetings gradually vanished. I did continue to meet Lilie, my waitress friend, occasionally.

Looking back at all of this, I did have the opportunity to see and learn new things. I also went by train to see the world-famous Casino de Monte Carlo, hoping that some of the ideas from there could be applied to the casino back in Nepal.

1.2 ON TO AND IN PARIS

Au Revoir Marseilles, En Route To Paris

I had already received some money from Al Mattocks before leaving Marseilles. I told Jean and Lillian that I was leaving for Paris and would do whatever was necessary there. They agreed and let me go. Jean and his wife Lillian were relieved, as well as saddened to see me leave. Jean told me that I could stay at his grandmother's place in Paris for a few days. He explained to me that she was eighty-two years old and therefore had to make my own arrangements within a few days after arriving in Paris. This made me so delighted, and I boarded the night train for Paris.

During the journey, I alternated between falling asleep and staying awake. The train went through the underground time and time again, which was the first experience of its kind for me in my life. At dawn, the outskirts of Paris began to appear. There were many twenty and thirty-story buildings, and I knew I was about to arrive in a big city. After a while, the train reached Gare de Lyon station in Paris.

'Gare' means train station in French. Most of the trains that came from the southern side of France were stationed here. The passengers that arrived here went down to the underground to get the metro for different parts of the city. They also took medium and long-range trains to reach faraway places. The metro station that took me to my destination was close. I had to leave the main station and change the metro after five stations. At that time, I had no idea of how to get to Jean Michel's grandmother. Therefore, I asked some people at the station and showed them the address. They guided me as to where to go, where to change, and which direction to follow to get the correct metro. Since they were speaking French, I understood most of what they said and boarded the metro.

The door made an alarming noise as it closed. It was just like Milan, the rucksack on my back had remained outside of the door. Some of the passengers shouted 'bag, bag.' Suddenly the door opened itself and somebody pulled my rucksack inside. I was dumbfounded. I remembered the incident in Milan with Maria.

Finally, after changing stations, I arrived at 'Sato Do' metro station. Leaving the underground, I reached the main street Boulevard De Strasbourg and started searching for Michel's grandma's address; house Number Eighty-Six. On my left were the even numbered houses while the odd numbered houses were right beside me in serial order.

I went through the houses and found house Number Eighty-Six.

French Cultural Lessons

Just as Jean had instructed, upon reaching house Number Eighty-Six, I climbed to the first floor, went to the apartment on the right side, and pressed the bell at the door, then waited; no one came. Had something happened to Jean's grandma, who was already an eighty-two-year-old lady? Where do I go if I don't meet her? What would I do? Many questions started coming to me.

I pressed the bell again, after a while, no one came! I heard nothing inside. I just kept standing there. After a long time, the door opened slowly for a few inches. An old lady with scanty eyes peeked at me from inside. I mentioned Jean Michel and said to her in French, 'I am Shyam, Jean Michel's friend.'

After that, she opened the door wide and invited me in. I was so relieved; otherwise, I would have begun to worry about where I would be able to eat and sleep in this new and strange city of Paris.

I talked to Michel's grandma for a while. Although I was hungry, I dared not ask her to prepare food for me. Grandma brought coffee while we were seated there. After the coffee and a few more minutes of chat, I left to find a restaurant and have some food.

I found one nearby on the right side of the street which had the sign 'Self-Service Restaurant'. Inside the restaurant, you had to get your own tray, pick up a plate of prepared food, place it on the tray, and then get water, wine, or juice as desired. You would pay accordingly at the end of the buffet table at the cash counter.

This was another first kind of experience for me, and I found it accessible and efficient. Unlike other restaurants, you did not have to wait long after ordering your food, there were no waiter services, and the meal cost was cheaper. It was an appropriate place for someone traveling on a low budget with less time. I went back to the self-service restaurant frequently.

When I was returning to Grandma's apartment after visiting the city all day, I saw on the street lines upon lines of girls exhibiting their breasts and thighs to lure customers towards them. The street Bd Strasbourg was the center for women who were involved in the profession of prostitution. They were in groups of eight or ten along the street.

Whenever a man passed by, they would say, 'Tu Viens, Cheri?' 'Do you want to come with me, darling?' Most of the girls were of African descent, and there were quite a few white girls too. During my first few days, I was a little scared of them, but later I became accustomed to the scene. Sometimes there were beautiful girls.

If you gave a slight look, they immediately said 'Tu Viens, Cheri'. After a few days, some of them recognized me as a local resident. They smiled at me without saying a thing. I replied with a smile too.

Michel's grandma couldn't walk very well as she was quite old, however, her brain was sharp. The next day after meeting Grandma, I kept some of my money for expenses at her apartment during my visit to the city. I wanted to leave a five hundred Franc note for safekeeping with her. I was afraid the money might become lost or stolen.

Just as I was leaving the apartment, she asked me to wait. Grandma went inside the room without saying anything. She brought a pen and paper from inside the room. I was curious to know what she was doing. She requested that I sit down. She shakily wrote the following thing on the paper: 'On this date today, Shyam Shrestha has given me five hundred Francs for safekeeping at my house, this money belongs to him.' She then folded the paper, put it into an envelope, and showing me, placed it in the safe.

I was surprised and said to her, 'You didn't need to write this, I trust you.' In response, she said, 'If anything happens to me, what proof will you have that this money belongs to you? That's why I have written this for you.' I was awestruck to hear this. I was impressed with how honest and careful she was even at her age. My heartfelt respect for Grandma was enormous.

This was an example of French culture with honesty; I had experienced this for the first time. Later, after I started working in France, I learned a lot about French culture. While staying at her apartment for four days, she taught me how to sit at a dinner table and how to behave with people according to French tradition.

Michel's grandma also taught me that I should sit straight at a dinner table and not place my hands on the table while eating. If we did have to place our hands on the table, she showed me the correct position.

She also taught me that when you go to someone else's house for dinner, you should not start eating before the hostess of the house. While drinking wine or water, you should wipe your lips with a napkin so that an oily substance doesn't stick to the edge of a glass. This would prevent other guests from being in discomfort with the site of a dirty glass.

Grandma also told me how to properly set a wine glass, spoon, and fork on the table. I also learned from her what types of spoons, knives, and forks to use while having different types of food.

For someone like me who was from Nepal, habituated to eating while using hands and sitting on the floor, Grandma was the first one who taught me how to eat in French style while seated at the dining table. I also learned how to place specific guests in their appropriate seats at the dinner table.

As a host, you had to be seated at the far end of the table, towards your right the highest honored guest's wife would be seated. Towards your left, the wife of the second highest honored guest, while your own wife would be seated at the other end of the table. On her right would be the highest honored guest and the second highest honored guest would be on the left of the table.

During my stay in Paris, I learned simple but valuable lessons in life. For example, you must always greet a person well whether you know them or not using the words: good morning, thank you, and sorry at every opportunity. Later, I also taught my children these table manners and other similarly practical things.

Michel's grandma also shared with me knowledge about other French cultural practices and rituals. For example, if a person requests another person to deliver his letter, then that person should deliver the letter keeping the envelope open. This means that the letter doesn't contain anything offensive. Meanwhile the person receiving the letter must close the envelope in front of the deliverer and keep it in his pocket. This means that the receiver wants the deliverer to believe that he trusts him, it doesn't matter if the letter is open. In this manner I was able to learn the ritualistic behaviors along with the modern traditions in the lifestyle of France.

Staying at Youth Hostel

Jean Michel had told me when leaving Marseilles that I could only stay for three or four days with his grandma. It was time to find my own space; his grandma was too old, and I didn't want to give her more trouble.

After a few days of staying at Grandma's house, I searched for a youth hostel in the center of Paris and stayed there. I have forgotten the name, but I do remember that it was right in the center of the Latin Quarter, near Sorbonne University.

I got a first-floor room at the hostel. The stairs to the other floors were going up right past the front of my room. I could see people passing in front of my window. It was cheap to stay in that hostel. It was crowded with different types of youngsters from different parts of the world just like the previous hostels I had stayed in. Therefore, I felt comfortable staying there.

There was the provision of cooking gas and other kitchen utensils. In other places there had been a separate spacious kitchen which was common to all. I bought some items like rice, soup packets, some vegetables, and meat from the outside to cook in the kitchen. I decided to have rice and soup on the first morning of my stay there. I cooked the rice and a young foreigner stood on the stairway and asked me what I was cooking. I replied to him that it was rice.

He said 'alright' and headed upstairs smiling. After my morning food, I would visit famous and important places near Paris. Upon returning that evening I cooked rice again along with the packaged vegetables. The same guy was taking the stairs again that evening. He asked once again what I was cooking. I replied that it was rice. He then replied to me with surprise, 'You are cooking rice again!?' and I replied yes. Then he continued upstairs laughing.

The next day I thought, I would rather cook here at the hostel so that I don't have to go to any restaurants, and in that way, I won't spend a lot of money. Once again at around eleven am I decided to cook rice, soup, and some meat.

The same guy was going upstairs after buying his lunch outside. As always, he asked me, "What are you cooking today?" I said, "rice and meat". He was stunned. Then he asked, rice again? I told him that we ate rice every day, all year long in Nepal. It was our staple diet.

He looked at me cluelessly and went upstairs smiling once more. In the following days he stopped asking me the same question while I was cooking and eating. For ten days I ate all my morning meals at the hostel before heading out to visit various important locations in Paris, returning to the hostel in the evening.

Paris: The City Of Art And Beauty

Paris, the capital of France, was beautiful. It is spread on both banks of the river Seine. Paris was also known by different names. Among them, it was also called "La Ville-Lumière', which meant the city of lights. The development of Paris started around two thousand years ago and was established by the Celtic tribal community.

By 1200 AD, the University of Paris had already been established. Due to all these factors Paris had become the center of education, culture, and art from the Middle Ages. The Romans at one time had captured Paris. This evidence is found in the remains of houses and palaces of the Latin Quarter. The Latin Quarter is very famous for mixing with young people as It has many educational centers, cafés and the Luxembourg garden and most importantly the Sorbonne University.

Many types of revolution occurred in France at different times. Among them the revolution of seventeen eighty-nine during the rule of King Louis the sixteenth had brought a significant outcome and established France as a republic. That revolution had ended the feudalistic and autocratic monarchy which then established the republican system. As a result of this revolution, the king and queen both received death sentences.

As the revolution was the first of its kind, it has created a long-lasting impression for the global fight for freedom and is therefore considered one of the most important worldwide events. During my stay in France, I regularly visited historical monuments. Some of those places have been discussed below.

Notre Dame Cathedral

My visits to the historical monuments in Paris began with this Cathedral. I arrived at the cathedral after walking directly south for half an hour from Michel's grandma's apartment. This cathedral in Paris was a heritage site built in France during the Middle Ages. It is a grand monument filled with art, stained glass windows, and sculptures.

The foundation of this church was laid down by Pope Alexander the Third in the year eleven hundred sixty-three AD. It is known that the entire construction took almost ninety years to complete. In this very church built in the Gothic style, Napoleon Bonaparte declared himself the king of France and put on the royal crown in the year eighteen hundred and four AD.

The height of this cathedral is two hundred and thirty-three feet. I was really stunned when I went inside for the first time; it looked like you could fit the Dharahara of Nepal inside.

Eiffel Tower

One morning after breakfast I went out to see the world-famous Eiffel Tower which was considered the signature monument of Paris. From a distance, the structure looked like a tall electric transmission tower made from iron truss; it was the symbol of Paris. This tower represents the recognition of the city of Paris. It was designed by French engineer Gustave Eiffel. This structure was made for the World Exhibition Center which opened in Paris in eighteen hundred and eighty-nine AD.

Ten thousand tons of steel pieces were used. It was constructed with the plan of dismantling it after the exhibition. Later, because of its beauty and tourist attraction, it was decided that it would be kept intact. The tower is nearly three hundred thirty-three meters tall. It is amazingly beautiful, below the tower is a garden area as big as the Tundikhel in Nepal which is well decorated and covered with trees on all sides. I spent hours visiting this place. The view of the city from this tower makes anyone exclaim with joy and wonder.

I met a Japanese girl there. She spoke very little English. We visited the tower together and then went down to the street. She had arrived only a few days earlier with her group. This was her second visit to the tower as she was really impressed by it. I felt a little lonely after she left. While visiting with her, the environment felt calm, the conversation was polite and civilized and the time was well spent. Most of the French girls I had met were skittish and too talkative. I wondered how nice it would be and fun for us if we could spend three or four more days visiting different places together. But the hope was shattered.

After that, I crossed the bridge over the Seine River in front of the Eiffel Tower. Climbing up from there you arrive at Esplanade De Trocadero. There were two dozen water fountains spraying huge amounts of water towards the top of Eiffel Tower. This scenery and the overall structures constructed in the pond were breathtaking. Some people were playing with water under the fountains. Seeing them up close I was even more surprised; the size of the water sprouts was as large as cannons.

From there, climbing the stairs which were made of huge stones and then reaching Esplanade De Trocadero you find a huge exhibition square with the flooring made of white, sleek, and square granite. You could see a very beautiful view of the Eiffel Tower from there. This area was constructed eighty to a hundred meters away from the River Seine. Hundreds of people were taking pictures in this square with the Eiffel Tower as a background. I had a wonderful time as a tourist at this place and finally returned to my hostel in the evening.

Montmartre Hill

The topography of Paris is almost all flat, but some places also consist of small inclines and hills. Among the highest was a small hill called Montmartre which was situated in the northern region of Paris. One early morning I left my hostel early and planned to reach this hilltop. The place is at the highest elevation in the city of Paris. It is at a height of one hundred meters above sea level.

On top of the hill was a religious church named Sacre Coeur Basilica. The construction was begun in eighteen hundred and fourteen and concluded in eighteen hundred and seventy AD. To reach the top of this place you could either walk the hundreds of stairs or take a vehicle. From the vantage point of the Basilica, you could see the eastern, western, and southern parts of Paris. The view included grand heritage sites along with the Eiffel Tower.

The outer walls of the Basilica were covered with granite rocks. Anyone viewing Paris while standing at this place is sure to become spellbound. Sketch artists and painters crowded the area. There were hundreds of people capturing the city of Paris on their canvases, sitting on the stairs or sitting on the grass. There were also artists who sketched people and then charged them money.

Montmartre was full of small restaurants, cafes, and souvenir shops. Some people spent their entire day in this famous place having lots of fun.

During the following days, I gradually started walking more, looking at the map and then going to the monuments nearby the hostel: Place de St. Sulpice, St Placide, Sorbonne University and the Luxembourg Gardens. I also visited the palace along with the Pantheon and finally a very large tomb with Dome style roof.

One such day I was walking along a footpath. It was spacious and less crowded. Suddenly a huge black Mercedes car stopped right in front of me; a middle-aged man opened the door and invited me in. I asked him why. He said that I looked like a tourist, and he could give me a free tour of the city. I had a cold feeling about it and said, no, thank you. Still, he slowly followed me. I ignored him and kept marching ahead. Later, I understood that these people preferred boys instead of girls. This type of incident happened a few more times as well. Later, I stopped making eye contact when such vehicles stopped in front of me.

Most of the time I ate my meals at the hostel. For convenience, I cooked pasta sauteed in butter along with a couple of eggs. I found it so delicious that I always ate more than was required and then had to lay down flat on the bed. One day I ate so much my stomach was swollen to the point that I had to vomit. Suddenly I remembered an incident that had happened during my stay at Bhimphedi in Nepal. I had seen a snake with a piece of stone in his stomach that he obviously couldn't digest. I imagined myself in the same situation as the snake lying in the bed for hours. I cursed myself for my stupidity in eating so much.

I had already become familiar with the Latin Quarter which was considered a famous center for the gathering of youth in Paris. People also visited many cafes in the area. My three-month visa was about to expire so I had to extend. I was a little anxious and began to think about what I would do next. All plans of going to the United States had been shattered.

In the hope that the staff of the Nepali Embassy in France would shelter me for a few days, I went there. I searched for a long time and finally met with the First and then the Second Secretary. There I knowingly or unknowingly made a mistake. I almost always wore T-shirts and pants. That day I was wearing a Daura without sleeves along with pants. I suddenly realized as I reached the Embassy that the staff would question seeing me in such clothes! Since I had arrived in France, this was the first time that I had worn this type of clothes. To change, I had to return to the hostel, it would cost me hours of time.

I headed inside the Embassy ready to face any situation there.

The first secretary then was Mr. Sundarnarh Bhattarai. I explained my situation to him. He asked me to meet with the Ambassador and sent me upstairs to his room. I reiterated my situation with the Ambassador. His name was Shardul Shumsher Rana. He was listening to me while smoking a cigarette that was in between his middle and index finger. He asked me why I had come to France without a return ticket to Nepal.

I explained to him that I had arrived in France taking the land route and had planned to go on to America. I also explained that the friend who had invited me hadn't responded to my letter. That was why I was in trouble. I also told him that I was returning to Nepal via the land route and didn't have a single return ticket. Finally, in contrast to my faint hope he said, we can't do anything about this here. I left there feeling very frustrated.

Later, I came to know that the help I was expecting from the Embassy was impossible. There were rumors spreading around the Embassy that a Nepali guy named Shyam Shrestha had become penniless after arriving in France. A dark stain for me was put on all my French discoveries. This rumor had finally reached my parents in Nepal, which caused them to panic. The Nepali Ambassador had also heavily criticized my attire on that day. Bihari Raj Rajbhandari who was also living in France at the time told me all about this forty years later.

After leaving the Embassy I went directly to a cafe called Le Petit Cluny in the Latin Quarter. There was a gathering of youths from Vietnam, Cambodia, as well as local French. There was a group of French and Vietnamese youth near my table. We slowly began talking after saying hello to each other.

They asked me which country I was from and invited me to their table when I said Nepal. They had assumed that I was from Vietnam too but became excited when learning my nationality. They asked me a variety of questions about Nepal. Some of them also asked me about the political system in Nepal.

I said that there was an absolute monarchy. I was embarrassed to say that I belonged to a country with such an old political system in such modern times.

Then during the conversation, I told them of my visit to the Embassy and the situation I was in. An older Vietnamese named Daniel said to me, "Don't worry, we are here for you. We have all come from Asia."

Then I shared with them that I had no problem for a few days. I did want a cheaper place to stay so one of the Vietnamese invited me to live with him at his place. He said that he had a spacious room along with a good kitchen and toilet facilities. This provided me with such a relief.

I spent a lot of time with them in the cafe. Then they made a program to go to another place and asked me if I wanted to join. I agreed as I had nothing else to do. Even though most of them were Vietnamese, there were some French boys and girls in the group. All of us left and went to another place across the street which was called Le Grand Clunny. It was a larger café and restaurant than the previous one. In fact, as the group became larger the group that had gathered at Le Petit Cluny moved to Le Grand Clunny.

With or without my new friends, Le Petit Cluny became a place for me to rest and keep my mind occupied when I didn't have anything else to do. The waiters and waitresses had become like friends to me. In those days, the waiters were referred to as 'Garçon', which means 'boy' in English. However, I never used that word; I always said, 'excuse me'. Over time, this tradition of calling a waiter 'Garçon' has disappeared. Instead, they use the word 'Monsieur', which means 'Sir' or 'Gentleman'. I have been really impressed with this cultural development in use today.

People were not allowed to stay too long in the youth hostels. So, I shifted to Daniel's apartment, my Vietnamese friend. He provided me with his space for two weeks. There was one large room along with two beds: one large and one small. I got the small one. It was convenient for me to cook as well.

Once again, I wrote to my friends in Nepal to repay me the money that I had loaned them, but I never received a reply. I was already beginning to worry that I would have to leave Daniel's room within a few days.

The area in which I was staying was called The Latin Quarter. It was frequented by many tourists. There was also the world-famous Sorbonne University. There were many French and foreign students from different parts of the world studying there.

In the youth revolution of 1968, the students at this university had actively participated and were later able to dethrone the then President Charles De Gaulle using a referendum.

Some of the Vietnamese friends were students while others had jobs. Even though I thought of asking them to help me find a job I never did.

There were many Vietnamese people frequenting The Latin Quarter area. There were innumerable tiny Vietnamese, Chinese, Indian, and Arabian restaurants in the gullies there. As I visited Le Petit Cluny regularly, I made friends with Vietnamese, as well as French youngsters.

I also developed a friendship with an African man who was much older than me. He loved flirting with girls but didn't dare to talk to them. Therefore, he took me everywhere with him and made me talk with the girls! I wasn't courageous enough to talk to girls, however, I talked to them without hesitation upon his requests.

Our initial point of conversation was, "How are you? Where are you from?" If the girls responded well and smiled, then we'd say, "Would you like to go with us to a Jazz Bar?" Some of them said 'Sure' and some others responded with a 'No' and left smiling.

Since the African guy had no shortage of funds, he spent his money in the bar on both of us. We used to ask many girls at night if they wanted to join us. I had to approach the girls exclusively. We mostly spoke with foreign girls. Even when they didn't want to join us, they were not rude.

It was a little more difficult to flirt with the French girls. American and Scandinavian girls were much more fun-loving and often joined in with us. We had a good time, although, occasionally, and suddenly, I would feel like a vagabond.

Then one day I said to my African friend, "How long will I be the only one to begin the conversation with girls, you should try as well."

He replied to me, "Listen Shyam! I am an aged guy, and I am not as good looking as you are. The girls do not respond to me very well when I talk to them."

I kept quiet after hearing this. A few girls were in that café sitting nearby us and having coffee when my friend tried to initiate a conversation with them saying, "Do you think my friend is handsome" and pointed at me. I was amused as the only time I had seen him initiate a conversation was because it was focused on me.

Fortunately, the girls were smiling and said., "Yes…Yes…! He is very handsome."

Then he used my sentence and said, ""Would you like to go to a Jazz Bar with us?".

This time the girls said, "We are sorry, we are busy."

This was the way I spent some of my days with my African friend. I spent most of the other days with my Vietnamese and French friends. Sometimes we went to a disco at night to dance. There were an equal number of boys and girls, so when it got too late in the night we separated into small groups and slept at different friends' places in cramped spaces.

Sometimes I would go alone to other friends' houses. The environment and atmosphere of The Latin Quarter was so much fun.

One day I was introduced to a Danish girl at the hostel, who was quite fun. During the conversation I asked her if she had a boyfriend. She said that she had a boyfriend, but she also said that Danish girls never believed in having a single boyfriend.

We both laughed very hard and then spent the day walking and visiting different areas of Paris. I wanted to continue my relationship, but I knew that with the little money I had this wouldn't be possible.

One evening Daniel and I were having dinner at a small restaurant. Two Swedish girls were also enjoying their dinner at an adjacent table. They were stunningly beautiful. We knew their nationality after we started the conversation with 'hi' and 'hello'. They had just arrived earlier that day.

As Paris was a new place for them, they asked many questions about the city, and we answered their questions. Later, during the conversation, they agreed to go to a dance party with us, so after dinner we went to a discotheque nearby. We added a colorful spectrum to the night along with drinking and dancing.

During the dance, we felt like we were couples, enjoying the moment together. We reached their hotel much later in the night and stayed there for a while. We also drank the wine that was in their room. It was already five am when Daniel and I returned to our place with very fond memories.

The next evening, we went to the hotel where the girls were staying. They weren't there. We waited for a while, but they never arrived, so we left.

That night we went to the same discotheque. The Swedish girls were dancing with some other boys. Daniel became frustrated upon seeing this and he shouted out. I consoled him by saying that Scandinavian girls love their freedom.

One night, feeling very bored, I found myself wandering near the junction heading off to Pigalle. After five minutes, I encountered a woman on the footpath. She was strikingly beautiful, with a well-proportioned figure, a hint of lipstick on her lips, and captivating bright eyes. We exchanged smiles, and she asked, "Hello, which country are you from?" I replied, "Nepal."

She approached me, and we engaged in conversation. After a few minutes, she invited me for coffee at her place, and I followed her without hesitation. In a matter of minutes, we were climbing the stairs to her apartment, which overlooked the street. She led me to her room. Upon entering, I felt a pang of unease. The room was bathed in a red light, overly decorated. Despite my initial impression, I didn't think she was a professional sex worker; her demeanor was different. Unlike street prostitutes who wear excessive makeup and provocative attire, she showed no such signs.

She removed her coat and hung it on a hanger, her body language suggesting an invitation. She spoke, revealing that she wasn't a professional, but sometimes engaged in such encounters out of necessity. Then, in broken French, she requested fifty francs. I hesitated, feeling a mix of emotions. Addressing her, I noted that she was still wearing her skirt suspenders, which bothered me. She responded with affection, calling me 'darling,' and mentioned that removing them would cost an additional ten francs.

Despite my reservations, I was drawn to her warmth. Our intimate encounter provided a temporary respite from my depression, leaving me feeling rejuvenated both physically and mentally.

French Visa Was About To Expire

Even though I was enjoying life on the outside, my real problems were weighing me down. I had always been anxious about what to do and where to go next. The fear of being caught by the police for overstaying my visa loomed over me constantly. One day, while visiting the banks of the Seine River, I witnessed a police officer questioning a black man and scrutinizing his documents. Witnessing this scene filled me with a sense of dread. I quickly averted my gaze and hurried away, pretending not to have noticed. Seeking solace, I retreated to my regular coffee shop, where I sat down and pondered why I had left Nepal without a solid plan. I questioned why I hadn't brought enough money with me and why I had lent my own funds to others just before departing. Lost in thought, I spent two hours sipping coffee and reflecting on these matters.

One Of My Godfathers Came In

In 1969, while working as a croupier at a casino, I met a French couple named Jean and Anne who were visiting Kathmandu. They had come to the casino to gamble, and we struck up a friendship. Knowing that I planned to visit France, they became closer to me. When they faced a difficult situation after their money was stolen at the hotel, I helped them by giving them five hundred rupees.

Despite their misfortune, I showed them around Kathmandu and invited them to restaurants several times. At that time, five hundred rupees was a significant amount of money. I remember distinctly that ten grams or one tola of gold cost around one hundred and sixty-five rupees. This is etched in my memory because I crafted my first gold ring at the age of eleven, using thirty-three grams of gold that I purchased with my own money.

After spending some time together, Jean and Anne returned to France, and I became absorbed in my own work, gradually forgetting about them.

While drinking coffee at Le Petit Cluny, I suddenly remembered Jean and Anne. I searched for Jean and found his name in the phone book. He came to visit me at Le Petit Cluny the very next day. He was quite shocked and very happy to see me in Paris; I was very happy and relieved to see him.

Jean took me to his home and introduced me to his parents the same day. They had a huge mansion that looked like a palace. His father was a senior medical doctor. Jean gave me five hundred Francs the very same day. He told me, "Don't worry, I will help you." After five days, he invited me for lunch at his house and gave me another five hundred Francs.

I spent around two weeks having fun, visiting places, and dancing at parties with my Vietnamese and French friends. Then slowly my mind began to wonder about what to do in the upcoming days. When I went to the visa center, I got an extension for only fifteen more days. This was discouraging so I decided and was determined in my heart that I would contact Al Mattock and try to head towards England.

'Es Tu Pédé? (Are You Gay?)

My mind was a bit worried for a few days because of the uncertainty of getting the English visa. My shortened French visa, my dwindling finances, and the lack of accommodation were always on my mind.

One day I was in the same Le Petit Cluny having coffee with a Vietnamese friend and a woman named Brigitte who was sitting by my side. I was lost in my thoughts about my own problems when suddenly she started talking to me and asked, "Es tu pédé?" (In the French language, Pede meant "gay" which I did not understand at the time).

I didn't understand the word she was using. Suddenly, I heard my Vietnamese friend Daniel scolding Brigitte, "Why are you talking like that to a foreigner? Shyam is a very genuine person."

Brigitte replied, "I don't know! Shyam has never shown any interest in me. I have tried to get his attention many times, but he never responds. That's why I was asking him if he was gay."

I understood this and said, "I am very stressed these days. I'm messed up. I am focused on only these issues." During the conversation, the Vietnamese friend went his way asking us to continue our conversation.

Then slowly, I explained to Brigitte about my visa and accommodation issues, and this brought a change in her facial tone and emotional state. When I was with my friends, I had never properly noticed the affection expressed from Brigitte. I was really surprised to hear this. I had a small idea that perhaps she was attracted to me because when I would catch her looking at me time and again. We didn't meet regularly, so I had forgotten about it.

After listening to my side of the story, she said, "If your visa work is complete, then you won't have any problem with accommodation, do not worry about it." I thanked her. She had previously thought that I was Vietnamese.

As it was already evening time, we ordered some food together. She told me more about her family and work, and I also told her that I was a tourist in Paris. I explained that I was planning to go to England after my visa was sorted out because my previous boss lived there, and I was going to meet him.

After a pleasant conversation with more coffee and food, we hugged each other and then went our separate ways. That night, I felt like a real loser.

UK Visa

I had already informed Al Mattock about my problems and the situation I was in. He told me that he was coming to Paris very soon and asked me to apply for a British visa.

I went to the British Embassy and asked for a visa application form. The staff at the Embassy took me to the office of the vice consul. The consul officer looked a bit old. He looked at my passport and asked me how and why I had come to France.

He also asked me where my return ticket to Nepal was. I explained to him that I had arrived in France by road and planned to return the same way. I also told him that I had no plane ticket. I didn't know whether he understood me or just pretended that he didn't understand me. He continued to ask me repeatedly why someone would come to France without a return ticket.

I told him that I was going to England for one month and planned to return to Nepal after that. I also informed him that I had a friend in London, and I planned to stay at his place for the duration. The officer didn't listen to me at all. He put a small stamp on my passport which mentioned "visa applied for UK". Then he said, "Come back to apply for your visa again after you have the return ticket!"

I left there. I tried to meet the consul once again the next day. After a few more requests, the staff finally took me to the consular office. I explained to him that my boss is arriving in Paris. I asked him if it would be possible to visit England if my boss wrote me a guaranteed letter.

The consul paid no interest in what I had to say and angrily responded, "You must show the return ticket." I was about to speak again when he said, "Leave me alone, please!" My visa was rejected once again. I was compelled to leave quietly.

After a few days, Al Mattock arrived in Paris and stayed in a star hotel named Place de la Republique. I went to meet him the very next day. I found a significant change in his attire, and his walking and talking style. He looked like a billionaire. I told him everything concerning the incident at the British Embassy. Mr. Mo-hen, apparently the British pronounce Mohan as Mo-hen, as he always called me Mr. Mo-hen back in Nepal. This pronunciation reminds me of the past.

Then he said, "Don't worry I will take you with me even without a visa and I will try to get the visa directly at the airport." Then he bought tickets from France to London for the both of us. The following day we boarded a bus and went to a small airport called Beauvais, a little outside Paris. From there we flew to the airport in Ashford near the city of London.

When the plane reached the sky, I was very curious. I was also very worried about what was going to happen once we landed there. I was going back and forth between two different thoughts. On one hand I thought that they would let me enter because I was being guaranteed by such a personality like Al Mattock. On the other hand, I remembered that they wouldn't allow a Nepali to enter without a visa.

Along with this, the Embassy in Paris has already stamped "visa applied" in my passport. How I wished that it was not stamped. During this time, I then realized that the plane was already above the English Channel. The scenery was amazing, but my heart continued to beat even faster. After a few minutes the plane descended towards Ashford airport and landed.

Arriving near the terminal I saw that the police were checking everyone's passports and letting them enter the terminal building. When my turn came, they stamped my passport and let me enter. I was a little encouraged and thought this is great that they let me enter too, it must mean that I will be allowed to enter the city.

In the arrival hall an immigration officer was checking every passenger's passport and then letting them enter. He stopped me and asked me where my visa for England was. I explained to him that I had come to France via overland and planned to return in the same way. I also explained that I didn't have a return air ticket, therefore I was not given the visa.

Al Mattock was right beside me. He explained to the officer that I was his friend, and that I was going to stay at his home during my time there. He said he would give me a guarantee. The officer then insisted that I should have already received the visa and that a Nepali won't be allowed with "visa upon arrival" in the UK.

Al Mattock suddenly became heated and shouted, "I can write a 'guarantee' letter for him. I am the manager of a Casino in London. Why can't you give him a visa?" Then the officer responded, "I can do nothing about it, I will ask my boss". Al Mattock said, "Alright!"

Unfortunately, this incident then happened, Al's voice was loud and clear, the same as it was back in Nepal. The officer was just a few meters away from us when Al said, "These government employees earn less money than many people, therefore they try to exhibit their authority." I felt a prick in my heart hearing this. I realized that my visa approval may go wrong because of this.

The officer returned after a while and handed me my passport. He said that he was sorry, but I must go back to Paris. My boss said that he didn't agree. I felt like falling off a cliff and I was speechless; I couldn't utter a word. By then it was already time to board the same plane back to Paris.

I was ready to return after all hopes were lost. Al handed me all his money and six packs of Benson and Hedges cigarettes which he had in his pockets. He expressed his sorrow and sympathy. On my return to Paris even the bright sky felt like it was covered with a dark blanket of clouds.

What will I do back in Paris? Where will I stay? These types of questions kept coming to my mind. I was confused on whether to go to Daniel's place or to Brigitte's, which is a little further from Paris. Should I search for a youth hostel? By the time the plane had landed at Beauvais airport, it was already evening time. Paris was a sixty-kilometer bus journey. Therefore, I decided to go to' Bd Kellerman', a youth hostel.

This was a very large hostel situated on the southern edge of Paris. In the Cité Universitaire canteen young people and students could get a good lunch for five Francs. This was why I didn't prepare my own lunch during the day. Many young boys and girls frequented this hostel, so it was not difficult to pass the time.

From Beauvais, I took a bus from the airport and arrived in the center of Paris. By the time I had taken the metro and reached the hostel it was very late, I was completely exhausted, so I went to bed immediately.

The next day I headed back to central Paris and in the evening arrived at the same Le Petit Cluny. I met up with my friends and told them what had happened. They were sad to hear my story. I stayed in the youth hostel for a few days and then at some other friends' place. I spent quite a few days with my friends roaming around purposelessly.

During the following days I was focused on deciding whether to return to Nepal from Paris or to find work somewhere. If I was returning, what should I take with me? Should I extend my French visa for another month? First, I went to the French immigration office to extend my visa. Although I had requested a one-month extension they only stamped my passport for fifteen days. At that time the officer told me that I could return to France again after leaving for a few days.

I decided to go to Switzerland and got a one-month visa from the Swiss Embassy. Since there were only a few days left for me in France I went to the French Immigration office again and asked for another visa. They stamped my passport with the Visa de Sortie (visa to exit France) for fifteen days and for the last time.

After getting the Swiss visa I met with my Vietnamese and Cambodian friends and informed them of my return plans. Some of them proposed to find work for me in their companies if I wanted to work in an ordinary job. I was not interested in anything else since my passport had already been stamped with "last visa for France".

During my last few days in France, I met with a few good friends several times to spend time together before I had to leave. One evening all of us had a farewell dinner. Since there was no chance for me to extend my stay in France, we talked about meeting in Nepal. In fact, all these friends had shown an interest in visiting Nepal.

One Vietnamese friend gave me a second-hand camera so that I could take photos during my return journey. Another friend gave me one hundred Francs and said that he had never seen a dollar, so after you return to Nepal, send me dollars equivalent to one hundred Francs. For me the closer I came to leaving France the more my heart ached.

Finally on August eighteenth, nineteen hundred and seventy, I boarded the train for Zurich, Switzerland.

My cabin had only one other female passenger. She was an air hostess with Swiss Air. She was returning to Switzerland after a few days of vacation in Paris. We introduced to one another, joked around and laughed all night. She said she had never seen another Nepali in her entire life.

In the morning, the train arrived at the Swiss city of Basel situated on the French-Swiss border. The police stamped the entry date of August nineteenth, nineteen hundred and seventy on my passport. Forty-five minutes later we arrived in the city of Zurich. Although it was fun talking and laughing with the Swiss air hostess, I took a long breath upon arriving at the station.

The air hostess said, "I will take you for breakfast and a tour of the city for two hours. After that I must go home. I must prepare myself for the flight this evening."

We kept our bags inside the railway lockers and went to a café for breakfast. She took me along the road by the side of the Limmat River near the station. She said, "You are quite entertaining and courageous". I took a photo of her before we separated with the second-hand camera I had received as a gift. I felt quite nostalgic after she left.

After that I headed straight to the train station and from the information center, got the map of Zurich plus the address of a youth hostel. I then headed back towards the hostel. Due to exhaustion from the previous night's journey, I stayed in the hostel and rested that day.

The next day I remembered that there was an office of the Swiss Association for Technical Assistance (SATA) in Zurich. One of my Nepali friends, who was an engineer, named Mahendra Shrestha, had come to SATA for technical training. I went to the SATA office hoping to find his address and inquired about his presence. The officer there told me that Mr. Shrestha had already returned to Nepal, but another Nepali named Laxmi Bahadur Manandhar was still in training. He also happened to be a friend that I knew from Nepal.

I asked for his address and phone number and found out that he lived a forty-five-minute train journey from Zurich in a city called Schaffhausen. I thanked the officer and returned to my hostel. From the hostel I went to visit the center of the city.

Zurich is the largest city in Switzerland. It was an international city full of corporate houses and banking institutions that was situated on the bank of Lake Zurich. Walking in the streets you could see numerous banks and many watch shops. Most of the watches were quite expensive. That day I began to think again that there was no one to help me if I was in trouble or in need. To reassure myself that I did have friends in France to help, I went back and applied and received the visa to visit France again.

While visiting the central part of Zurich I called Laxmi Manandhar's number from a telephone booth near the SATA office. I told him everything about me. He asked me to visit Schaffhausen city where he stayed. He provided me with all the details on how to reach his place. I boarded the train from Zurich the very next day and went to meet him. Using the telephone, I informed him of my arrival at the station. He provided me with the details concerning the bus I had to take and where to stop. I followed his instructions and by the time I had arrived at the stop he was already there to receive me.

I had long hair and was wearing a Parisian outfit. Laxmi gazed at me from head to toe. After that, we went to his rented place on foot. We were walking slowly and conversing at the same time. I felt like the women in Switzerland were quite tall in comparison to the ones in France. I said, "Oh! The girls here are so tall. How so?"

He replied, "You are short yourself and therefore you must have found the girls here to be taller." I had noticed it correctly. The women in Switzerland were taller and more muscular in comparison to the women in France. I also remembered that the Swiss Air air hostess I had traveled with on the train was also significantly taller than me.

During our walk, Laxmi asked me why I wasn't wearing a watch. I was not sure what to say. I just kept quiet. After a while, we arrived at his house. There we discussed my travels and his work. He had rented two rooms in a house owned by an older lady, and it had the facility of both kitchen and toilet.

I had no issue staying there for a few days. Laxmi went to the training center in the morning. I used to be alone at that time as the landlady was at home all day. I would often go out to explore the city. One day, I ventured a little farther and visited the largest waterfall in Europe, the Rhine Fall. In the beginning, the landlady behaved well with me, but gradually, she seemed to grow irritated by my presence. Sensing her discomfort, I would often head out to the market or spend my day having coffee in a nearby café. Sometimes, I would also explore the villages located a little farther away. The Rhine Fall was particularly captivating, so I found myself returning there on occasion to marvel at its beauty and the rush of its waters. Moreover, on the path that was made to visit the falls, there were restaurants where they grilled delicious Swiss sausages on an outdoor fire. You could smell these grilled sausages from a distance, and it was amazing. I always fully enjoyed eating them. In the evening, I synchronized my return time with my friend and came back home accordingly. I prepared the dinner most of the time as Laxmi arrived tired.

I stayed for many days in Schaffhausen. During the stay, Laxmi sometimes took me to dinner or lunch with his friends. We also visited other places. One time we went to Inter Laken and the next time we visited Lucerne.

On one occasion, I arrived back at the house before Laxmi. I rang the doorbell, and the landlady opened a small portion of the door to peek outside. She shouted at me, saying that my friend had not arrived yet, and then abruptly slammed the door shut. I was left shocked and speechless, feeling deeply ashamed. As she shut the door, I resolved to find a youth hostel and stay there for a few days. I left and returned later when Laxmi had arrived. I recounted the incident with the landlady in detail to him, explaining my decision to stay at a youth hostel for a while.

Though I wanted to return to Nepal, I lacked sufficient funds. Despite having a French visa, my eagerness to return home remained strong. I shared with Laxmi that if he could lend me the money, I would repay him upon my return to Nepal. He said he would consider it. The next day, I moved to a nearby youth hostel. The lively atmosphere there lifted my spirits, with a vibrant crowd, singing, and dancing every night. It provided some much-needed joy during those uncertain times.

One night, a strange incident unfolded in the common bathroom on the first floor of the hostel. As I was washing my hands, an Asian-looking guy entered the bathroom but immediately left. He then attempted to enter another bathroom, only to find it designated for women. After some confusion, he returned to the gents' toilet where I was still washing my hands. Sensing a familiarity in his appearance, I asked him in English where he was from. His response filled me with excitement - "Nepal." Overjoyed, I exclaimed that I too was Nepali. We both got excited and started talking loudly.

Amused by the misunderstanding, I inquired why he had been switching between the gents' and ladies' toilets. His explanation was simple yet hilarious - "Since I saw you from the back, your long hair made me assume you were a lady, and I thought I entered the wrong toilet. So, I went to the other one, but there was a woman's sign there too." His candid response had us both erupting into laughter.

As we exchanged names and addresses, we delved into conversation about our reasons for being there. He introduced himself as a Newar with the last name 'Jonchhen', studying engineering in Russia. Despite my own Newari heritage, I had never encountered such a last name before. It seemed our boisterous conversation had attracted attention due to the echoing acoustics of the concrete hall.

Suddenly, two people from nearby rooms emerged and scolded us, "What's all this noise? Can't you talk in a lower voice?" After that, we retreated to our respective rooms.

He had already departed by the time I woke up the next morning. Thirty years later, after meeting him in Nepal, I found out that he had become an engineering professor at a top American university. I was really impressed.

Standing at five feet four inches tall, he appeared even shorter than me. How could such a short man be a professor to six-foot-tall Americans? Later, I discovered that he had settled near my father-in-law's house in the United States.

I stayed in the youth hostel for another week. Despite not having any friends of my own, I found it interesting to observe the different types of students and young people coming in and out of the hostel.

One day, a group of German boys and girls arrived. In the evening, they started dancing, each seemingly paired off. From a distance, I watched them and noticed one girl dancing alone. She approached me directly, took my hand, and led me to the dance floor, where we danced energetically. Dancing helped me release all the pent-up stress I had accumulated over the past few days.

Her friends observed us closely as we danced. Afterward, though we remained near the group, we sat separately, exchanged beers, and engaged in conversation. The next day, they departed.

Later, I learned that most tourists visiting the city only came to see the Rhine Falls, typically spending just one or two days at most.

After a week, I returned to Laxmi's apartment. My friend Laxmi wasn't the politest guy you would come across, but he was practical and had a helpful attitude towards others. Therefore, he was able to help me, saying, "Return to Nepal, and I will give you the money you need. You can pay it back when we meet in Nepal again."

One day, when he had a day off, we sat down to discuss the lending and borrowing of money. He asked me to prepare a fulfillment paper. I prepared a simple type of money receipt. After reading it, he said, "What good is this paperwork? Wait, and I will write it." He prepared a legal promissory note and asked me to sign. I put my signature on the paper without any hesitation and received three hundred Swiss francs from him, which was equal to two hundred American dollars. It was more than I needed.

Then Laxmi said to me, "Listen, why have I prepared this paper? If you don't return my money in time when I get back to Nepal, I will put you behind bars with the help of this paper!" I agreed and thought that he was a strict but methodical guy! Yet, he had been such a helpful person. I wanted to return home very soon after I received the money from him. I didn't want to return to France even though I had the visa. I said goodbye to Laxmi and left Schaffhausen with a plan to stay in Zurich for two or three days.

1.3 RETURN JOURNEY TO KATHMANDU

Zurich and on to Venice, Italy

With the aim of returning to Nepal, I went to the Zurich train station. There were a variety of shops. I bought a light suitcase, which was a little bigger than my previous one. I then went to a watch shop and bought a newly designed watch. Laxmi's voice kept recurring in my mind when he observed that I wasn't even wearing a watch on my wrist.

After that, I went to the youth hostel I had stayed in before. There, I transferred the goods from my rucksack into my new suitcase. I was happy because there was still some space left, and I was thinking about buying a few items for my friends and relatives. I went to the Globus Department Store, situated on the main street of Zurich, at around noon and spent hours shopping there. I bought light high-neck sweaters and some shirts. Then I returned to the hostel.

The following day, I left the hostel early, planning to visit other places in Zurich. You could see a large church-like building on the other side of the Limmat River, and you had to cross the bridge to get there.

In terms of transportation, there were buses and trams in Zurich. Trams were the main form of transport, and they were everywhere.

One day, I was going to the city center on a tram when a group of young students from Spain came on board, making loud noises. Everybody looked for a seat and started to sit down. Those who didn't find a seat had to stand. The tram started off again.

One of the girls looked at me and giggled. Since she was looking at me and smiling, I smiled back. After a while, a man who seemed to be the leader of the group came to me and said that his friend, Sofia, wanted to have a date with me because she had never seen eyes like mine.

I looked at the girl; she was beautiful and ever smiling. I said yes. The girl approached me and spoke in fluent Spanish. I spoke in English and explained that I knew French but not Spanish.

The leader said she was sixteen years old. "How old are you?" he asked. I thought, I am much older than she is. If I said I was twenty-two, would she be turned off? I said that I was eighteen years old. Sofia kept on giggling.

As I was near the river, I had to stop at two more stops to reach Rathaus (Town House). I told this to the group leader. Sofia got out with me when we arrived at the stop. We moved ahead, giggling with each other.

After we walked for a few minutes, Sofia stopped me, called me 'Eh,' and with her index fingers pushed her eyebrows back and showed me. Then she laughed hysterically. I smiled gently at this. Language was the barrier in our communication. She knew no English, and I didn't understand any Spanish. She did know one or two French words.

We walked along, and after a while, Sofia teased me again and started giggling. The third time she teased me, I gave her a tight hug. She didn't protest; she just kept smiling. For a while, she walked with my arm on her shoulder. She kept on talking and giggling.

I couldn't make her understand a single word; I wasn't able to tell her my plans for the day. I could only say "right," "left," and "front" in French and help her to understand that I wanted to know which city she came from. Apparently, she was from Madrid.

We arrived at Rathaus laughing, fumbling, and wobbling. We visited the area and followed the riverbank towards Lake Zurich, where the crowd was slowly thinning. I realized that our company with each other was becoming more soulful and romantic.

We were hungry and exhausted because we had visited many places. We had coffee and a sandwich at a café. I was so elated that I didn't want the day to end. It was nearly three o'clock in the afternoon. I was worried that she would leave me.

As we moved along Lake Zurich, I realized that we must return to the other side of the river. That was the only place where trams were available. If we stayed too long here, it might be too late for her if she wanted to meet her friends. Thinking about this, I half-heartedly proposed that we return to the main street.

We slowly returned, sometimes holding hands, sometimes hugging each other, and sometimes talking to each other without understanding each other. Since it was summer, the sun would be shining until nine p.m., and there would be sunlight for even longer. I didn't feel as though it was too late in the day.

We started to look around the inner areas of the city near Bahnhofstrasse, which was the main street in front of the Zurich train station. I assumed that Sofia was very happy that day as she had teased me many times with her eyes. Then she slowly stopped.

It was already around six in the evening as we walked along, staying closely together. Slowly and independently, we moved our feet towards the Bahnhof train station. From there, we could find a tram to any part of the city. I thought that she would take her tram from there as well. However, she had shown no interest in leaving me, and I did not want to be apart from her. We said nothing but stood there silently.

It was a very crowded area. Since it was the central tram station, there were a lot of people getting on and off. After a while, I pointed to the rear of the station and proposed that we go there. She came along without saying a word. Although the station was long, we eventually reached the rear section where nobody was. We became absent-minded for a while, hugging each other without saying anything.

Then, before leaving, as if she wanted to kiss but was too shy and too frightened, and then again wanting to kiss, Sofia finally, having no idea of what to expect, gave me what was probably the first kiss of her life.

I quickly sat down right on the floor. I had no interest in leaving that place. Instead, I wanted to be rooted there, shedding a few tears. After that, I returned to the hostel. Later, when remembering our parting, I was surprised to realize that a person can become so emotional in such a short time. Thinking about it now, I feel lucky to have had this experience. I had taken her picture during our time together, which I look at these days with fond memories.

I reached the hostel at night and went straight to my room. While trying to get onto the top of the bunk bed to sleep, I heard two American guys discussing Nepal. This immediately caught my attention, and I asked them why they were talking about Nepal.

They answered that they were going to Nepal by the land route. Then I said out loud that I was Nepali and that I was going back to Nepal as well. They were happy to hear that and meet a Nepali before reaching Nepal. We planned to have breakfast together in the morning, and then I went to sleep.

Just as we had agreed the previous night, we sat down at a breakfast table and started discussing the schedule for reaching Nepal. During our conversation, I was more than delighted to find that their route was almost the same as mine. They were first headed to Italy, and then Greece, Turkey, Iran, Afghanistan, Pakistan, India, and finally Nepal. I decided to take the same route as well.

Our first stop would be Venice and then on to Rome, finally reaching Brindisi, which is situated on the southern coast of Italy. From there, we would take a ferry to reach Greece and after that, Turkey. In Turkey, we would improvise concerning the route ahead and what means of transport we would take. We decided to leave Zurich that same evening.

We boarded the train for Venice, Italy, leaving Zurich at night. Among the two young men I was traveling with, one had a beard and mustache; his name was Michael. His friend was Jack. The train traveled all night long with a few stops in between. We arrived at the Venice station in the morning. Michael had already collected information on where to go and where to stay. Accordingly, we went to a hotel by boat on a canal, which was the main mode of transport within the city.

The hotel was like a youth hostel. I was delighted to see a big crowd of young people. Though I was in a new city with new friends, I often thought about Sofia from Spain.

I would have been in a hopeless state if I had been alone. New friends, new places, and a new environment helped me to rejuvenate and become energized. I was able to move ahead again. During the day, we went to see Saint Mark's Basilica. This church was at the center of Venice and was constructed nine hundred years ago. In front of the Basilica was a large area like Tundikhel in Nepal. It was paved with stones and filled with thousands of pigeons and tourists. In the square was a tower as tall as Dharahara in Kathmandu.

We also visited the Grand Canal, which was lined with antique buildings on all sides. We visited the most famous bridge, the Ponte di Rialto, by boat. It was a unique experience to visit all these places traveling on canals by boat. Venice is among the favorite places for tourists around the world. Even though we had a short period of time, we were able to visit the city and many of its monuments.

Venice To Rome

After spending two or three days in Venice, which gave me a completely different perspective of Europe, we bought tickets from Venice to Rome as we had planned. We boarded the morning train, and inside the moving train, there were different types of people selling a variety of counterfeit goods. They kept on insisting that we buy something even if we didn't want to. Since there were the three of us, I was not worried because Michael and Jack handled them easily. After riding the train all day long, we reached Rome. We stayed in a youth hostel near the station.

I had not trimmed my hair in the last three months. The next day, I went to a barber. When I looked in the mirror after getting my long hair trimmed to a proper length, I felt I was ready to enter Nepal.

There were many ancient religious monuments in Rome, plus ruins that represented thousands of years of heritage; Rome was flooded with tourists. Sometimes I visited famous places alone and sometimes with my friends. I also visited the Colosseum, which is what remains of a two-thousand-year-old round stadium. During that era, this stadium could house up to eighty thousand people so they could enjoy sports and other entertainment. This was an example of the Roman Empire, and the Colosseum is now considered among the Seven Wonders of the World. I also visited places like Piazza di Venezia, Fontana di Trevi, and Piazza Spagna. The place I was most impressed with was Saint Peter's Square, which was inside Vatican City. The Basilica temple there is world-famous. You could spend hours visiting this place without wanting to leave.

Rome wasn't as clean as Paris. Most of the outside walls of the houses looked like they hadn't been cleaned in decades and were covered with black spots. Although the ancient places and heritage sites had been kept clean, the footpaths were dirty and dusty. Overall, Rome became my second favorite city in Europe.

Rome To The Port City Of Brindisi

After visiting Rome for three days, we boarded the train and headed to the port city of Brindisi. The train ride took all day long. There were facilities to buy food and drinks inside the train, so we drank tea, coffee, and Coke as and when we wanted. From the train windows, you could see plains and sometimes hilly regions that reminded me of Nepal. Throughout this journey, I felt as if I was returning home after a successful venture.

When we arrived at Brindisi, we went straight to a youth hostel. We met other Americans there and quickly became a group of friends.

Although it was a comfortable environment, I was not the type of person that talked all the time. The others chatted without a break.

The following evening, we prepared to leave Italy for Greece. We bought a ferry ticket from Brindisi to Athens. Brindisi wasn't a particularly large city. We spent the day looking around the area. My suitcase was heavy by the time we had arrived in Brindisi. I had heard that the port was nearly a kilometer away from the city, and I was worried about how to transport my bag to the ferry. But the next day, Michael, Jack, and another American took turns carrying my bag to the ship. I felt that the Americans were helpful people. This was my first experience of having an extended friendship and companionship with American citizens.

We reached the port on time. Since this was my first ferry ride, I found the ship to be huge. We were relieved as we boarded. There were seats for passengers inside the ferry. I went to look for my seat number in the inner hall and was really surprised. There were large rooms just like in a house. You had to pay more money for a single room. For a normal ticket, there was a hall larger than a cinema theater, where hundreds of seats had been arranged.

Once I was on board, I realized that the ship was half cargo, half passenger. These kinds of ships took passengers from Brindisi to Greece at cheaper prices than normal passenger ships. I believe the ticket price for this ferry was only ten dollars.

The ship slowly picked up speed. After a few hours of travel, land became invisible. There was blue water as far as the eye could see. Traveling on such a huge ocean and on a ferry made me a little nervous. Thoughts went through my mind: I didn't know how to swim, and if the ship were wrecked or in an accident, who would come to save me? The waves below the sea deck were massive. Other thoughts went through my mind: How would I ever be able to survive such huge waves? A simple push from this ship would send me to the heavens!

There was a spacious restaurant for dinner. After dinner that night, I immediately went back to my room and lay down on my comfortable seat. From the window, nothing but darkness was visible. A few hours later, after waking up, I went to the balcony deck and looked at the remote blue Mediterranean Sea. I really felt like I was on an adventurous journey.

Later that morning, the ship arrived at Patras Port. Some passengers left the ship as it stayed there for a couple of hours. Patras was a large island belonging to Greece. Many tourists then boarded the ship. Once the new passengers bound for Athens had settled, the ship started moving again. I climbed the deck once more and looked at the beautiful blue surrounding sea with its waves. I was traveling with a flurry of emotions.

Later, I found that there was a swimming pool above the deck, and the scenery from there was even more enchanting. Since it was summertime, I went into the pool. Even though I didn't know how to swim properly, I was good enough in the water to avoid drowning. I also clicked a few pictures for memory. Later, I sat at a restaurant for coffee. In the meantime, I received information that the ship was about to arrive at a port called Piraeus. I began my preparation to leave. I didn't know where Michael was during the entire trip, but we did exit the ship together.

Piraeus was the main port for the Greek city of Athens. It was ten kilometers from the port to the city center. There was a bus service to reach the city, so we boarded the bus to Athens. We looked for a youth hostel and registered there. That day, we visited the area around the hostel.

Michael then decided to take an airplane to Istanbul and said that we could meet in Istanbul. I advised him to stay in the same hostel I had stayed in while heading to France and gave him the address. The next day, he left Athens.

The environment of the hostel kept me from feeling bitter, alone, and sad. After breakfast that day, I looked at the map of Athens and found my way to important heritage sites and monuments. I walked to all those places, learning that Athens was a very ancient and historical city that was established nearly five thousand years ago.

My first stop was Syntagma Square. It was an interesting large open area. Below street level, there was a small garden with some cafes and a resting area. Above the street was an amazing, massive pink parliament house that looked like a palace. As I had already walked for more than an hour, I sat down at a café and enjoyed the surrounding environment with a sip of coffee and a sandwich.

I found this city to be different from Istanbul and Belgrade. The streets of Athens were pretty much straight, and the seven-storey houses looked modern and consistent in their structure. After spending around one and a half hours there, I slowly headed towards Omonia Square with the help of the map. Walking slowly, I reached there within an hour. It was a purely commercial area, with shops, department stores, cafes, and restaurants. I looked at the shops and then went inside a Greek restaurant and ordered Moussaka, a brinjal-based meal. I then looked for my bus route and returned to the hostel in the evening.

The next day, I went out to see the most famous and historical site of Athens: the ruins of the Parthenon temple situated on top of the Acropolis hill. I also went there on foot with the help of my map. The magnificence of the remains there dazzled my eyes. There was a huge temple made of white granite pillars with some empty spaces and very large stone pieces. The pillars were the only structures of the ruins still standing. The rectangular-shaped temple had been constructed almost twenty-four hundred years ago. Thirteen thousand four hundred pieces of large white stones had been cut into shapes and joined together to construct this monument.

From there, one could see the mesmerizingly beautiful view of Athens. You could see faraway places with straight roads cutting through them. As the Acropolis hill was at a higher altitude than the city, there was a constant breeze. The weather was perfect, and it made you want to spend a longer time there. After spending around an hour, I slowly climbed down and went through the ancient stone-laid narrow street, looking at the old houses, restaurants, and shops while heading out to the city center.

I went into a small restaurant and ordered my first Greek salad, Greek beer, and a steak. I enjoyed my meal in a relaxed manner, taking it easy for a long time. From there, I went back to the hostel in the evening and fell asleep very soon because of the miles of all-day walking. Even fifty years later, I vividly remember this time.

Daphne Wine Festival Of Greece

The next day at the breakfast table, I heard some young people talking about a wine festival. This immediately caught my attention. I tried to learn more from them and found out that there was a wine festival in a small village outside Athens called Daphne. This was where the wine produced from different parts of the country was brought for people to taste. There was also an exhibition because this festival was very well known. The group had planned to visit the place in the morning. They had already collected information on how to reach there and return to Athens. During the conversation, I had already revealed to them that I was Nepali. When I asked to join them, they immediately agreed.

In the morning, I boarded the bus to Daphne along with the group. With a few stops, the bus took an hour to reach there. From the bus, we went directly to the festival.

The venue of the wine festival was below a pine forest. An entrance gate had been erected where you had to pay one dollar to enter. We all went in together. As the crowd inside was huge, I informed one of the members of the group that I wished to return with them and requested that he not forget me so that I would avoid getting into trouble if I returned to Athens alone.

As soon as we entered, we saw many barrels of wine with the place of origin mentioned on a paper glued to the wine barrels. There were also heaps of small plastic cups. Along with that, there were olives, cheese, and bread pieces. You could pour the wine of your choice from the barrels into the plastic cup and taste olives and cheese as you wished. These wine barrels were all over the park, infinitely spread around. There were a lot of young volunteers in Greek attire to help the incoming guests. In some parts of the festival, there were Greek songs, Greek music, and Greek dance.

This wine festival was a first experience in my life, and it was unique. I had tasted a variety of wines during my stay in France, but at the festival, I had the opportunity to taste thirty types of wine in the same place. I was careful enough to pour only half a glass of wine each time and drank them slowly. So that I wouldn't get drunk, I was also eating olives, cheese, and bread. Slowly, my eyes were beginning to flutter. The fun and entertainment kept on going. For a while, I didn't eat or drink so that I could watch the songs and dances of the Greek youths. Then I started tasting more wine unfazed.

I had no idea where all my friends were at the time and, to be honest, I didn't care. The more wine I added to my system, the more I forgot about them. I lost count of the number of glasses I emptied. I only remember walking wobbly amongst the crowd. From what I do remember, I stayed there till late into the night. I had no idea with whom and at what time I returned to my hostel. Upon waking up, I was clueless as to how I ended up in the right bed. I could only remember looking out of the window every once in a while, as the trees passed me by. I had no other memories. Moreover, I saw none of the friends in the morning that were with me the previous day. That final part of the festival is still a mystery to me.

Athens To Istanbul

Michael had already left Greece for Istanbul two days earlier than me. As I was traveling by train, I went to the station the day after the festival and bought a night ticket to Istanbul. That day, I visited as many places in Athens as I could on foot. I left the hostel on time in the evening and headed to the station. I ate some food before boarding. The train left the station at eight in the evening.

I couldn't sleep very well. Sometimes in the dark, you could see small and large, well-lit vessels in the middle of the sea. The train sometimes stopped briefly at other Greek stations, but I paid no interest. Finally, at around four a.m., the train stopped at the Turkish border. Slowly, three Turkish soldiers entered the train with heavy guns. They began to ask for and inspect everyone's passports, checking whether the foreign passengers had proper visas and passports.

I didn't have a visa for Turkey. I had consulted some people about needing a visa for Turkey but was told that we could apply for a visa upon arrival. They were probably talking about air travel, but I hadn't paid much attention. I had no idea where or how far I had to go to get the Turkish visa in Greece, so I had lazily avoided it. Now the Turkish army told me in sign language that I couldn't enter Turkey because I had no visa. Even though I tried to explain, they kept uttering "No" and took me off the train along with my suitcase. Then they took me to a little dark office room. The train I was on took off after a while. I was dumbfounded; I could neither smile nor cry. I sat on a chair.

The room was small with faint light and two giant army men. I felt very insecure. I suddenly remembered that German old man from Kabul and therefore didn't even look at their faces. In the middle of this, one of them pointed to their watch indicating six o'clock, and I interpreted that I would be able to talk to an English-speaking officer at six a.m. With this hope, I patiently sat on the chair.

Just as I had hoped, uniformed railway staff arrived at the office at six a.m. He first talked to the army officers and then asked me why I had come without a visa. I told him that I understood that I would get a visa upon arrival at the entry point. He then explained that this was incorrect but said, "It's okay for now, we will let you leave. You must get the visa at the immigration office as soon as you reach Istanbul. If you don't follow these instructions, you will get into big trouble." I was relieved and assured him that I would do as he said. He then told me that the next train was due at seven o'clock and that I could get on that train to head toward Istanbul.

I boarded the seven-a.m. train and arrived in Istanbul at two p.m. I went directly to the hostel where I had stayed before; Michael was also staying there. We talked for a while, and then he said that he had good news. He had bought two one-way bus tickets from Istanbul to Delhi directly. The bus would leave Istanbul the day after tomorrow and would arrive in front of our hotel at 8 a.m. We must be ready. I asked him to show me the bus ticket. He didn't have them; there was just a receipt that read, "Fifty dollars for each ticket, one hundred for two, passengers' names: Shyam and Michael." I felt cold as soon as I saw it. "This must be a fraudulent ticket," I said to him. "How can a ticket be like this? There is neither the company's name nor the address or phone number!"

He then said, "It won't matter, I guess; many others have bought it as well."

I told him that the bus probably wouldn't arrive the day after and that we were scammed. He was dumbfounded! I had to reach the immigration office on time, so I looked for a taxi and went there. They gave me a visa easily because they saw the visa that I had received six months earlier. After that, I went back to the hotel. Michael was sitting there.

My attention was focused on the travel that lay ahead after my arrival in Istanbul. In the middle of all this, I was taunted by the memory of the mother and daughter duo from my first trip through Turkey. I felt that they could suddenly appear at the hotel and surprise me. I felt some frustration for a while. There was, however, no possibility of finding them because I had already lost their address. There had been no letter exchange in between. I had not even imagined I would be back in Istanbul this way. I had only arrived here after my US dream collapsed.

That night after dinner, I shared all my experiences with Michael and went to bed with a heavy heart.

As I was an early bird, I left the hotel in the morning and went to visit the Blue Mosque. I imagined Emel with a guilty heart. How happy she would be if we met again, but there could also be a problem. What if her mother asked me to take her daughter with me as I was going back home? These thoughts kept playing in my mind. That day I was also talking to Michael about the journey ahead to Nepal. At that time, Jack, Michael's friend, who I had met in Zurich and had also visited Venice with, was also staying at the Istanbul hotel. We had to wait until the next morning to see if the ticket Michael had bought was real and then prepare for the journey.

That day, we visited the Grand Bazaar and the rest of Istanbul together. Jack had a lot of information about the city, so we went wherever he took us. Most of the places we passed were through the gullies of the old city. At one point, we arrived at a red-light district on Zurafa Street. There were queues of prostitutes sitting outside their homes, especially on the left side of the street. They were calling on potential customers. We slowly walked past the area looking at them. At one place, there were three women smoking, laughing, and talking to each other. As soon as we stood there for a second, my eyes fell on a mature, beautiful woman. Suddenly, she looked at me and said, "Oh! So now we have kid clients coming here! Let me see if you have the thing!" She approached me to pull at my pants and pulled me into her courtyard. Jack and Michael had been similarly pulled in by the others.

After leaving there, I could also see my friends slowly coming out in a delighted mood. We left and went above the gully without saying anything to each other. We had only begun walking for a few minutes when other women approached me, took hold of my wrist, and said, "What a beautiful watch. Give it to me and I will take you to paradise!" She kept on grabbing my wrist. I slowly got my hand out of her grip and asked my friends to leave there in a hurry. They laughed and came slowly as I hurried away. We went back to the hotel after leaving the red-light area. At dinner, we talked and laughed about the incidents of the day and went to bed tired.

Istanbul to Kabul

Michael and I had to be ready at eight a.m. for the bus. We had completed all our preparations; our bags were ready to travel. Just as it was mentioned on the paper sheet, the next morning we headed out into the street at a quarter to eight and waited for the bus to Delhi. It didn't arrive. It was already nine-thirty a.m., but there was no sign of any bus. I said to Michael, "I told you about this the day before yesterday, I told you that the bus was not going to arrive."

There were seven other passengers along with us waiting for the same bus. They screamed and then scolded one another. By ten a.m., all the other passengers had left without getting on the bus that never arrived!

Michael and I returned to the hotel and sat for hours like two lost people. We finally discussed how to move forward. The day before, after having breakfast, I had talked with some other passengers and found out that there were two options: you could take a direct bus from Istanbul to Tehran on a five-day trip, or you could go to Erzurum by train and then take a bus to Tehran. The second option was the cheaper of the two, so we chose option two.

After lunch, we saw a notice on the hotel board that said some people were searching for a passenger to go to Kabul from Istanbul. This person should also have driving skills to assist in driving the vehicle during the journey. The passenger didn't have to pay any fare or bear any of the fuel expenses. It was a Nigerian named Abdul who had published the notice and was staying at the same hostel as we were. He had requested the interested passenger to contact him. Seeing this, Michael said that he was ready to travel as a passenger and driver in that vehicle. I had no intention of denying him and therefore said that it was alright.

As soon as we met Abdul, we cracked a few jokes, and the deal with Michael was fixed. We prepared to travel the very next day. Abdul said, "Shyam, you are such a good-looking guy. Please help me to marry one of your sisters when we reach Nepal." I wanted to laugh and then thought, "What does this guy think of himself? Will any girl be ready to marry him just because he likes her?"

I said to him, "First of all, let's reach Nepal, and then if my sister likes you, we can talk about it." Then we all laughed. The next day, they left the city. I was alone again.

I had to get a new Iranian visa as the previous one had already expired. That day, I spent almost all my time getting the visa and then spent some extra time around the Blue Mosque area. I realized that I would keep on thinking about the mother and daughter if I stayed in Istanbul, so it was best to leave the city as soon as possible. After I got the visa to Iran, I went to the train station, bought a ticket to Erzurum, and left Istanbul the same evening. I had already planned to meet Michael in Kabul, Afghanistan.

Even though the train looked ragged from the outside, it was clean and well-maintained on the inside. In comparison to Indian trains, I found it more fun and more comfortable. As the train slowly left the station, I thought it would pick up speed, but to my surprise, the train wasn't fast and stopped at various locations along the way. We only reached Erzurum the next day in the afternoon. I thought this was the reason for the ticket being so cheap.

That day, I bought the bus ticket to Tehran for the following day and slept at a nearby hotel. Upon boarding the bus, I saw that there were many European and American citizens. There was also an Indian Sikh among them. We introduced ourselves to one another. I was happy to meet an Indian guy. He was a little older than me and was a talkative fellow. He was seated on the right-side window in the middle row right in front of me. The Sardarji didn't have his turban on and kept on talking to me even though we were sitting in different seats. He was returning to India after working in Germany.

The bus was constantly moving at its own pace. Smoking was allowed inside the bus, and the Indian Sardarji kept on lighting his cigarette from time to time, carelessly throwing the matchsticks outside the window. I was a little paranoid about what would happen if those matchsticks got to the fuel tank and caught fire. I tried to convince him not to do so, upon which he replied, "You're such a gentleman, my friend." I was confused about what to say. As far as I could see, he didn't throw the matchsticks outside the window again.

The Punjabi guy kept on sharing his experiences in Germany. He explained that some Germans made a mockery of his nation, Hindustan. He explained that some of his German friends used to make fun of the physical appearance of his country's prime minister; he had kept quiet after a few hours. He repeated the same story and laughed as well.

The bus continued at the same pace; I got a little sleep. Then the bus stopped abruptly. I heard loud cries and screams. The people in the front rows were getting up and going outside in a hurry. When I tried to understand what had happened, I was told that there had been an argument between the bus conductor and an American passenger. The conductor, who was Turkish, had attempted to stab the American with a knife, and the other passengers had gotten hold of the conductor to bring him under control. Apparently, the American passenger had scolded the conductor; when the conductor got angry, he tried to stab the American.

Then I remembered what I had heard about Turkey before: it wasn't unusual to be stabbed in Turkey. I had chills in my bones for a while, even though I wasn't directly involved in the incident. After that, we reached Tabriz without any other problems.

At night in Tabriz, I slept at a hotel close to where the bus was parked. I ate dinner with the Indian guy. I was relieved to have his company. He also told me that if I needed, he could arrange a few days of stay for me in Delhi at his uncle's house; this made me feel even better.

After leaving Tabriz early in the morning, we reached Tehran with only a single stop for lunch in the middle of somewhere! During my return bus trip to Nepal, I had a friend to talk to and a camera to take photos of different places along the way. More importantly, I had the opportunity to click a picture of Mount Ararat.

It was evening by the time the bus arrived in Tehran. I stayed at the same hotel as I had before. I don't know where my Indian friend stayed. During my stay in Tehran, I had to get another visa for Afghanistan, so I decided to stay and visit Tehran for a few more days. After getting my visa, I went to visit the places I had missed on my previous visit.

During the tour, I saw an advertisement for a restaurant that was fifteen stories high, from where you could view the entire city of Tehran. I went to the restaurant, and the view was as magnificent as advertised. It wasn't a very expensive restaurant, so I was able to spend hours there after having my lunch. I made a commitment to come back to the city again. Unfortunately, even after fifty years since my second visit to Tehran, I haven't been able to return.

The next day, I left Tehran on a train to travel to Mashhad, which was on the border of Afghanistan. After spending a night there, I went to the immigration office of Islam Qala, which was situated on the border between Afghanistan and Iran. Surprisingly, I met my American friend Michael and my Nigerian friend Abdul at the immigration checkpoint. I was happy and felt secure to finally meet them after spending several days alone. Since they were in their car, which had come from Istanbul, I had to take a bus to reach Kabul.

I arrived at the city of Herat after crossing the border, and after a one-day bus journey, I reached the city of Kandahar in Afghanistan. The following morning, I took another bus and headed for Kabul. On reaching Kabul, I stayed in the same hotel as I had before. Michael and Abdul hadn't arrived yet, but I had already given them the address of the hotel. The afternoon of the next day, I obtained a visa for Pakistan. Michael and Abdul arrived in Kabul the same evening. We stayed in peaceful Kabul the next day for touring and resting.

The following day, Michael and I headed by bus towards the city of Peshawar in Pakistan. The date was the eighteenth of October, nineteen seventy.

Kabul to Delhi

A few hours after leaving Kabul, our bus started taking the uphill road toward the Khyber Pass. I had already heard about the Khyber Pass, an important and ancient trade route from eastern to western Asia, reaching even as far as Europe. For centuries, it had been considered a crucial part of the Silk Road to and from China, as well as from India to western Asia and Europe. The pass looked barren, with no greenery on the mountains. It resembled a very dry desert.

After climbing for hours, we reached the border city of Peshawar, Pakistan, on the nineteenth of October, nineteen seventy. As soon as we arrived in this city, it felt as though we were in India. It was crowded with hawkers' shops, paan shops, rickshaws, and a lot of noise. I didn't feel as though it was a good atmosphere for a visit. We stayed at a hotel for one night.

Early the next morning, we went to the train station to travel to Lahore. It was crowded with a lot of noise and there were hassles just like in India.

We bought normal tickets. As the train was leaving, we hurried to board on time. There was a huge crowd of passengers also trying to get onboard. We were finally able to get on the train after a lot of struggles. The train slowly began to move and then it slowed down and stopped at different stations along the way. Looking outside from my window, it was difficult for me to distinguish between Hindustan and Pakistan. After an unpleasant full day's journey, the train arrived at the Lahore station that evening.

Since I had left Zurich, the suitcase I had bought was giving me problems. I had wanted to buy a smaller suitcase that could easily fit all my belongings, but the actual suitcase was a little bigger for more convenient travel. I had also purchased and added things along the way, which obviously made it heavier. It was therefore difficult while getting onto the buses and trains.

Michael and I didn't have any hotel or hostel address to look for in Lahore. We were both standing in the station looking confused. We didn't know who to ask or how to find information. In the meantime, three young men, who looked like students, approached us and asked what we wanted. We replied that we needed a youth hostel or a nearby hotel to spend the night. They said, "It's alright, why would you need a hotel? We are students, and we stay in a hostel. You can spend the night there; you won't have to spend any money if you come with us." Michael then said that it was OK, but I didn't feel comfortable about the situation and was not sure what to say. The boys insisted that we go with them. We slowly followed, thinking that their hostel was nearby.

We left the main street and took the road in front of the station through a huge group of rickshaws, with many people selling cigarettes, tobacco rolls, fruits, and paan. We told the Pakistani students about our nationality and our destination while walking to the hostel. We finally reached there, and they told us that we would stay on the first floor. We went upstairs, where there was a concrete balcony before the entry to the other rooms. After we arrived, other Pakistani students rushed towards us. They asked their friends who we were and where they had met us. Suddenly, one of the boys who had escorted us to his hostel replied loudly in Urdu, "Hey! Don't you disturb us? We have scammed them with great difficulty." They thought that we couldn't understand a word of Urdu. My ears popped up and chills ran down my spine after hearing this.

I whispered to Michael that neither the place nor the people were genuine and that we had to leave immediately. Michael still didn't seem to understand me clearly and was quite confused. Then I slowly asked them, "Which room are we sleeping in?" One of them replied, "You'll be sleeping right here on the floor; we will arrange some straw mattresses for bedding." I was still having shivers in my bones because of fear. Suddenly, another student from a distance rushed to us, pulled us aside, and said, "You better get out of here immediately; otherwise, these boys are going to rape you if, you stayed here tonight. hurry up, get the hell out of here!"

This guy was speaking in English, which finally opened Michael's eyes to our dangerous situation.

We told the students who brought us there that we were not staying in such a place. Some of them tried to convince us that there would be better arrangements, but we rushed down the stairs without giving them any attention. We quickly left the campus even though we had no idea where we were. After we left, we were not followed anymore by those students. We caught a rickshaw outside the hostel, went far away from there, and finally found a hotel. The city of Lahore looked ragged to me, and this incident made me even more disgusted, more disgusted than any other place in the world.

The next morning, we went to the Lahore train station and boarded the train to Delhi. In the afternoon of the twenty-first of October, nineteen seventy, we arrived at the immigration office in Hussain Wala, India, which is situated on the Indian-Pakistani border. We stayed on the same train and reached Delhi that night. After arriving in Delhi, I promised myself never to visit Lahore again. That incident still makes me wonder if there were many more gullible people who had been scammed or exploited by those students!

I called the Sardarji I had met in Iran after arriving in Delhi. He had already returned to Delhi before me. He invited us for lunch at his home; we then had a memorable rendezvous. In Delhi, we stayed at a youth hostel. It was my third time in Delhi, but since it was Michael's first time, we decided to stay in Delhi for a few days and visit places during our free time. He also had to get his visa for Nepal at the Nepali Embassy.

My heart was filled with excitement about returning home after such a bittersweet journey. I felt like flying to my country like a bird. After spending five days in Delhi, we bought a direct train ticket to Patna, along with a berth, which was leaving that evening.

Delhi to Patna

We reached the station one hour before departure that evening and went to a restaurant for dinner. I ordered chicken and rice. Somehow, a small piece of bone got stuck in my throat. I tried to swallow it at first but couldn't. I tried to spit it out but still couldn't. I slowly drank some water, and the bone went down slowly. However, there was still a bone fragment stuck in my throat, and it hurt terribly each time I tried to swallow, even my own saliva.

In the meantime, the train was signaling to leave. I was clueless about what I should do. Should I board the train or go to the hospital? I couldn't make sense of what might happen inside the train. What if my throat got worse? If it got more serious, how would I be saved in the middle of the night? I informed Michael about my situation. After listening to me, he was also clueless about what to do. The train had already blown the last whistle. My hurry to get back to Nepal urged me to board the train. I was also concerned about what Michael would think if I canceled the journey. He couldn't give me any concrete advice, so in the end, I decided to take the risk and boarded the train along with Michael.

As there was a rush while boarding the train, the stuck bone fragment caused me more and more pain. It was difficult even to swallow my own saliva. The train had already picked up speed by then. There was no question of going back anymore. I was worried and wondered how I would travel in this condition for the entire night. I avoided swallowing as much as possible. Sometimes I took a little sip of water and breathed slowly. I slept for a while and was awake for the rest of the night, always in pain. We finally arrived at the Allahabad station in the morning after a six-hour journey.

I knew that this was a major city, so the train would stop for a while. I wasn't moving from my berth due to the pain caused by any body movement. So, I said to Michael, "Go have some tea on the outside platform and please bring me some tea and puri when you return." He did as I had asked him. Along with the sip of tea, I tried to swallow a small piece of puri as I was hungry. To my astonishment, the pain I had endured to swallow the puri had opened my food pipe completely. I was out of trouble just like that. I cautiously took another bite, and there was no issue and no pain. I offered tons of thanks to God and ate the rest of the puri with full taste. I felt like I had jumped from the zone of danger to the zone of happiness in just a few hours! The train then arrived at Patna station.

Patna To Kathmandu

There was nothing significant to see in Patna; there were empty fields everywhere. The main city must have been somewhere else, as we couldn't see anything. We spent that day in Patna. I had experienced the hassle and trouble of taking the road from Patna to Kathmandu, so I informed Michael that it would be easier for us to take a flight from there. He was convinced, and we took an airplane to Kathmandu.

Originally, Michael had planned to stay in Boudha after arriving in Nepal, so we went there directly after landing in Kathmandu. I arranged a hotel for Michael, and as it was late, I took another room at the same hotel. I had left Kathmandu by land on the twenty-third of March, nineteen seventy to reach France. I had returned to Nepal after seven months and seven days using the same land route except for Kathmandu-Patna-Kathmandu.

The next day, I went home and met my mother. This was a moment of surprise and happiness for her. My father had already gone to his office. After having lunch at home, I went directly to meet my Dad at his office at the Supreme Court. I hadn't written to anyone about my plans to return to Nepal. I went inside his office; he was seated on a chair and was very surprised to suddenly see me standing in front of him. Not a single word came out of his mouth; he just kept looking at me, not even bothering to ask when I had arrived.

My hair was long, and I had on clean western attire. My pants were bell bottoms, which hadn't been popular in Nepal. I looked different from the other youths in Kathmandu. After a while, I started the conversation, telling him that I had arrived late the day before and had stayed in the hotel because of the delay. Dad didn't talk very much. He was probably very happy to see me but didn't express it in words. I felt a little awkward because of his silence. In confusion and desperation, I suddenly took out a cigarette from my pocket, lit it, and then asked for his forgiveness. I said that I had also learned this bad habit from France.

My dad looked at me, and he was even more stunned. This time he didn't look so happy. After some time, I left, saying that I would meet him back at the house that night. Outside, I felt uneasy and uncivilized for lighting up a cigarette in front of my dad. After seeing my dad, I went to meet my close friends. However, the afternoon incident with my father bothered me deeply.

PART II:

MY LIFE AFTERWARDS – FRENCH CONNECTION

2.1 TAKING THE AIR FRANCE JOB

Desperate Search For Work

After returning from France in early November nineteen seventy, I spent the entire month visiting friends and relatives, sharing my travel experiences. I then spoke with the new management of Casino Nepal for work because the ownership had changed. They promised to inform me of a possible job in a couple of weeks, but I was never called. I tried once more but was unsuccessful.

Upon returning from France, people looked at me with awe. Seeing my soft skin, people used to tease me by calling me 'Baby Face' and 'Lady Face'. I had long hair and fairer skin, and some uncivilized chaps even spread the rumor that I had altered my sex. That rumor and some people's behavior disgusted me. My close friends defended me and rebuked those who were talking ill about me.

In my free time, I enjoyed the company of my old friends, although I was always thinking about finding a job. At one point, when I was without any stable job, my father took me to the home of Gopalraj Raj Bhandari, a prominent businessman on Durbar Marg. He was the chairman of The Mercantile Corporation. My father had a good relationship with the Raj Bhandari family at the time. Mr. Raj Bhandari had acquired the agency of Burma Airways in Nepal. My father requested that Mr. Raj Bhandari employ me somewhere in his organization.

I let Mr. Raj Bhandari know that I was very interested in working for Burma Airways. He told me that an airline job would be too difficult for me to handle because I would be responsible for keeping an account of all the incoming and outgoing flights. Therefore, he didn't offer me the airline job. I was looked down upon by him at that time. My father and I left feeling frustrated. For a young man who had just returned from an adventurous journey to and from Europe, I felt hurt at being underestimated. My father's high hopes of finding a job for me were shattered.

I was having difficulty paying back my loans as I was unemployed. At the same time, Laxmi was regularly pressing me for the money he had loaned me in Switzerland. With no other options, I paid Laxmi with the help of a few close friends. (Later, in about a year, when I had permanent employment at Air France, I slowly paid back my loans to everyone I owed.)

Sometime after that, Larry Dornacker, whom I had known in Bhimphedi as a teacher for the American Peace Corps, returned to Nepal to pursue his Ph.D. He had a scholarship from The Fulbright Program in America. The subject of his Ph.D. thesis was "Teacher Training in Nepal." He needed someone to translate his documents and questionnaires from English to Nepali and vice versa. He also had to meet and interview teachers from various schools throughout Nepal. Along with that, the answers to the questionnaires from those schools had to be translated into English.

Since I had no other fixed job, I decided to work with Larry on his project. Consequently, I was able to visit different places in Nepal: Pokhara, Palpa, Bhairahawa, Biratnagar, Dharan, etc. Larry covered the cost of the airplane tickets, as well as other expenses. He also paid me a daily wage. What I disliked about this job was that I was only paid on an hourly basis. The workplace was very uncomfortable and mismanaged. Our office was on the top floor of the US Education Foundation's building. There was nothing except a few tables and chairs, and it looked like a warehouse. It was excruciatingly hot, and I felt sleepy all day. This made it very difficult to properly focus on work. Therefore, I enjoyed the job much more when we had project trips out of Kathmandu.

I also searched for other jobs while working for Larry. There was a vacancy for a single staff member to work for the General Sales Agent of TWA Airlines, which had been recently acquired by The Soaltee Hotel. Once again, I had high hopes because I had good relations with Prabhakar Rana, the manager, due to my former job at Casino Nepal. I made an appointment and went to see him. Mr. Rana told me that they were especially interested in hiring a female for that job. I returned home feeling hopeless again.

After my disappointment, I began to believe that I wasn't going to get any job in Nepal. This really infuriated me. I decided that I would search for a job in a much larger city, like Delhi. When working in Casino Nepal, I met the Director of Sales and Marketing of Oberoi International in Delhi. He had visited the casino during his Nepal tour.

I had met him multiple times and had maintained a good relationship. His name was Datoo Telang. I planned to visit him and ask for a job, thinking there must be some opportunity for me in such a grand hotel. I also planned to visit Air France, Japan Airlines, and Alitalia in search of a job there. I stayed with my friend Lal, who worked for the United Nations Development Program.

After making this decision, I informed Larry about my plans and went to Delhi. Upon reaching there, I telephoned the Oberoi Inter-Continental and arranged an appointment with Datoo Telang. During the appointment, I told him my story after I had left the casino job to go to France. He expressed his happiness to see me but told me that there was no suitable job for me in his hotel at that time. However, he promised to introduce me to an American filmmaker.

As promised, he introduced me to the American filmmaker Conrad Rooks. I had no idea whether Datoo had explained my situation to Conrad or what I wanted from him. I met Conrad at the same hotel at three in the afternoon. I introduced myself briefly and informed him that I was looking for a job. Conrad told me that he was already familiar with Nepal. He spent an hour explaining to me how to start a discotheque in Nepal, how to paint the mandala art on its ceiling, how to decorate the floor with copper flooring, and how to place all the lights. We had finished a couple of cups of coffee by then. At first, I found his explanations interesting, but later I started to wonder how it would be possible for someone like me, who was looking for a job, to gather money for such a big investment. I also wondered if he was planning to be the full investor for the project. It felt as though he didn't understand my position.

I left Oberoi Inter-Continental, as my first day of job hunting was totally unsuccessful.

The Almighty Descended, Employment With Air France

The next day, I was near a telephone booth on the sidewalk at Connaught Place. I made the decision to call Air France using the telephone directory kept in the phone booth. I called Mr. Jean Claude Rouyer, who was second in command at Air France's India office. Fortunately, his secretary easily connected my phone call to his line. In my introduction to Mr. Rouyer, I said that I was a Nepali youth, recently returned from a trip to France. I know a little French and I am looking for a job. I would like the opportunity to work for Air France. In response, he said that there were no jobs in Delhi, but he did tell me to visit his office the next day for a more detailed introduction.

I went to the Air France office the next day at nine a.m. sharp, which was in Scindia House. I introduced myself to the receptionist and informed her of my appointment with Mr. Rouyer. A staff member approached me and handed me an examination paper containing four pages; the staff member asked me to answer all the questions. There were questions about the English and French languages along with questions about the history and geography of France. I filled in all the answers. I had hoped that I would be ninety percent correct because I had filled in ten percent of the questions based on wild guesses. Coincidentally, all the answers were correct. It took me thirty minutes to complete the questionnaire. Fifteen minutes after my questionnaires had been taken, I was called into Mr. Router's office.

We exchanged a brief introduction. Then he informed me that there were no jobs available at that time in Delhi, but as Air France was opening an office in Kathmandu, I should try there. He asked me to leave my Kathmandu address so that we could remain in contact. Happily, I left my address there and decided to return to Nepal. I had a feeling that my Delhi stay needed to be longer, but I needed some more money if I wished to stay. I started to think about what I would do.

Then I remembered a friend of mine who was working in the far western region of Nepal. I bought a map to find out the shortest route from Delhi to western Nepal. I had also known that the easiest route was from Delhi to Lucknow and then to the Gaurifanta border checkpoint. Since it was a long route, I then looked for a shorter one. I headed towards Dhangadhi, looking on the map at the cities along the way. I had no idea how to proceed or what kind of transportation I would find to get there.

I did find buses at regular intervals along the way. Sometimes I had to take a rickshaw to go from one village to another, and sometimes I had to walk. I also had to find shelters along the way. I was frustrated, thinking that I was a stubborn fool and that I was digging my own grave. The farther I got from Delhi, the more I felt like I was heading into a remote place. In some places, I was treated like an alien or an uncivilized, uneducated guy and was laughed at and teased. Later, I realized it was because of my appearance. I had long hair, and I was wearing bell-bottom pants and a very tight shirt. I'm sure they thought I was a strange person, which is probably why they were making fun of me.

I reached Dhangadhi after many struggles. I met my friend Sagar there and asked to borrow money. He gave me three hundred Nepali rupees. The Dhangadhi village I visited was one street with a few houses. Some of the houses were small cottages on a semi-concrete road. After receiving the money from Sagar, I headed for the Gaurifanta border and then on to Lucknow, finally reaching Delhi four days after leaving the city.

Upon returning to Delhi, I didn't feel like searching for another job; rather, I enjoyed myself exploring the city and watching movies. I also had a few shirts and pants made. Three days later, I returned to Kathmandu via Patna.

After returning to Kathmandu, I resumed work with Larry Dornacker. As usual, it was quite tedious work, but I had no option other than to continue.

A few months passed, and I figured it was time to follow up based on my interview with Air France in Delhi. I wrote to Mr. Rouyer immediately for any news concerning my case. To my surprise, I received a prompt reply from him asking me to contact a certain Mr. Robert Rieffel in the RNAC building. Mr. Rieffel was, at the time, General Manager of the Royal Nepal Airlines Corporation. He was finishing his tenure and was going to establish an Air France office in Nepal. Thank God, I received the letter in two days once it was posted in Delhi, which shows the efficiency of the postal service in the nineteen seventies.

I contacted Mr. Rieffel based on the letter I had received from Mr. Rouyer. It had been six months since my father's passing. My appearance was probably the worst it had been in all my life: a white shirt, a clean-shaven head, gray pants, and white tennis shoes. The right shoe had a hole poked in it by my long toenail. I had no option but to present myself in this condition because of the clothes that were worn by family members to observe someone's death.

The meeting with Mr. Rieffel was going to determine my success or failure in life. Even though I was not very confident, I still spoke with him in French. I also confessed to him that I had no prior experience working in an airline or in a travel agency. Luckily, based on my language skills and my travel in France, he decided to offer me the job with a six-month probation. He then said that he had already accepted me from his side, but the final approval was still to come from Paris. I agreed to this and returned to work with Larry.

A month later, I went to meet with Mr. Rieffel. He told me that there had been no decision from Paris. Upon hearing this news, I was stunned and frustrated. He asked me to return in two weeks for news. Thereafter, I began to count the days for the two weeks to finish. When the due date finally arrived, I appeared at his door. When he saw me, he placed his two hands on each side of his head, pulled his hair, and screamed, "Oh Mon Dieu!" (Oh my God!) Witnessing this scene, I became scared to death. He then calmed down on his own and exclaimed that his people in the head office were useless, doing their own thing and not paying much attention to issues outside of Paris. He apologized and asked me to come back in another two weeks' time.

I left there feeling very disheartened. I was going to go back to my work with Larry, but I didn't see anything on the street. Even though the sun was scorching hot and bright, the street that I was crossing seemed all dark to me.

The next day, I went to work for Larry halfheartedly. At ten o'clock, a clerk from the United States Educational Foundation came up to the third floor where I was working and announced that there was a lady at the reception asking to see me. I wondered who it could be and rushed down to the reception. There was no one there, but I found a note left for me that said: "Please come to see Mr. Rieffel tomorrow at ten o'clock."

I was concerned about this message. On one hand, there was hope and happiness, but on the other hand, I felt fear that Mr. Rieffel might announce his regrets concerning my job. That entire day and all through the night, I felt anxiety and desperation. The next day, I went to see Mr. Rieffel at ten o'clock, and he asked me if I could start work on that very same day. I replied that I couldn't do so because I had to give notice to my current boss, but I could join Mr. Rieffel the next day. He agreed with that.

The next day, I went to the Air France office on time and met with Hannah, the secretary at the front desk. I later learned that Hannah had to return to her home in Malaysia because of some important issues. She briefed me on all the major work that I was responsible for. She also told me that Mr. Rieffel was a very nervous man but good at heart, and not too scary! One month after the interview, Mr. Rieffel finally gave me the job. Many people, such as travel agents and Royal Nepal Airlines staff, were competing for the Air France position that I had received.

There was no proper work schedule and no lunch break as Mr. Rieffel was busy. I was working all day and hungry all day. Our office was in the RNAC building, and my friends there said to me, "You seem like you've lost two kilos in the last two days! Doesn't your boss give you a lunch break during the day?" I went to the bathroom and looked at my face in the mirror. My friends were right—my cheeks were caved in and looked hollow. I mustered the courage to ask Mr. Rieffel about the lunch schedule. He then asked me, "You haven't been going to lunch at all? You can take a one-hour break at any time during the day according to your convenience." Only then did I start taking lunch.

I discovered that Mr. Rieffel had the habit of shouting if a job didn't go according to his instructions. One of the older men working at RNAC said to me, "Mr. Shyam, this guy is not Mr. Rieffel; this guy is Mr. Rifle. He blasts like a gun and walks like a bullet. It is tough to satisfy him."

One time, Mr. Rieffel was typing in a very clumsy manner because the typewriters were old: the letters kept getting jammed, and the lines didn't move freely even if you tried repeatedly. Finally, Mr. Rieffel angrily grabbed the typewriter and threw it out of the RNAC window!

He left the office yelling loudly. Another time, Mr. Rieffel was traveling to his office by car. The driver of the car had to stop at a busy traffic light between Mahankal Stan and the Army Hospital. When the driver reached the airline office, he opened the door for his boss, but Mr. Rieffel wasn't there! The driver was shocked and later realized that Mr. Rieffel had gotten out of the vehicle at the crowded traffic light and walked to his office!

Mr. Rieffel also went trekking many times with his friends. He must have been about sixty years old at that time; he was very active and powerful. He trekked with younger friends, as well as friends of his own age. His friends would tire very soon on the trek and took many breaks. However, Mr. Rieffel was very hasty and strong, so he kept moving ahead and then would wait for his friends. When his friends didn't arrive after waiting for a long time, he would go back on the trail to meet them.

One time he was on a similar trekking journey with his friends. His friends walked along with the guide, but Mr. Rieffel decided to move further ahead. He missed the correct route and went the wrong way. He was lost. The group he was trekking with, upon not meeting him, waited for him at the main road junction. Lunchtime had passed, but Mr. Rieffel was nowhere to be seen. The guide went in search of him. After hours of searching and questioning, the guide finally found him waiting for the group on the wrong route. Due to hours of hunger and thirst, his body was in a miserable condition. The guide took help from other people and brought him to the place where the rest of the group was anxiously waiting for him.

With the passage of time, I slowly learned the job with the help of the staff of Royal Nepal Airlines Corporation. This was vital for the progress of my airline career. I also learned more of the French language during my time at Air France.

Back in nineteen seventy, Michele's grandma had given me a receipt for the money I had given to her for safekeeping, even though I didn't ask for it back. Three years later, when I asked for a loan of two hundred francs from Mr. Rieffel, he happily gave it to me. However, he also made me sign a paper stating that I had taken a certain amount of money as a loan and that I would return it as soon as I received my first salary. What amazed me was the way the French conducted any economic exchange, maintaining proper proof.

My First Training In Paris And First-Class Travel

Three months after I joined Air France for a probationary period of six months, Mr. Rieffel confirmed my job with the company. He then announced that he would send me to Paris for a training program. I couldn't believe my ears when he said this to me. I was going to France again! I flew to Delhi for my first training in December nineteen seventy-two, en route to Paris. Upon reaching the Air France check-in desk, I had to wait for my boarding pass. I found that even though my ticket was for economy class, Mr. Rieffel had made a provision that I could travel in first class if there was a seat available. This created an outrage in Delhi. They wondered how this Shrestha guy who had recently joined as a category two staff got to travel in first class. In the end, the Air France airport staff were in no position to deny my entry into the first-class cabin.

From Delhi, I flew to Paris. The airplane I was on was a Boeing 747, which could accommodate nearly five hundred passengers. Two years earlier, when I was living in Marseille, France, I had seen this plane from a distance at the airport. I couldn't believe my eyes that I was now entering the same airplane. From that time in Delhi, I once again thought about where my fate had taken me. In a mere span of two years, from two different corners of the world, I remembered that my first trip to Paris was overland with buses and trains because it was the most economical way to travel west. Now I was returning to Paris on an Air France plane in First Class! This experience made me delve into a deep state of mind with the realization of how much a man's fate can change.

The air hostess showed me to my seat in the airplane. In all honesty, I was feeling a bit awkward sitting in a seat covered in red leather upholstery. It was a large seat, and I felt like a small child being hugged by his large mother. After sitting down, I glanced sideways at the other passengers. The first-class area was filled with high-end businesspeople.

I was a little uncomfortable in front of them but still managed to keep my calm and stay there with growing confidence.

As I sat down, the hostess gave me a warm wet towel. I wiped my face like the other passengers did, then folded it and placed it on the armrest of my seat. I felt fresh for a short while. All the sweat and dirt collected outside had been wiped off my face. Within a few moments, I was presented with a champagne glass brought in a silver chalice. I slowly picked up the glass and began to sip. In a short while, she also brought a variety of French snacks on a silver tray.

The dinner service began as the airplane gained full altitude. The air hostesses kept bringing varieties of food time and again. I also peeked at other passengers to learn how to properly eat the kind of food that was being served. The hostess spent nearly two hours serving different varieties of food six different times. They also continuously served champagne, whiskey, wine, and finally cognac. Since I had eaten many cashews and peanuts along with the whiskey, I was full by the time they were serving the dinner course. I was already full, and then came other types of fruits and desserts. Still, I managed to eat small portions of each item just to look like a normal civilized passenger.

Later, when I tried to go to the restroom, I could not get up from my seat. With great difficulty and leaning against the seat, I finally managed to get myself up and headed for the restroom. On returning to my sofa-like seat, which reclined backward, I was able to sleep well for three to four hours. When I was awakened by the hostess, the beautifully lit city of Paris was visible from the window. I looked at the magazines in front of me, and after a while, a grand baked breakfast began to be served. My food from the previous evening had not been properly digested, and I was wondering how I could eat all this breakfast food. Once again, to act as a civilized passenger, I pushed the breakfast, with great difficulty, into my mouth. After landing at the airport, I took the bus and then the metro to reach the hostel that I had booked earlier.

The next day, the training period began; it started early in the morning and lasted until five in the afternoon. The training was conducted entirely in French, and as I was not too proficient, I felt sleepy during the entire training. To get rid of my sleepiness, I would sometimes pinch myself and go to the bathroom to splash cold water on my face. During the introduction, people were surprised to learn that I had come all the way from Nepal. In the evening, I met with some of my old friends and partied until it was late. The next day in training, I kept feeling drowsy. Fortunately, there was no pass or fail certificate at the end of the training; the conference ended with fun and a champagne toast.

After concluding the training in Paris, I returned to Kathmandu. At that time, Bangladesh had recently won independence from West Pakistan. The West Pakistanis who lived in East Pakistan came to Kathmandu in the tens of thousands to fly back to their homes in West Pakistan. They needed to fly to Yangon, Burma from Kathmandu on board Burma Airways and then from Rangoon, take the Air France flight to Karachi in West Pakistan. The plane that arrived from Bangkok belonged to Air France and then went to Karachi from Rangoon, and then on to Tehran, Tel Aviv, and finally Paris. Therefore, thousands of Muslims from West Pakistan visited our office to get their tickets. These tickets arrived directly from West Pakistan as prepaid tickets; the tickets were forwarded to our office via telex. We then had to issue the passengers their tickets. Due to staff shortages, there was a heavy workload for me. At that time, Royal Nepal Airlines was the General Sales Agent for Air France. It was a huge relief for me when RNAC designated two of their staff members to help handle the huge influx of Pakistani passengers.

On another occasion, I went to Tokyo for training. One day during the training, there was a rumbling sound in the room. The cupboard furniture and the lights started shaking violently. It was a huge earthquake. The people who had arrived at the training from outside Japan were all pale-faced and started screaming. But the Japanese just sat there laughing. Because they experienced a lot of earthquakes, they were not really concerned about minor shakes.

Mr. Rieffel set up the Air France office in Nepal in May 1972 and then retired in 1974 Before he left, I had begun to regard him as my godfather. He was replaced by another French manager named Jean Chaland. Within one year, Jean Chaland was called back to Paris as part of Air France's campaign to begin austerity measures. I was appointed as the manager of the company thereafter, three years from the time I was first hired as sales staff. With this new change and structure, Nepal came under the general management of South Asia with it headquarter located in Delhi, covering North and South India, Bangladesh, Sri Lanka, and the Maldives.

In 1984, a new regional manager was appointed for North India and Nepal. His name was John Paul Tabarly, and he was a harsh manager who was always screaming. He ruthlessly threatened the staff that worked under him. I was really scared of him, but I lived in Nepal. According to my Indian colleagues, I was lucky to be working far away in a different country. Mr. Tabarly regularly came to Kathmandu to check the office and inquire about business. During his inspection visits, I faced him with strong determination on all business matters and answered all his queries on bookkeeping. Sometimes, in the middle of the conversation, he mentioned how fearless the Nepali people were. He said that Nepali people would confess if they made mistakes without any hesitation, but in India, it was not the same. During a regional meeting in Delhi, he once stated, in front of all the participants and fellow colleagues, "I have no reason to shout at Shyam because he easily confesses his mistakes, but here in Delhi everybody tries to put the blame on others."

On another occasion, he called a North India, Nepal, and Bangladesh regional meeting at one of the meeting halls of the Ashoka Hotel, where Mr. Tabarly's office was located. The meeting was supposed to begin at nine a.m. Everyone arrived on time and waited for the meeting to begin, but John Paul Tabarly didn't start the meeting. Fifteen minutes passed, but there was no sign of the meeting starting. One of the senior Indian managers asked Mr. Tabarly what the holdup was. Then he announced that the king of Nepal (Shyam) hadn't arrived. While everyone was waiting, he was handed a Telex message that notified him that Shyam had missed the flight and would only arrive the next morning. Mr. Tabarly got up and announced that the meeting was adjourned for that day and would take place the next day, at the same time and the same place. The following day when I reached Delhi, all my Indian colleagues were making fun of me.

During my tenure of fifteen years after I first joined Air France, different kinds of managers came and went. There was also a woman regional manager whose name was Mrs. Barbier. She was brought in from one of Africa's Air France regional offices by Mr. Paul Leborne, who was the Director General of South Asia. They were friends and had worked together in a few countries. Unfortunately, we didn't get along very well because anytime there was something wrong, she would always ask me why I had done that before checking with me. So, I got angry and snapped at her.

Highest Level Promotion Instead of a Warning Letter

On one occasion, I flew to Delhi to pay a visit to the general manager, Mr. Paul Leborne. As soon as I entered his office, he said, "Hey Shrestha, so now you've started shouting at your own boss!"

I was shocked and said, "I believe you are talking about Mrs. Barbier."

I quietly explained to him, "Sir, the thing is, whenever something goes wrong, she directly starts pouring down on me without understanding whether I was responsible for the wrongdoing or not!"

As soon as I said that Mr. Leborne said, "I know, I know, don't worry." He then pulled a piece of paper from his drawer, showed it to me, and said, "Your boss Mrs. Barbier has recommended that I give you a warning letter, but I have just kept it inside my drawer. This is because I know you well."

During my next visit, six months later, before leaving India for good, Mr. Leborne pulled his desk drawer open and gave me a letter. This was not the warning letter that Mrs. Barbier had wanted to give me; rather, it was a letter announcing a huge promotion for me which advanced me to a category six level. This is the highest level worldwide for Air France local staff. Mr. Leborne then said to me, "If I do not give you this promotion today, you'll never be a category six officer." This category six position is equivalent to an executive officer in Paris. This also gave me access to travel in first class if seats were available. For this, I have been thankful to Mr. Leborne throughout my life. I don't know whether he is alive or not today, and despite many efforts, I haven't been able to find any information on him.

After Paul Leborne, Mr. Mark Benedetti replaced him as the general manager. I found him to be a person who was extremely friendly and spoke with people using a great deal of patience. I had a sound relationship with him from the very beginning. Even after thirty years, I still have a very good relationship with him. He is one of my godfathers. Every time I visit France, I meet him and his wife, Francois, for dinner. He ultimately became the Vice President of Air France.

Air France Training And Responsibility In Retrospect

When I was a young man, I was returning, as always, from the general post office at Sundhara when collecting my mail from Post Box 630. I was walking on the sidewalk towards the RNAC building. The street was almost empty, covered with tall trees on both sides, it was a clean and wide footpath that provided a unique pleasure when walking. I still remember those days. I saw an envelope lying on the footpath floor, I picked it up, wondering why and how and who could have dropped it there. After opening the envelope, I saw that there was a timetable of Air France Flights with a lovely picture of an extremely beautiful Air France air hostess. Two things boggled my head at that time. One was the western attire and glamor exhibited by the lady in the picture. Another was the name "Air France", the airline name itself emanated so much grandeur.

My imagination started flying. I thought, if I could work as a sales manager in such foreign companies, how much my life would be meaningful and prestigious. In the years after this dream was planted, miraculously and coincidentally, it became a reality on Durbar Marg in Kathmandu, Nepal when the Air France office opened there in 1972. I got employment as the ticket and cargo agent. In the course of time, in 1975, I became the Sales Manager of the Company.

I began my job with Air France with a salary of six hundred rupees a month. At that time, Robert Rieffel was around sixty-two years old. Even though he shouted a great deal and was always moving around the office, I felt like he really liked me in his heart. On one occasion, when our office was still in the Royal Nepal Airlines Corporation building, I heard him screaming from the toilet. I ran towards him. He had opened the tap in the sink to rub off the ink on his hands and was desperately searching for soap. After not finding it anywhere, he screamed, "What kind of a toilet is this? It doesn't even have a single piece of soap. Alright, I'm going to do it the Nepali way!" Then I saw him begin to rub his finger against the wall. He was so annoyed that when he rubbed his finger too hard, blood started oozing. He tried to stop the bleeding by placing his finger inside his mouth. I couldn't help him as I was dumbfounded by the entire scene that had unfolded in front of me. I didn't even have a handkerchief to give him so that he could wipe off his blood.

While working in Nepal, Mr. Rieffel wrote a guidebook in French called "Namaste Nepal." This made it easy for incoming French tourists visiting Nepal. This book was sent to different Air France offices throughout France. During my visits to France, I carried the books and distributed them to many offices there. Later, this book was translated into English and published. "Namaste Nepal" was helpful in promoting European tourism in Nepal.

After retiring from Air France, Mr. Rieffel spent many years as Honorary Consul General of Belgium to Nepal for his continued service in the promotion of Nepal. The Nepali government gave him a permanent lifetime visa for Nepal. I have considered him my godfather from the beginning. Even today, when he's resting in Heaven, he still holds the same place in my heart. My first child was a son, and we named him Robert after Mr. Rieffel. After that, his wife wished for us to have a girl as our second child. Fortunately, our second child was a daughter as Mrs. Rieffel had wished. Therefore, we named her Cecile, the same as Mrs. Rieffel's first name. Compounded with this fact, Cecile Shrestha was also born on the same day as Cecile Rieffel, which was Christmas Day in nineteen eighty. This made Mrs. Rieffel unboundedly happy.

Sometimes Mr. Rieffel cracked jokes during work hours. Once, he told me and my colleague Anne Marie about an interesting incident. One of his Italian friends had shown an interest in visiting Nepal. His name was Mangia Vaca. In response, Mr. Rieffel said to his friend, "Hey, don't you dare come to Nepal. As soon as you arrive here, you will be arrested and put in jail." His Italian friend asked him why, and Mr. Rieffel replied, "In Italian, Mangia Vaca translates to Beefeater. Here the cow is considered a goddess, so if they find out that you eat beef, they will put you straight in jail!"

2.2 GENERAL SALES AGENCY OF AIR FRANCE

As a result of continuous losses in the business of Air France in the early nineteen-nineties, Air France began to downsize the number of staff worldwide by proposing voluntary early retirement. The company asked for my suggestion about the scheme in Nepal. My colleagues and decided to go into an enterprising job of creating our own challenges of market development and revenues. Thus, instead of salaried staff, the Air France office in Nepal became a General Sales Agent in which income would be given on a commission basis. I became the chairman of the agency in Nepal, and we were also given the facility of an unlimited number of heavily discounted tickets for staff and their families until the year twenty-thirty.

With this shift in the structure of my job responsibility, I no longer had to go to the office at nine or count the number of holidays and leaves I had throughout the year. I was independent and able to go anywhere I wanted. I traveled often to France and other European countries engaged in business. I was able to increase my income and elevate my financial status, which translated into acquiring a beautiful apartment in a high-rise building on the bank of the Seine River. Many friends from Nepal and India were able to take advantage of this while in Paris. In the meantime, I was able to broaden my business opportunities.

2.3 MARRIAGE, LOVE AND FAMILY

In nineteen seventy-five, returning from a trip to Bangkok, I went to the Kathmandu Guest House to meet some Australian friends, John and Peter, whom I had met on the Bangkok flight. At that time, Nepalis were only allowed to buy two bottles of duty-free whisky; since I was always entertaining friends and clients, I asked John and Peter to purchase some whisky and gin for me. We met at The Tashi Takay Restaurant to see one another again and for me to collect the alcohol. They were sitting at a table with an American woman named Kathy who was also saying good-bye to John and Peter. Our paths crossed briefly.

In mid-December of 1975, I was busy at my job in Air France. I went to The Annapurna Coffee Shop for a cup of coffee and a break. Mr. G. Singh, manager of Air India to Nepal, was with a group of foreign ladies at a table. When he saw me entering, he asked me to join him at his table. He then introduced me to these three women. Two of them were British while one was the American woman that I had met at The Kathmandu Guest House. She reminded me that her name was Kathy. During our conversation, I found out that the two British ladies were leaving Nepal the very next day. Kathy was very friendly, and at the end of our conversation, she gave me the address of the hotel she was staying in.

One day after office, I didn't have much to do. I went in search of Kathy's hotel and found her in her room, all crouched up on her bed under a Nepali quilt because of the cold. She looked very happy to see me. After a short conversation, we decided to go out for dinner. During the dinner, I found her to be a very cordial and entertaining woman. Our friendship grew day by day. I also introduced her to my brother and sisters and later invited her to stay with me at home. A few days after that, some of my younger brothers suggested that I should not invite Kathy to stay with me because I had unmarried younger sisters living at home. I then realized my inconsiderate act and gently told Kathy that from then on, I would meet her outside my house. When she heard that, she appeared startled and asked me, "Yes, but where and when?" I realized inside that she had already made a space for me in her heart. I replied to her without any reservation, "I will meet you at your hotel, The Kathmandu Guest House, where you have a room of your own." Then she said that two days would be just fine if she could see me. After that, I began to go to the guest house and spend the nights there.

As I frequented there regularly, I met some of her European friends who had traveled with her from London to Kathmandu on an overland expedition in a Bedford truck. These friends found out that she was dating me and asked her, "How is your local Nepali boyfriend?" To which she replied, "Not bad for a local!" During my stay with her at the guest house, my friendship with Karna Shakya, the owner, was also growing, and we became good friends.

Our relationship was becoming deeper and sweeter every day. One day, we were riding in a taxi heading towards Thamel, and I began to think, how would I ever be able to pay back the love that she has showered upon me? I suddenly said to her, "Since your next destination is Australia and I have my annual vacation, you can come with me at that time. If I declare that you are my wife with Air France, you can get free tickets to anywhere in the world. We can first go to Australia and then after that, we will travel to America, we'll go to New York, then you can stay there, and I will return to Nepal."

In response to this, she said honestly, "I'm only getting married once in my life." I was not sure what to say after that. If I ignored her statement, she might feel hurt, and if I said OK to the marriage, even though I hadn't really given any thought to the question of marriage in my life, she would feel assured. Embroiled in this difficult situation, my soft heart pushed me, without any preparation, and I said to Kathy, "All right then, we can get married." After this sudden development, we became even more intimate. My mother, who was on a four-week pilgrimage in India, had just returned to Nepal. She was very happy to hear the news as she had already tried to arrange many marriages for me.

On March 8th, 1976, we were married to one another at Surya Binayak temple in Bhaktapur. The following day, we had arranged a reception party for our wedding guests in the Rotary Club building. There was a huge incident before the party had even started. Before Kathy, I had had a relationship with a woman who was really interested in me; however, I was not very serious about her. My only attraction was for physical pleasure. Moreover, she was a married woman with two children. In one of our previous conversations, I had told Kathy a little about her, and she was furious with her even though she hadn't even met her.

On the day of the reception, I had also invited this married woman just like any of my other travel industry friends. She came fifteen minutes ahead of the invitation time. I was preparing to welcome the guests and Kathy was with me. She immediately made a frowning face upon seeing this woman arrive. I greeted her normally and tried to divert her attention elsewhere. I had hoped that she would go inside and join the other guests. She went towards the other guests but returned towards the welcome gate carrying a chair in her hands. She placed it right by my side and sat down. Kathy's face suddenly turned red with anger, and she aggressively pointed at me and said, "Why is she here seated along with us? Please tell her to leave immediately!"

I was clueless about what to do, then I gently asked her to mix with the crowd. She didn't move a muscle. On the other hand, Kathy's anger was beginning to reach its limits. She angrily said to me, "Is she going or not? Otherwise, I'm going to push her to the ground and sit on her body and choke her down." I sat down feeling quite nervous and dumbfounded. Fortunately, after the threat, Kathy slowly got up and walked away. After that, I felt a little more comfortable and thought to myself, I have made a huge blunder by inviting this woman.

Every year during the month of June was my holiday time; therefore, Kathy and I began our round-the-world honeymoon trip. We traveled first to Singapore, then on to Australia, where we met John and Peter, and finally to America. Our first stop in the United States was in Los Angeles. Kathy's brother, Dr. Jon Amsden, and his wife, Dr. Alice Amsden, lived there. Dr. Alice was a little rude, so I had my first bitter experience in the United States with her.

After Los Angeles, we went to a village called Avon, south of Rochester in Western New York State, where Kathy's father was living. We also had a marriage reception there. I got a chance to meet all the family and was treated warmly by everyone. The only negative experience for me was from one of her aunts who during the conversation asked me, "Shyam, when you joined Air France, you must have started work by cleaning the floor, right?"

This was a huge insult for me, and I didn't know how to reply. I was hesitant to give any precise answer, so I just said "Hmm." When I told Kathy after the reception about the incident, she explained to me that it meant that you must have started the job as all beginners do. My aunt was not trying to underestimate you in any way. After her explanation, I was able to sleep peacefully that night. I also realized that it is necessary, in order to understand what people, mean to have proper knowledge of the many cultural differences in language.

Since our first meeting, Kathy was always soulful to me; lovely and possessive. Whether it was inside the home or outside, she always held my hand, kissed me time and again, and called me "my baby." Whether it was my family members or my friends, she always kept me close to her. Sometimes, I felt like she was treating me as a child. Fortunately, my mother, brothers, and sisters were all very liberal in their thinking. They never showed any resistance toward her behavior. Likewise, in the US, she also behaved in the same way with me in front of her family. Her behavior and attitude towards me were always uniform. During our wedding reception party in the US, she said to me, "Tonight you cannot dance with any other women, only me. If you must dance with someone else, you can only dance with Aunt Nonnie." Later, I found out that Aunt Nonnie was an eighty-year-old chubby lady.

After spending a week with my in-laws in New York State, we returned to Nepal through London, Frankfurt, Paris, and Delhi after thirty-five days of travel. We were able to meet with many common friends. On returning to Nepal, Kathy began her job hunt and started to learn the Nepali language. One day, while returning from the office, she asked me in Nepali, "Tapaiko bichko junga kahan gayo?" In English: "My dear husband, where has the middle of your mustache gone?" I laughed hysterically in surprise.

Fortunately, later that year, Kathy got a job at Lincoln School, an international school that had been started by the Americans. My life

Kathy's Family

Kathy's father's name was Horton Amsden. He worked for a book company. Her mother, Margaret, was a teacher by profession. She had a very tragic death due to a gas furnace explosion in the cellar. Kathy was still a small girl at the time. Therefore, her father single-handedly raised all his children without getting married again. Along with her dad, her uncles and aunts were also vital in raising her and her siblings.

Kathy's elder brother is Dr. Jon Amsden, a professor at the University of California, Los Angeles, with a rebellious outlook. Sally Amsden, their younger sister, works as a psychology consultant. After our marriage, Sally was the first family member to visit us in Nepal.

A Drama I Will Never Forget In Avon, New York

In the summer of 1981, we visited the US to attend the marriage ceremony of my sister-in-law Sally. The ceremony went quite well, and the reception was grand. We returned home late in the evening after the party was over. Sally's husband, John Ramberg, was a lovely, cordial person. He was always smiling and easygoing with everyone. We were having a good time with some beverages and snacks. Everyone was picking up their cups and plates and taking them to the sink. Finally, the newlywed son-in-law, John Ramberg, was taking his turn to bring the cups and plates to the sink. Suddenly, I heard the father-in-law exploding, "God damn it! Don't just place them in the sink, wash them as well!" I was scared and didn't know what to say. I knew Horton, my father-in-law, was a funny and angry man, but I didn't know he would go to this extent. John Ramberg, hearing this explosion, just gently laughed and said, "OK, OK, Butchy (Horton's nickname), I will do it," and he started doing all the dishes that were there. I was more than shocked by the scene that had unfolded that evening, and I thought to myself, what a difference between countries like Nepal and the USA. Here in the USA, I see a father-in-law scream at his son-in-law on the very first day of his daughter's marriage. Then there is Nepal, where the son-in-law is respected and is expected to bow down to the in-laws' feet. The scene between Mr. Amsden and his son-in-law may not be normal even for American society, but this was an incident that would never be erased from my memory.

Miraval, My First Home

Kathy had an American salary after she joined Lincoln School. Apart from my Air France job, which I had been doing for nine years, I was also earning money working as a consultant for various companies. With this combination of salaries, our living standard improved. We started planning to build a house together. As our family house in Tyauda Tole was old, my father had always wished to buy a new one. He went to the heavens without fulfilling his desire. So, with our combined incomes and the wish to fulfill my father's dreams, we set the plans in motion.

The location of the house came from our friends, Mr. Ken Jones and his wife Una. Ken was the principal of The Budhanilkantha School, and Una also worked at Lincoln School. In the late seventies, we were frequently invited to their house in Budhanilkantha. On one such occasion, while we were strolling around the area above the Budhanilkantha temple, we found the region beautiful and serene. 1977, we bought two ropanis and eight annas of land at the rate of sixteen thousand rupees a ropani in that area. (Currently, a ropani of land in the same area costs eighty million rupees!)

With the land purchased in what is today known as Budhanilkantha Heights, we started to build our house in nineteen eighty. In the meantime, I had been looking at many houses to model our home after while traveling to different European countries. Finally, at the end of nineteen eighty, we started to build our house resembling those in the Spanish hills by the Mediterranean Sea.

Today the area is very developed, but back then, being at the edge of Kathmandu, it was very rural and rustic. To reach our home, we had to leave our vehicles at the parking area near the Budhanilkantha Sleeping Vishnu Temple and walk five hundred meters uphill from there. The road was so bad that it resembled a rocky riverbed. We walked back to the parking lot the next day to go to the city. It was difficult even for trucks to maneuver up and down that road. After we began construction, we leveled the roads so that the trucks carrying the materials could easily reach the construction site. We had to bring all our construction materials on trucks from the city.

The house was nearly finished in two years; the job of welding began, but there was no electricity! Since there was no electricity in the village at the time, I had to play an important role with the Electricity Authority in bringing the connection to the entire village. Since our home was at a high altitude and there were only a few houses, the view of the entire Kathmandu Valley could be seen from our house. There were mainly paddy fields between our house and the town, so Miraval could be seen from any vantage point inside Kathmandu, Lalitpur, and Thimi. The construction of the house began in nineteen eighty and was completed for residence at the end of nineteen eighty-two. I was surprised that the house turned out to be an outstandingly beautiful example of architectural combinations. Inside and outside, Miraval was loved by all our friends and family.

Every day for two years, when we came back to the house from the city, we would have a couple of staff members carry our two children in Dokos (woven bamboo baskets), as well as our shopping, uphill to our home. Between the early eighties and the year twenty seventeen, we had innumerable invitations to our home and hundreds of different kinds of guests. We were the first ones to introduce Budhanilkantha as a desirable place to live. Those hundreds of guests discovered Budhanilkantha during their visits to our house. The villagers there still remember and talk about our parties.

Pandemonium And Confusion From Our Cross In Cultures

Every marriage is a work in progress of understanding, learning, patience, and compromise. In marrying Kathy, we brought together two very different cultures, each with its own set of unique viewpoints on marriage and family. Throughout the years, we experienced many occasions that demonstrated the vast differences between us. For example, for our wedding reception dinner, I had managed to arrange imported alcoholic beverages with the help of one of my diplomatic friends. However, the Nepali government had issued a notice that we were not to use foreign alcoholic brands during parties and receptions. Therefore, I served all locally available liquor at the reception.

After a few days, I sold most of the bottles to a few of my friends. Once in bed during a conversation, I told Kathy about this, and she suddenly turned very angry. She shouted at me, "You are a very immoral man. You immediately get those bottles back from your friends and return the alcohol to your friends from the Embassy!" I replied, "She has already given the alcohol to us, and we didn't use it because we didn't need it!" Kathy responded, "This is unacceptable. This is immoral.

I cannot spend my life with an immoral person even if I was married to him yesterday!"

After hearing what she had said, I immediately responded, "I will do whatever you have asked me to do. I'll take those bottles back from my friends tomorrow and return them to my embassy friend." Therefore, despite feeling uneasy, I did what she asked me to do. I then spent a few days in mute silence and finally apologized to her.

La Vache Qui Rit, (The Cow Who Smiles)

One day when I had just returned from France, I brought tiny cubes of cheese used as an appetizer. In France, they were called La Vache Qui Rit, meaning "the cow who laughs." In the evening, both of us were having drinks along with eating the cheese cubes, spending time happily. Kathy doesn't drink alcohol. In the process, there was only one piece of cheese left in the bowl. I picked it up and ate it myself. She then shouted at me, "Why did you have that last piece alone, without even asking me? What if I wanted to eat the cheese too?" I got angry and said, "Oh, I can't even have one more piece of cheese than you?" She then said, "You gave no consideration to my presence here. Our co-existence should be fifty-fifty, which you obviously didn't respect."

Our argument escalated to such a scale that it became a fiasco with crying and tears. Our loud screams traveled into the houses of our neighbors, attracting their attention. We screamed at each other for more than half an hour. After that, she started to try and make me understand, "Shyam, I love you so much that I could give you the whole bowl of cheese to yourself and not just one extra piece if you had just asked me before you ate the cheese. We must communicate and share opinions on each topic. Otherwise, it'll feel like you are undermining me!" I felt like I had suddenly fallen from a huge cliff when she said that. I finally understood what she was trying to say and agreed with her in my heart. After that, we shed some tears of joy and spent the evening in love.

During the year 1979, we stayed in an apartment in Kamal Pokhari owned by Mr. Gokarna and Rita KC. We were both very busy at our jobs but also frequently invited our friends and other guests. Even though our kitchen wasn't spacious, we had installed all the necessary amenities. I regularly brought new kitchen accessories whenever I returned from France. On one such occasion, I brought a grinder used for grinding coffee and other spices. It became very useful in the kitchen.

The Grinder Dispute

One afternoon, my mother visited me in my apartment. Kathy was already at school. While my mother was looking around the apartment, she went into the kitchen, saw the orange-colored grinder, and asked me, "What is this, son?" I replied, "This is a grinder. It easily grinds coffee beans and spices." Then my mother said, "Wow... I would love to have one of these for my kitchen." I realized that I often go to France and could bring another one on my next trip to Paris. I wanted to see her happy, so I said, "You can take this now; I will buy another one for us another time." Mother said, "No, no, you can bring one for me on your next trip." But I insisted that she take the grinder with her. Mother returned home very happy with her new grinder.

A few days later, the grinder was needed, and Kathy asked me to find it. I told Kathy about my mother's visit and how I had given it to her. Kathy immediately burst out in anger and said, "This time also you gave it to your mother without even asking me! Why did you do that?" To this I replied, "Can't I give a ten-dollar grinder as a gift to my mother, which I bought myself? Why do I have to ask you? Do I need permission from you even for that?" She replied, "Every item in this household belongs to you and me equally. It is wrong that you gave it to your mother without even asking me." Hearing this really enraged me, and I thought to myself, what a troublesome woman she is! After that, I screamed loudly at her. She screamed equally loud right back at me. There were many screams and cries that followed. Full of tears, Kathy said that she would be so happy to give our dear mother not one but many other items as well. She continued, "The grinder itself is not the issue here. It's just that you did not feel it important enough to ask me about it. This is how you disregarded my identity." After a while, both of us cooled down. We realized that we had misunderstood each other once again. Then we spent the night peacefully without compromising the extent of our love for each other.

In the year 1979, the first guest from Kathy's home country was her younger sister, Sally, who came to visit us in Nepal. I went to receive her in Bangkok. She was a very modern and advanced type of woman. It was a great atmosphere in the family because of her arrival. After that, we invited our friends and organized a party at our home. We were drinking a lot of alcohol and having a lot of fun. I cracked a joke as the alcoholic spirit was working in my head. I told Sally, we have a proverb in Nepal, "Sali kasko Venako," which means the younger sister-in-law belongs to her brother-in-law. When Kathy discovered what I was saying to her, she started to yell and almost slapped me!

One trouble during Sally's stay with us was in the neighborhood. She always went jogging in the morning dressed in her jogging gear from the US. She wore very short shorts and revealing t-shirts. The women in our neighborhood said, "Alas, what a shameless woman (Nakchari)!" Meanwhile, the men on the streets seemed to have enjoyed peeking at her legs. These days a lot of young Nepali girls dress like Sally without any problem. It is amazing how a situation can change with the flow of time.

Screams That Scared My Neighbors In Budhanilkantha

One morning, my neighbors near Miraval in Budhanilkantha woke up hearing screams and cries coming from our residence. After twenty-five years of living there, we had grown a large number and variety of trees in the garden. Some trees towered fifty feet. Unfortunately, some trees along the main road were Uttis (Scientific name Alnus Nepalensis) trees, which don't have a strong trunk; therefore, they can easily break during fierce storms. The trees could also fall onto high-tension lines on the main street, which could be life-threatening for our neighbors and other residents. The neighbors had been warning against this for several years, but Kathy never allowed the trees to be cut or trimmed. She was a tree hugger.

Finally, one summer before she left on her two-month holiday in the US, she allowed me to have the trees trimmed. I also left for the US to join the family. Before I left, I hired some tree cutters, asking them to chop just the tops off the trees. I came back after three weeks and saw that they had overdone it. I said, "Oh my God!" but it was already too late!

Two months later, after she finished her holidays in the US, Kathy arrived in the evening and was unable to see the state of the trees. Early the next morning, she went to the garden and saw that the trees were almost chopped in half. That is where the deafening screams roared into the sky. "Shyam! What have you done to my fucking trees?" She kept on screaming at the top of her lungs. I came out to see her and found that she had a stick in her hand. I couldn't even imagine how to handle the situation. I tried to explain what happened, but it made the situation worse. All the neighbors had come out of their houses and wondered what was happening to this foreign woman who had been one of the friendliest and most cheerful women in the village for two and a half decades. As the situation was getting out of hand, I quietly went to my room, picked up some of my clothes, nightwear, toothbrush and paste, and put them all in a bag. I quietly called my driver who lived next door and drove off to my hotel in Dhulikhel, forty kilometers east of Kathmandu. I stayed for six days at the hotel, hoping that she would call me with an apology, but she never did. So, I came back home quietly on the seventh day.

After five years of marriage, we were both very busy with our own lives. At her Lincoln School job, Kathy's responsibilities were growing by the day. She was among the most well-liked teachers in her school and took on more responsibilities than she had to. Due to a few incidents that I would like to keep confidential, the pressures on our marriage made things quite turbulent. These incidents kept us more and more distant from each other.

Separation Kathy and Shyam

As the distance between Kathy and me was continuously escalating, I accidentally in a bizarre situation met a young woman named Diki Lama from Sindhupalchowk. She was the youngest daughter of the head Lama of a monastery in Sindhupalchowk, Mr. Kalsang Lama, and his wife, Mrs. Karchungma Lama. Diki and I developed a very deep relationship in a very short period. There were many hurdles in this relationship because, on one hand, Kathy was pressuring me to get out of the situation, and on the other hand, her own family and sisters were pressuring her to break up with me. But it was not so easy, and I personally played a dramatic and maneuvering role to continue with her instead of letting her go.

After Kathy found out about this affair, she did everything possible to break us apart, and finally, to preserve her sanity, we were legally separated. In the days leading up to this, Kathy didn't know my whereabouts and had been searching desperately for me every day. One day she found me outside my friend's house in Naxal, she immediately slapped me hard and then asked me to come home with her. At first, I checked to see if anybody had been watching us on the street or from the windows above. After I was sure that nobody had seen me in this situation, I felt relieved. After that, I talked Kathy into leaving me alone for that day and promised her that I would come to see her the following day.

As promised, I went back to our Miraval residence. She had been angrily waiting for me. A heated debate started after I arrived. She then started to physically attack me, pulling my hair. My hair had already started to fall out naturally by then. I was horrified and thought, Oh no, all my hair is getting plucked out today. To save my hair, I let my head go in whichever direction she was pulling it. I spent that night at Miraval. The next day, when I was preparing to go to my office, I opened the cupboard to pick out my favorite shirt, only to find out that she had cut my shirt into small stripes from top to bottom. I didn't know whether to laugh or cry. However, I felt satisfied that I was alive even though my shirt wasn't! That night, I made an agreement with Kathy that I would, from that point on, live at Miraval four nights a week and three nights in the town in a new house I had bought to live with Diki.

The next morning, I stopped by Diki's house in route to my office. When she heard of the new arrangement, she blasted and said, "No way, you must spend five nights in my house, and you can spend two nights at Miraval!"

In the years that followed, my marital and family life remained full of struggle. Along with that, there was work pressure, foreign training, and several meetings, which kept my professional life very busy. My area of work and business has been expanding day by day. Along with my Air France job, I was also working as a consultant for other French companies to help them expand their business in Nepal. We finally decided to legally separate.

After the separation, our friendship and affection continued. Sometimes we came together, inviting our friends for dinner, cracking jokes, and laughing together. On one such occasion at the dinner table, she said, "Do you guys know Shyam's full name? His name is: the random-phantom, high-maintenance, high blood pressure, high blood sugar, attention-deficit-disorder, Maharaja with a bit of narcissism." Everyone at the table then laughed uncontrollably. Since then, Kathy addresses me in this way even now.

I don't Give a Damn about your Friends

Though we were separated, our lives were still intertwined, and sometimes our unique situation would lead to some very explosive situations. One day, an Indian named Sachdeva, who was the General Sales Agent for Air France in Southern India, visited Nepal on the recommendation of Air France. I had ongoing issues with him and Air France, Delhi. Sachdeva had sneakily been given the General Sales Agent of Cargo in Nepal. All the other cargo and travel agencies in Nepal, including me, were strongly against this. Mr. Sachdeva was visiting, along with his family, to settle the issue with me. He wanted to know if there could be some kind of cooperation. I invited him and his wife to dinner at our home the same evening of his arrival. The Delhi office had also requested a meeting between us in the hope that there would be some positive progress.

I had already informed my chef to prepare dinner. In the evening, I took them to Miraval and had them seated in my room. Kathy then arrived home from her school. I informed her of the guests' arrival. I was also aware that she was angry with me for all that had been happening in the past. I informed her that I was hosting a dinner for my Air France guests. According to the scheduled agreement I had with Kathy, that night I was to stay in my Kathmandu house. However, that same day I had also organized dinner at Miraval house with Mr. Sachdeva and his family. Kathy then asked me if I was going to spend the night at Miraval after dinner. I said to her that according to our schedule, I must return to the city this evening. Then she said, if you're going to invite your guests and serve them dinner at this house, you must also spend the night here as well. Then I repeated our agreement and said that according to the schedule we have agreed on, tonight I must go back. Kathy then screamed, "If you are calling your guest here for drinks and dinner, then you are not allowed to leave this house and return to Kathmandu!"

After realizing the heat of the situation, I quickly rushed to my guests, took them from the drawing room to my room, and shut the door. I went to find Kathy to try and make her understand, but by this time, she had also arrived in the lobby from her room. She was carrying a big bamboo stick and started banging it on the floor, creating a loud noise and screaming at me. I slowly whispered to her, "Please speak a little lower, I have foreign guests here." As soon as I said this, she shouted again, "Go to hell with your friends, I don't care…!" My heart started to tremble because of shame and fear. Then I told Kathy, "Oh, OK, OK!" She slowly went into her room. I went to my room to see my friends, who of course had already heard what had happened. They had gone pale. I apologized to them and said that things were messed up and we would be heading for dinner elsewhere. I took them to the Yak and Yeti hotel and hosted dinner there. Throughout the dinner, the incident at the house kept banging in my head, and I couldn't enjoy the food. My conversation with them became distorted and uneasy.

My Son And Daughters

On the 20th of July, 1978, I took Kathy to Santa Bhawan Hospital, now known as Patan Hospital, in Patan. It was midnight, and she was beginning her first stages of labor. Upon reaching the hospital, I took her to the delivery room. There was a young American doctor named Dr. Matern. After the nurses took Kathy inside, I was asked to wait outside. Kathy asked me to come inside the delivery room with her, but the nurses denied my entry. The doctor understood the situation and said it was okay for me to come in, but the nurses continued to deny my entry and said to the doctor, "How can a man be allowed to enter the delivery room?"

Hearing this, the doctor explained that I was the husband, so it wouldn't make any difference if I was in the delivery room. After that, I was allowed entry. During the delivery, I held one of Kathy's hands and tried to provide courage and strength. The nurses still had frowning faces. Later, this became a non-issue as our first child, Robert, was born that day, healthy and without any complications. This was a matter of great joy for the whole family.

Robert Ryan Shrestha was born on the twentieth of July, nineteen seventy-eight. He graduated from Lincoln School in 1996, where he won a civic award, and went on to study film at Loyola Marymount in Los Angeles. Currently, he is working at Sony Pictures Entertainment as an executive director in global creative marketing.

Once again, on the 25th of December 1980, I took Kathy to Santa Bhawan Hospital for the delivery of our second child. It was during the midnight hours as well. Dr. Matern had been replaced by another doctor by this time. The nurses, therefore, absolutely denied my admission into the delivery room this time. I didn't try to force my entry either. Our second child, Cecile Ann, was born in the early morning of Christmas Day on December twenty-fifth.

My daughter Cecile Ann Shrestha was born on Christmas Day in 1980. She graduated from Lincoln School in Kathmandu in 1999. After completing her undergraduate degree at the University of California, San Diego, she received a two-year scholarship provided by the French government to study at a renowned university in Paris named 'Sciences Po'. She received her master's degree and is now working as one of the managing directors of Planned Parenthood Federation of America. She resides in New York City with her partner, Jeff, and daughter, Siena.

My second daughter, Angela, was born on the 24th of April, 1994r to my spouse Diki Lama. She has now completed her two-year master's degree from one of the top ten private universities situated in southeastern France called Grenoble Ecole de Management and is now working for a multinational company in the same country. A kind, hardworking girl, she regularly asks, "Dad, do you need any money?"

2.4 PROFESSIONAL VENTURES

Mirabel Resort Hotel: *Curse of Insurgency Called People's War*

During the winter, I regularly visited Dhulikhel, a town in the Kavre district, 30 km east of Kathmandu, with my friends. From there, you could see a magnificent view of the Himalayan range. Every time I visited, I thought, "If I could buy a couple of ropanis of land and build a house, I could happily and peacefully spend weekends here." I often visited the Himalayan Horizon Hotel for lunch and sometimes spent the night. After frequent visits to Dhulikhel, I finally found three ropanis of land, which was more than enough to build a beautiful house with a big garden.

During my search for land, I found a good spot on top of a small hill. Among the other owners, the owner of Araniko Hotel in Dhulikhel had also bought a piece of land there. Including that piece, I eventually bought a total of six ropanis in two stages. As I kept adding more land to my property, by nineteen ninety-six, I had acquired around thirty ropanis of land.

After acquiring all the land I had wished for, I began to conceive a plan to build a resort hotel resembling Mediterranean French architecture. However, the political situation was unstable due to a Maoist insurgency rising in the far western region of Nepal. Despite suggestions from friends and family to stay away from the hotel project, my stubbornness led me to begin construction. I invested my own money and obtained loans for this purpose. I personally made the conceptual design, landscaping, development, interior design, and decoration. To make this an exemplary and memorable hotel in all of Dhulikhel, I brought all the interior decorations from different countries such as India, France, and Thailand.

The hotel was inaugurated by the late Prime Minister Girija Prasad Koirala on the nineteenth of September, nineteen ninety-eight. One outstanding memory I have is the speech given by the Prime Minister. In my welcoming speech during the inauguration ceremony, I thanked him for traveling such a great distance from Kathmandu and gracing the occasion of the inaugural celebration of Mirabel. In response, he said, "A house is built with the combination of several small bricks, so each small thing has its own value. If such small but beautiful resorts are built all around the country, it would be helpful in the promotion of the Nepali tourism industry."

The prime minister enjoyed himself and stayed for hours, sipping chilled beer and smoking Shikhar cigarettes, while his assistant was greatly troubled that they were very late for another event in Kathmandu, thirty kilometers away.

Once the hotel opened for business, a large influx of clients and important individuals, as well as big businessmen, began to pour in. Many people from the diplomatic corps also came to Mirabel. I was also able to welcome seven other prime ministers of Nepal to the hotel. Among various high-level individuals and professionals, I have kept everlasting memories of some of the excerpts from these notable visitors. One big hotelier of Nepal and a friend of mine Mr. Karna Sakya told to the French Ambassador during their visit to Mirabel, "What I did in thirty years, Shyam did it in one!" Another big hotelier said, "Mr. Shyam, you have built a palace."

One famous actress Manisha Koirela while visiting the hotel made comment in the hotel note book. "This is the most memorable place I have been to. Please, Please do maintain it."

As explained earlier, after the inauguration, the hotel enjoyed massive success in the first two years. The capacity of the hotel, both in the rooms and at the restaurant, was always overwhelming. This led me to think about opening another sister hotel of Mirabel in Pokhara. I flew there along with a few friends of mine on an exploratory visit for new land in the lakeside area. This all took place despite my heavy workload at Air France.

Unfortunately, the hotel business took a downward turn as insurgent activities escalated in the country. This insurgency went on for almost twelve years. Mirabel, in the following ten years, had to bear excessive losses. Therefore, the hotel couldn't pay the bank loan and interest, the taxes, and the salary of the staff on a regular basis. On one occasion, after I came out of the office of the CEO of my bank, I almost fainted, remembering his words of threat in acting against me. I had to lean against the wall to keep myself from falling on the floor! Because of a crooked plan hatched by banking professionals, including some of my friends and brothers, the rumor spread in town that the Mirabel Hotel was in the process of being auctioned. Considering the adversity of the time, I thought it would be best to sell the hotel to protect myself from bankruptcy. Therefore, I initiated talks with different parties interested in buying.

Trip to Ho Chi Min City in Search of Hotel buyer

Among them, here is an incident with a potential buyer that constitutes an unforgettable story: A Vietnamese guy named Peter fooled me to an extent I never imagined could happen in my life. When he agreed to pay the price of the hotel, which was set at around two million dollars, he said, "That's fine if it is under ten million dollars!" I decided to visit Vietnam to see his purchasing capability. I was picked up outside Ho Chi Minh City at the airport terminal. As I rode to the town, I was convinced neither by the car nor by its driver. During the ride, he continually talked highly of Peter and what a big businessman he was. In the town, his office was even less impressive. During the three hours I spent with him that afternoon, he never talked once about the purchase of Mirabel. He only showed me the design and pictures of a big resort hotel that he was building on an island on the Vietnam seaside. After that, he told me he would come to pick me up from my hotel for dinner. I thought we would talk about the purchase of my hotel over dinner. I was expecting a candlelight dinner in a fancy restaurant. Sure enough, he and his driver came to pick me up outside my hotel, and we drove off for dinner. Just two blocks away, the car stopped, and we all got off. He took me into a restaurant that was a kind of fast-food joint. He kept talking and told me he owns ten acres of land in Paris and about the same amount of land in the US. Suddenly, he left the driver and me alone in the restaurant, saying he had to attend a meeting. We ate some fast food, and I walked back to my hotel without seeing him again that night.

During the day, when I was with him, he told me about the program for the next day, which was to go to that island where he had been planning to build his hotel. So, we needed to be ready for departure at eight am in the morning, having breakfast at seven on the top executive floor of Hotel Caravelle.

The next day, the breakfast was elegant and very filling, as it was a five-star French hotel. As per the plan, I went with him and his team of about seven other Vietnamese and one British man to the ground floor of the hotel to get in the vehicles and leave for the island. To my surprise, I saw about five vehicles lined up: all second-hand Mercedes, Toyotas, and Mitsubishis. I didn't know which vehicle to get into. I thought I would be in the same car as Peter, but he came and told me to get into the black Mercedes. When I entered, to my surprise, there was a beautiful and elegant Vietnamese lady adorned with lots of jewelry.

I was in a state of surprise. Neither Peter joined us in the back seat of the black Mercedes nor did the man at the wheel. Peter had introduced this man to me as a General and the husband of the beautiful lady in the back seat with me. If these two were husband and wife, I wondered why they weren't sitting together in the vehicle? Why was he the driver? I was disgusted looking at the General's attire. He had a very thin green shirt on top of which was a star stripe, and it was in serious need of some ironing. I hadn't seen such a ragged uniform even worn by the police in India or Nepal.

After the car started on the journey, the lady slowly began to speak to me concerning various business matters. Mainly, she wanted to know if my country's development was lagging because of a lack of river transport infrastructures. I replied yes. Then she said, "The large rivers in your country are connected to the Gulf of Bengal. From there, you can bring ships into your territory and build a land port. I am an engineer too. I can help you in the construction of such infrastructures."

I replied, "There have been talks in Nepal about this in the prime minister's cabinet, but we do not have the capacity for such a huge investment."

She then said, "I can help you manage the investment too."

When I told her about my association with Air France, she asked me if I knew French, and I replied with an obvious yes. We immediately began to communicate in French. She said, "I have some friends in Hong Kong. I'm going to call them."

I told her to wait because the economic situation in Nepal was not very favorable. In the credibility examination given by the World Bank, Nepal was at a very low rank, so getting an international loan would be very difficult. By then, she had already started to speak in Chinese with her friends in Hong Kong. After the phone call, she agreed with me, saying that I was right and that now Nepal could not be trusted with large investments. By this time, she had come very close to me and was only a centimeter away from touching my hand. I became cautious, thinking that this could be a trap. I had heard, via the media, of other Nepali men falling into such traps in Africa.

The woman seemed to be a very educated personality and exhibited a keen interest in visiting Nepal. I slowly asked her about Peter, to which she replied, "I do not know him well. I have only heard that he is a big businessman." When we were near the destination, Peter pointed towards the island and told me of his plans to build a five hundred-million-dollar resort. He also showed me the planned construction. I nodded yes to whatever he said without giving him much response. He did not discuss the idea of buying my hotel. When I pressured him to discuss our deal that evening, he said that he would sign the agreement papers on his visit to Nepal. He then stated that he could help transform Nepal into an industrial country just like Vietnam. He suggested that when I returned to Nepal, I was to ask the Prime Minister to send Peter an invitation letter. I was dumbfounded by this and then returned to Nepal without a deal.

After returning to Nepal and contacting him by telephone, he promised to come to Nepal and provided a date for his arrival. He again insisted on the invitation letter. I got angry and said to him, "Do you think a country's Prime Minister is going to send an invitation letter to some random foreign businessman to visit his country?" Later, Peter did visit Nepal, and I met with him. He said he would visit Lumbini and then get back to me, but I have never seen his face again.

The Hassles Of Tax And Vat In The Process Of Selling The Hotel

Due to the twelve-year-long Maoist insurgency, the hotel business fell into ruins in Nepal. I could not provide salaries to the staff nor pay tax and VAT on time. This led to the doubling of the payable amount, turning into a huge debt. Despite all my efforts, the amount cleared was insignificant compared to the requirements.

One day, I received a phone call from a very polite junior staff member at the Jagate tax office. He informed me that I had a huge amount of taxes remaining to be paid. After that, his voice grew louder as he said that if I did not deposit the required amount within a week, they would come to me with the police with siren and lock up my hotel. Numerous industries and hotels had closed because of the civil war. I panicked and borrowed money from my friends and relatives, depositing some of the amount due at the tax office.

Then, another unfortunate incident occurred. One of my newer staff had unknowingly submitted a tax statement that was over eight times more than what we had to pay. As days passed, that amount kept doubling, turning into a huge sum of payable taxes within a short period. When I visited the tax office, I was made to wait a long time. Deciding to see what was happening, I discovered that I had to pay eight times more than what I had calculated. I nearly fainted.

Upon checking the computer, it became clear that the mistake was due to my new staff member's miscalculations. I requested the officer correct this mistake, but he suggested that I pay what had already been calculated. He would then make the corrections and return the necessary amount to me. Despite having a recommendation from the tax department, I couldn't make the officer correct the miscalculation. Tears streamed from my eyes at the injustice.

After facing many fraudulent buyers, impersonators, and heavily exploitative potential buyers, I finally sold the hotel to a group of businessmen in Dhulikhel. Despite the difficulties, I thanked the director, the operator, and all the related staff for their unselfish help during this transfer. The last page of another chapter in my life had been turned over.

The Promotion Of Nepal-France Industry And Commerce

On the 21st of November 1995, the late Prime Minister Manmohan Adhikari of Nepal, along with Political Leader Ishwar Pokharel, arrived in France. At the time, I was involved in the establishment of the Nepal France Chamber of Commerce and Industry. In Paris, the late Maurice Herzog, the first summiteer of Mt. Annapurna I, who later became the Minister of Sports, had established the Paris-Nepal Chamber of Commerce under his leadership. He organized a business dinner in honor of the Prime Minister of Nepal. The Prime Minister himself, along with Ishwar Pokharel, his personal assistant, the late Ambassador Keshab Raj Jha, and I represented the Nepali side. From the French side, Maurice Herzog was accompanied by three other officials.

Initially, our conversations centered on the political situations of both countries. The topic then shifted to the trade and business potentials between Nepal and France. The medium of communication was English, which was probably a little difficult for the Prime Minister and Mr. Ishwar Pokharel. Due to limited knowledge of trade and industry, the Ambassador kept his communication to a minimum. In this situation, I had to bear the responsibility of communicating with all the French representatives. I spoke with them, utilizing my knowledge of Nepali trade and industry.

At one point, Maurice Herzog, looking at the Nepali delegates, remarked, "They don't seem to be saying much," and looked at them inquisitively. Still, there was no significant communication from any of the three except the Nepali Ambassador, who spoke a few words occasionally. I slowly had to re-enter the conversation. The Prime Minister listened intently to what I was saying. He suddenly rose from his chair, came forward, and exclaimed while pointing at me, "He is right!" Then he returned to his seat without further words.

The conversation between me and the French side continued, with the Prime Minister listening intensely. He occasionally rises forward and says again, "He is right!" Thus, the meeting continued with me handling most of the communication, and the Prime Minister affirming my statements with his repeated exclamations of "He's right!" The dinner ended in a very cordial way, even though there wasn't much direct conversation between the two parties.

This experience highlighted the importance of effective communication and the role I had to play in bridging the gap between the Nepali and French representatives. It also underscored the Prime Minister's confidence in my knowledge and ability to represent Nepali trade and industry interests effectively.

The French Minister of Commerce suddenly announced, "We have a man in Nepal called Shyam Mohan Shrestha!"

In November 2004, as the president of Nepal-France Chamber of Commerce I organized a Nepal Export Promotion Expo in Paris at the Rotonde Venue. The Nepali Minister of Commerce, Mr. Iswar Pokharel, visited Paris to inaugurate this expo with the President of the Paris Chamber of Commerce and Industry.

The next day, the Nepali Minister of Commerce and Dr. Niranjan Basnyat, Minister Counselor of the Nepali Embassy, paid a courtesy visit to the French Minister of Commerce.

During the visit, the French Minister suddenly informed the Nepali team, "We also have our man in Nepal called Mr. Shyam Shrestha." Dr. Basnyat was shocked! That evening, he called to report the story, saying, "Shyamjee, you are so popular in France."

Later, I received a call from Mme. Bernadette Vasseux from the French Embassy in Kathmandu. She reported, "Shyam, Dr. Corneille Jest, former director of CNRS, said your speech in French at the Expo opening was excellent."

Collaboration With Renault And Various French Companies

A variety of bilateral economic activities were added to the France-Nepal trade relationship due to a short official visit to Nepal in 1983 by the French President, François Mitterrand. His visit contributed to a gradual rise and promotion of trade between France and Nepal. With the success of various France-Nepal business activities, I acquired the sole dealership rights of Renault, a French automobile company, for Nepal and Bhutan.

I was also working as the District Manager of Air France in Nepal. Due to these various affiliations, I became extremely busy, which led me to become even more involved in the promotion of trade between Nepal and France. Renault cars were slowly entering the Nepalese market. Along with this, there was no direct flight to Europe from Kathmandu, so Air France was involved in carrying Nepali passengers from Kathmandu to Delhi via Nepali or Indian flag carriers. Passengers were picked up in Delhi and then flown to Europe and North America. Likewise, Air France brought thousands of French and other European tourists to Nepal via Delhi.

Because of my continued relationship with France, I had the opportunity to work with sixteen different French ambassadors beginning in 1972.

The latest one, Mr. François-Xavier Léger, honored me with one of the most prestigious awards from France called 'Le Chevalier dans l'Ordre de la Légion d'Honneur Nationale' for France and abroad. This is the highest civil award from the government of France, bestowed on behalf of the President. At the end of 2020, a new ambassador, Mr. Gilles Bourbao, who I am very closely associated with, continued to promote the social and economic relationship between the two countries.

From 1970 to 2021, I have had the opportunity to befriend ten Nepali ambassadors to France. Among them, the eighth one, Mr. Mohan Krishna Shrestha, is my younger brother. He served as an ambassador to France after completing his government job at the Ministry of Foreign Affairs. I have maintained a very sound relationship with all these honorable ambassadors and have always received generous help from them whenever needed in relation to France-Nepal activities.

These relationships and collaborations have greatly contributed to the enhancement of trade and cultural exchanges between Nepal and France. My involvement in various business ventures, such as the Renault dealership and Air France operations, along with my close association with French and Nepali diplomats, has played a significant role in fostering and strengthening the bilateral ties between our two nations.

Other Business Associations

Member of the Board of Directors at Nepal Airlines Corporation

One of the highlights of my professional career was serving for fifteen months on the Board of Directors for the national flag carrier, Nepal Airline Corporation (NAC), from 2008 to 2009. This experience was invaluable, allowing me to share my expertise and knowledge in the airline industry while acquiring a deeper understanding of NAC's operations. My knowledge was used to tackle various issues, especially advocating for staff members who had genuine problems.

Kathmandu City Area Cable Car Project

Today, many cities around the world, especially in South America, have made significant progress in developing urban cable car transport systems. In 2011, Medellin, Colombia, became the first city to install such a system. This innovation was later adopted by cities like Caracas, Rio de Janeiro, Mexico City, Santo Domingo, La Paz, and Bogota. Ankara, Turkey, also implemented the cable car system as a daily mode of transport due to its effectiveness in alleviating traffic congestion in narrow streets and reducing air pollution. I am relentlessly making efforts to convince the Nepalese authorities to introduce this system in Kathmandu, which has often been ranked as one of the most polluted cities in the world.

2.5 PROFESSIONAL CONNECTIONS

Dignitaries And Friends That I Met In Paris

In 1991, after I acquired the general sales agency of Air France in Nepal, I also received, in exchange for my salaried employment, the freedom to travel anywhere as needed. Air France also provided my family and me with ticket privileges until 2030. Consequently, my visits to France and other nations became more frequent. By this point, more than two decades had passed since my first visit to France in 1970. Due to these countless visits, I became intimately familiar with the streets and alleys of Paris. Whenever my friends were unsure of which way to go, they would exclaim, "Oh, ask Shyam; he knows the roads in Paris better than any of us!" During my stays in Paris, I had the opportunity to meet and welcome many people, including friends and VIPs, to my apartment. I would like to recall some of the incidents worth mentioning.

The Late Mr. Prabhakar Shamser SJB Rana

At the end of December 1991, one of Nepal's top industrialists and businessmen, the late Mr. Prabhakar Shamser Rana, along with his family, stayed in my Paris apartment. I had the privilege of escorting them to various historical sites in and around Paris. Among the sites we visited was the Château de Fontainebleau, a grand historical castle that belonged to kings and monarchs of the past. The construction of this castle began in the thirteenth century. Initially, it was built as a hunting and vacation shelter but gradually evolved into a palace over time. It was also used by Napoleon Bonaparte. The château houses very old and precious antique paintings and royal jewelry, exhibited on the walls of its well-guarded rooms. Château de Fontainebleau is very well-preserved and is a UNESCO World Heritage site and museum. A beautiful pond has been created just outside the palace, where we had a picnic lunch before heading to the Palace of Versailles in the afternoon.

Without a GPS system, I navigated the roads using a printed map, my own knowledge, and assumptions. Despite occasional confusion about directions, we managed to reach our destination. The Palace of Versailles is an incredibly beautiful and grand palace with numerous gardens and water fountains. Its grandeur, both inside and out, is hard to describe in words; it leaves visitors spellbound.

That evening, Mr. Rana and I dined at a fancy restaurant at Place D'Eina. While there, I had a flashback to twenty-two years earlier when I had visited Mr. Rana's office at The Soaltee Hotel in Kathmandu seeking employment. At that time, he had told me he was looking for female personnel, and I had left his office feeling very sad and disappointed. With the passage of time, I felt fortunate to be able to host him at a high-end restaurant: The Grand Corona at Place D'Eina on the bank of the Seine River.

My flashback continued concerning Mr. Rana. Within six months of my recruitment by Air France and one year after I had visited him at The Soaltee Hotel for employment, I received a call in my Air France office from Mr. Rana. He said, "Shyamji, please arrange a meeting for me with Mr. Rieffel. We want to make a joint venture between the Meridian Hotel chain of Air France and our Soaltee Hotel. Please talk him into it."

Manisha Koirala, A Successful Indian Cinema Artist

On the ninth of March 1993, I had the opportunity to meet Manisha Koirala and her mother, Sushila Koirala, during a dinner program at the residence of the late Ambassador to France, Mr. Keshab Raj Jha. At the ambassador's request, I welcomed them to stay at my apartment for a few days. The next day, I picked them up from their hotel in my car and took them to my apartment located on Rue Emerio, on the fifteenth floor of a high-rise building on the bank of the Seine River. The view of the city and the river from the apartment was magnificent and grand.

That night, we went to the famous Crazy Horse Cabaret Show in Paris for dinner and enjoyed a delicious meal along with an amazing show. There was also a flow of champagne. The next day, we visited many historical sites and other places of interest around the city. It was fun to drive around Paris with a rising Indian cinema star, but I must admit it was very difficult to find parking spaces, which killed half of our fun.

On the third day, due to a heavy delay in packing their bags and the very busy traffic on the road that evening, they almost missed their flight. Luckily, the station manager of Air India was waiting when I pulled in with the car and dropped them off at the airport just in time.

Mohan Gopal Khetan

Every year, as part of my professional work, I frequently traveled between Paris and Kathmandu. Cellular phones were not yet available. In Paris, I stayed with my friend Corneille Jest, whose house was ten kilometers from the city center in a suburb called Boulogne. One evening, I arrived home at seven after finishing my business in Paris. Upon reaching home, my friend informed me that The Intercontinental Hotel had been continuously calling for me. One of their customers, Mr. Khetan, had asked that I call him immediately.

Realizing it was Mr. Mohan Gopal Khetan, a renowned Nepali businessman and industrialist, as well as an important customer of Air France, I immediately called him. He informed me that I had carried his medicine with me from Kathmandu and requested that I come to him immediately as he was suffering. Despite the late hour and the distance, he insisted I come right away.

I hailed a taxi and rushed to The Intercontinental Hotel. When I arrived at his room, it was in disarray, and he was lying flat on the bed. I quickly retrieved the medicine from the bag I had brought from Kathmandu, and he took it. He then proceeded to inject insulin into his wrist by himself, leaving me amazed. After a while, he found relief and we resumed our conversation.

I urged him to return to Nepal immediately, but he insisted on continuing his journey to New York. Despite my shock, he remained resolute, stating that no sickness could discourage a businessman's business, and he must carry on.

Opportunities In My Life To Accompany VIPs During State Visits

During my professional life, I had the opportunity to accompany foreign entourages with various officials and even prime ministers.

On November 2nd, 1998, I had the privilege of accompanying Prime Minister Girija Prasad Koirala on his official visit to Japan. During this visit, I had the opportunity to meet with various industrialists and businessmen. One particularly memorable encounter was with Ms. Yuri Konno, renowned as Japan's first female entrepreneur. She offered valuable advice, suggesting that supplying Ayurveda medicines, especially those enhancing men's sexual abilities, could be a lucrative business venture.

Reflecting on that trip, one amusing memory stands out vividly in my mind. In Tokyo, where our first hectic meeting took place, all delegates, including Prime Minister Girija and members of the business community, were accommodated at the Hotel President. On one evening, Sujata Koirala, the Prime Minister's daughter, and I decided to explore the neighborhood, filled with quaint streets adorned with bars and Japanese restaurants. We enjoyed our evening out but returned to the hotel quite late. To my surprise, upon our arrival, I found almost all the business delegates gathered in the lobby, eagerly awaiting Sujata's return. Their surprised expressions suggested they were curious about our late arrival, leaving me pondering over what they might be thinking. After exchanging brief greetings, everyone dispersed gradually.

Another significant event occurred on July 31st, 2000, when I was part of Prime Minister Girija Prasad Koirala's entourage during his official visit to India. This marked my second participation in a high-level official visit. Though the trip didn't yield significant outcomes, it provided me with valuable opportunities to interact with Indian industrialists and businessmen, as well as attend official dinners.

Official Visit To France In 2001

When the Prime Minister was invited to France on an official visit in 2001, I was also included in the entourage. As the President of the Nepal-France Chamber of Commerce and Industry, I attended various business meetings during the visit. Riding in a car escorted by a government motorcade, I experienced the thrill of crossing red lights on the streets of Paris.

Former Prime Minister KP Oli's Official Visit to France

Once again, during Prime Minister KP Sharma Oli's official visit to France on June 13th, 2019, I was included as part of the visiting team with FNCCI. I have already briefly mentioned this in one of the previous sections.

Late King Birendra's official visit to France in 1994

I was in Paris when the King arrived in France, and I had the chance to meet with him. The Late Ambassador Keshav Raj Jha introduced me to the King as Nepal's Air France representative. The King asked me if I had come all the way from Nepal to visit him, to which I replied, "Yes, your Majesty. During this visit, I have the pleasure to meet with you, and I also have business to do in Paris with Air France." I will never forget in my lifetime that short meeting and the king smiling at me.

FRIENDS THAT I AM INDEBTED TO FOREVER

Jean Michel Binoist, A young French traveler, whom I first met in Kathmandu in 1965, became a friend with whom I began exchanging letters, thus nurturing our friendship. In 1970, I met him for the second time in the city of Marseille. During this visit, I stayed at his house for nearly two months. He has been a primary and major source of influence for me, giving me the courage to embark on the adventurous journey of life. We reunited again in 1980 and for the third time in the year 2000 in France, after having lost contact for twenty years. At my invitation, I met Jean Michel and his second wife in Nepal for the fourth time.

Al Mattock The British gentleman who trained me in the first casino of Nepal, "Casino Nepal," was Al. Although I was initially rejected in the first interview, Al served as the trainer and pit boss of the casino when it began in 1968. Initially, he was my boss, but over time, he became my friend. He's also the same person who flew me from Paris to London without a visa, although unfortunately, I was turned back and unable to enter the UK. Despite feeling extremely distressed by that unfortunate event, later in life, I realized it was a blessing in disguise. This incident led me to return to Nepal and seek out new opportunities, which I now recognize as the Almighty's blessing.

Michael Hoffman, A young American traveler in nineteen seventy who traveled from Europe to Nepal and became a good friend of mine for a Travel Company, as well as, during his one year stay in Nepal.

Jean Claude Rouyer, In the early 1970s, he was the Frenchman who served as the regional manager of Air France for North India, Nepal, and Bangladesh, under the general manager of the Indian subcontinent. Jean Claude was the one who opened the first door for me to enter Air

France. Later, he became a close friend. Even after his retirement, I visited him and his wife at his house in Chamonix, France, three years before he passed away.

Robert Rieffel, My first employer in Air France in May 1972 in Kathmandu, Nepal. Not only did he hire me for the Air France job, but he also taught me many life lessons. Eventually, I considered and regarded him as my godfather. After the birth of my son and daughter, I named them after him and his wife: Robert and Cecile. Due to his contribution to the promotion of Nepali tourism in France, the Nepali government granted him and his wife permanent residence in Nepal.

Paul Le Borne, General Manager of Air France in Delhi for the Indian subcontinent. In the late eighties, he was the first French royalist that I have ever met in my life. He acted like a royalist, and at times, he seemed to have disliked me due to my direct confrontation of certain issues. Later, I realized he really liked me because he tore up a warning letter that originated with my immediate boss. Instead of giving me warning letters, he gave me the highest level of promotion, Category Six, within twenty years of my service with Air France. Normally, people in Air France retire with Category Three or Four. After he retired and returned to France, I tried to locate him but without any success. I still miss his smile and kindness when he reminisced about his royal beliefs.

Mark Benedetti, The general manager of Air France in the Indian subcontinent following Paul Le Borne. He was jovial and soft-spoken with the local staff, which was opposite in character to Paul Le Borne. In our very first meeting, we became cordial, and he tried to help me in every way possible. He is the one who facilitated my transition from salary employment to the General Sales Agency in Nepal. Even after the GSA transition, he continued to help me in incredible ways, for which I am indebted to him for a lifetime. Thirty years later, we are still very close friends, and I visit him and his wife Francoise every time I go to Paris, spending quality time together. I also regard him as one of my godfathers.

Madam Bernadette Vasseux, Bernadette worked in the French Embassy in Nepal for forty years in various capacities. During her tenure, we became very close friends and associates in the service of France-Nepal relations. I make it a point to see her in Paris as often as possible.

Doctor Corneille Jest, He was among the first French citizens to visit Nepal, beginning in the year nineteen sixty. He was an ethnologist and an anthropologist. He also served as the Director for the Nepal Chapter in the French government organization called CNRS. Spending many months in Dolpo, the Karnali region of midwestern Nepal, he immersed himself in studying the local culture, history, and human development. His experiences culminated in the book "Tales of the Turquoise: A Pilgrimage in Dolpo." During his stay in Dolpo, he even learned the Tibetan language.

Cornielle was also an expert in Nepali language, culture, and architecture. Whenever he visited Nepal, I had the opportunity to learn new things about my own country's history and culture from him. There was always a room reserved for me at his home whenever I visited France, and reciprocally, when he visited Nepal, he stayed at our home in Miraval. It has been a few years since he passed away, and the country of Nepal, including myself, lost a very devoted and valuable friend.

Christine Montenbault, She came to Nepal on holiday in nineteen seventy with a friend called Lilie from France. I met them on New Road. They had asked me for directions to a certain place in broken English, and I replied to them in French. I told them that I had been to France the previous year on an overland tour. They were so excited to meet someone in Nepal who spoke French. We bonded immediately over our French connection. I found out that they were looking for a restaurant near Asan Tole in one of the alleys, where you could smoke hashish and eat Western-style food at the same time. I didn't know the place, but I was familiar enough with Asan to offer to take them there. We chatted and laughed all the way to the restaurant. To my surprise, as soon as we entered, I was shocked by the ambiance. The restaurant was full of long-haired Western men and women, who I now understand were hippies. It was an adventurous trip for Christine and Lilie; they wanted to try smoking and explore. We spent some time there drinking, eating snacks, and enjoying a few puffs. Even though I didn't like it, I wanted to keep them company and joined in with them. We had a wonderful time during their stay in Nepal. Later, I became very close friends with Christine, even after she got married, had a child, and then divorced. We remain very close friends even today. She tells my younger daughter, who lives in France, that she is her French mother. I visited Colmar in Eastern France quite often and became a family friend.

PART III:

INCIDENCES AND REFLECTIONS

3.1 Travel Experiences

I think my deep fascination for travel is mainly responsible for the ups and downs in my life, even though my weaknesses also play a big part. I am the kind of person who focuses on one purpose. I am not the person who sits at home thinking that he can do nothing. Instead of limiting my exploration of business opportunities with companies in France or elsewhere by using phone, fax, and e-mail, I focus on making direct contact by visiting them in their home country, whether it be France, Spain, Germany, or the USA. It is probably one of the reasons why I have traveled to the West nearly four hundred times in a period of forty-five years of being involved in business. The crossroad point has always been Paris, France.

When I visit a new country, I don't spend weeks there. It is enough for me to see the geographical and natural landscapes, the beauty of the place, along with people's ethnicity, customs, the cleanliness in the streets, people's fashion, houses, temples, and monasteries. I also like to learn how people behave with outsiders. After getting the prima facie idea and picture in a few days, I feel a sense of satisfaction. If I am on a longer vacation, I also enjoy visiting the major museums in those cities to learn about the legends and history of the place.

Air France, at the time of my voluntary retirement, gave me, my family, and some accompanying people with an ID card, heavily discounted tickets, which allow us to visit any country that we desire to see. This travel allowance is valid until the year twenty-thirty on any Air France flight. If I live longer and stay fit, I may eventually ask for an extension. Adding up all the distances that I have traveled through the air in my life, I must have traveled a distance equal to ten journeys to and from the moon.

Aftermath Of My Travel Craze

I remember now, that back in those days I was a youngster who lacked wisdom and long-term vision. I just kept on traveling around without any assessment of the situation and its limited possibilities. To fulfill my desire of visiting France, I hadn't done any proper thinking and assessment. It was only because one of my friends who was heading for the US had said to me, "Shyam, what can you do here in Nepal? Come to the US." Without properly analyzing the situation, as well as asking my friends and family about my plans I decided to follow my friend's suggestion and travel to the US.

Based upon the decision from my own thoughts, I was delving into a whirlpool of uncertainties. This is why I had to come face to face with various obstacles. Looking on the positive side, the experience of various types of achievement because of my own decisions was important.

The kind of entertainment and self-satisfaction that land-based travel provides cannot be achieved through flight. Traveling by land, you get to step into many countries one at a time, see many cities, experience various lifestyles and customs, and meet all kinds of people during the journey. These things make traveling by land highly memorable.

I returned to Nepal after spending more than seven months in France and other parts of Europe. I had planned to write a memoir about the land route travel, but I couldn't manage to write more than a half page. It feels unbelievable to myself that I have been able to do this fifty years later. This has given me immense pleasure.

3.2 UNFORGETTABLE EVENTS

Briefcase Stolen In London and the Panic …

In November 1988, I went from Paris to London. Upon reaching the arrival hall, I went to a telephone booth to call a friend, Uttam Amatya. Keeping the briefcase by my right leg, I made the call. After a few rings, he answered the phone, and I asked him for directions to his apartment. As soon as I hung up the phone, within one or two minutes of conversation, I looked down and noticed that my briefcase was missing. I was dumbfounded! Immediately, I looked for it, but it wasn't there. I scanned with my eyes within the perimeter of forty yards, to see if anybody was carrying my brown liver-colored briefcase. Unfortunately, I couldn't find it. I did not see anybody running away with my briefcase, nor did I see a briefcase that resembled mine. I asked myself, what should I do now? Everything was inside that briefcase. I only had a little cash in my pocket.

After that, I searched for the address of the Nepali Embassy and headed towards there directly. I explained everything to them. Based on my old passport number, they prepared a new one for me. It was already evening by then. The following day, I had to be in France, but my French visa was stamped in the previously lost passport. Therefore, as I needed a French visa now, I searched for the French Embassy's address and went there. It was already ten am in the morning, and there was a huge queue stretching for almost two hundred meters, with people who were there to apply for their visas. If I stayed in the queue, I would have reached the embassy gate by about one pm.

I jumped the queue and went straight to the embassy gate and told the security that it was an emergency. The people in the queue were shouting at me, but I was able to convince the security police and entered the consular office. There was another long queue there. I had no options there but to wait patiently. From the gossip that came from the applicants who were returning from their interviews, the consular asked them to come back in a month for another visa interview. My heart was beating like a drum because of fear and desperation.

After finally getting my turn, the clerk at the passport counter looked at my passport and said, "It might take you two months to get a visa. In your case, we must correspond with our Embassy in Nepal, and only after we receive clearance from there can we deliver your visa." On hearing this, my heart almost burst. I controlled myself and then said, "I am the manager of Air France in Nepal. I have a three-year multiple entry visa. Since I lost my previous passport at the airport yesterday, in fact, it was stolen, I have made a new one. I need the visa so that I can travel to France today. Please let me talk to your consul."

After that, he hesitated a little and then went inside to a room. Three minutes later, he came back and escorted me to the room and introduced me to the Consul. I told him everything; he repeated whatever his staff had told me outside earlier. After that, I asked him, "Please give me your name and telephone number. I will get my visa approval today from the consul of Nepal. The Consul of Nepal is a friend of mine." After that, he was confused and gave me the name and telephone number. In those days, there was no cellular service, so I had to go to a telephone booth on the street to make the call using coins. I said, "OK, I'm going outside the embassy to make a call to Nepal." It was nearly lunch hour by then.

I hurriedly went outside to a nearby cafe and made a special request to the owner to give me twenty, one Euro coins. I called Stefan Maicon, who was the Vice Consul at the French Embassy in Nepal. Fortunately, the call was received on the first try. I explained everything in a hurry and gave him the name and number of the Vice Consul in London. At first, he laughed and then said, "All right, I will call him right away; you go back to him now." After that, I returned to the embassy again. The problem of the queue was still the same. Once again, I jumped the queue and managed to directly get into the Vice Consul's office. He gave me a cheeky smile and asked me to wait a while.

After staying there for another half an hour, he handed me my passport with the visa. I went directly to London airport and had my ticket made at the airline counter. I boarded the flight just before the door was closing. When I sat down on the seat, I sighed with a long breath. When the plane took off, I thought to myself that I would not be returning to London anytime soon! I also wondered how I even dared to breach the queue and go directly to meet the Vice Consul. Sometimes, you naturally tend to become unruly because of the situation that befalls you.

First American Culture shock

Just after Kathy and I had been married in the year nineteen seventy-six, our friends Vergil and Barbara had their children. I found out that they had agreed to share the expenses of their children equally. This left a churning sensation in my stomach. It was probably because I was raised in Nepali culture that I couldn't digest this thought. But after forty-five years of being habituated with American customs and culture, I have unknowingly assimilated it. Today, whenever I visit my American family, and no one proposes to pay the bill in the restaurant, we all agree to share the cost along with the service charge. I realized that this practice ensures that nobody must carry a hefty burden alone.

In Brussels

I went to Brussels on July 11th, 1992, to meet with some of my friends. Just like in London, I went to the telephone booth to call my friends. This time, however, I kept my briefcase right in front of my eyes and my carry-on bag at the back nearby. After two minutes of conversation, I turned around to see that my very beautiful Samsonite bag was gone. Once again, I looked to the sides, nearby, and in the distance to see if anybody was carrying my bag, but there was no one! This time my briefcase, money, passport, and ticket were still with me. Therefore, I stayed in Brussels that day and returned to Paris on the next day feeling very stupid.

In Copenhagen

On May 11th, 1995, I went to visit my Danish friend Alice Marcus, who frequently brought travel groups to Nepal. After staying in Copenhagen that day, we went to another city called Aarhus by train and then by ship to where her mother was living. The journey was a very memorable one; just like my sea cruise from Brindisi in Italy to Athens, Greece in 1970.

After staying with Alice for two days, I returned to Copenhagen alone. There was some time left before the arrival of the train at the station. I kept my briefcase and handbag on the floor of the platform and walked around, with a constant look toward my bags. At one point, I went a little ahead. I looked back to see if my bags were in place, even though I had kept the passport, ticket, and some cash with me. The bags contained credit cards, and some money sent by an Indian businessman, Mr. Santa Chatwal, who was staying in New York at the time. He was sending the money to one of his aides in Banepa, Kavre of Nepal, along with some other documents. I had not been paying too much attention to them; there was also a gold chain inside!

Meanwhile, as the train was a little delayed, I looked at the time schedules of train arrivals and departures. When I looked for my bags from afar, they were not there, and I couldn't see anyone. There were no people on my platform. One more magic stroke of bad luck was on my head; the train had arrived by this time, and I had no choice but to get on. Fortunately, this time I didn't lose my passport, ticket, or cash, except the five hundred dollars I was carrying for a man in New York, Santa Chatwal. I was supposed to give the money to his employee called Bade in Banepa, Nepal. There was also my gold chain! Upon returning to Nepal, I had to pay this money back to Bade, which broke my heart because I was in dire need of money at Mirabel Hotel. From this experience, I have promised myself never to carry other people's money again!

Panic In Milan, Italy In Safeguarding My Bags And Wallet

Sometime during 1995, I traveled to Milan, Italy because of some work. I went into the city center in a shuttle from the airport, and my hotel was just across from where the shuttle bus stopped. Getting out of the bus there, I had to cross a very wide street to get into the hotel on the other side. The road was nearly empty of traffic, and there were not many people coming or going. I was trying to cross the street, carrying one briefcase with one of my hands and rolling another suitcase with the other hand.

Suddenly, I saw a group of gypsies. There were two or three small children and a woman who looked like their mother. They rushed up to me and spread out their hands to ask me for money. As soon as I uttered the words "No, No," they started screaming and shouting at me. They began attacking me; one of them started pulling my briefcase, another one was pulling my suitcase, and two of the boys started to push their hands into the inside pockets of my jacket. In fear and confusion, I was screaming, "Hey! Hey!" I had already begun to think that they were going to make a mess out of me that day. A single person could not defend the suitcase, the briefcase, and my pockets at the same time. I was clueless about what to do.

Suddenly, a vehicle stopped, and the person driving saw the extent of their harassment. They shouted at the gypsies. After this, they slowly let go of me and started shouting back at the person in the car. I hurriedly crossed the street, went inside the hotel, and took long and heavy breaths. Sometimes, even when you try to be completely vigilant, you can come face to face with unexpected troubles.

The Pandemonium At Charles De Gaulle Airport, 2000

In November 2000, I called a taxi from my apartment at La Defense in Paris to take me to Charles De Gaulle airport. Right from the beginning, the taxi driver struck me as impolite, muttering complaints to himself. Despite this, I managed to reach the airport on schedule.

Upon arrival, the driver demanded two hundred ninety-two French francs, which encompassed additional charges for my baggage. Unfortunately, I only had two hundred ninety francs with me. He insisted on those extra two francs (about .40 USD) and waited as I scrambled to find them. Feeling exasperated and wanting to end the situation, I gave him a ten-franc coin that I had saved for a coffee later at the terminal before boarding. Normally, I would have given a bit extra, following the French custom of adding five to ten francs. However, I lacked the extra coins and found it unnecessary to use my credit card for a simple cup of coffee at the terminal (That was the reason why I wanted to save the ten-franc coin.) His behavior left me irritated, and I couldn't shake off the frustration of the encounter. This very 10-franc incident led me to a devastating ordeal for the whole week and many months ahead.

While checking in at the Air France counter, a staff member offered an immediate boarding pass for economy class. But, for a business class pass, I had to wait half an hour. I opted for the latter and was told to bring my bags on the trolley with me. They assured me they'd check in the bags once I returned for the business class pass. So, I arranged my bags on the trolley, including my Lancel briefcase which I covered with my coat. Letting the staff know I'd be back in half an hour, I left.

Normally, I'd head to a nearby café for coffee post-check-in. However, the taxi incident left me short of francs. Instead, I decided to call my friend in my apartment to let her know I hadn't finished check-in yet. If I wanted my usual coffee, I'd have to go down to the arrival level 9with all my suitcases and visit a bank to get money. Maneuvering my trolley amidst other travelers' baggage and dealing with bank queues seemed like a hassle. This process would have taken more than one half hour. So, I abandoned the idea and decided to make a phone call.

As I headed to the booth, an African woman hurried ahead to reach it before me. Annoyed, I entered the booth before her. With my trolley covered by my topcoat, I placed it behind me instead of in front. After my call, something felt wrong. Removing the topcoat, I realized my briefcase had vanished in a matter of seconds. I knew no one could have moved more than twenty-five feet from my trolley. Stunned, I felt like screaming. Amid the crowd, the atmosphere was oddly calm, as if my bag had disappeared like magic from under my coat.

I looked at the African woman beside me, peaceful and calm. Her family managed their suitcases in a similar manner. I wondered if my missing briefcase could be hidden in one of their trolleys, but I hesitated to ask them to open their bags. Slowly, I distanced myself from the scene and went to the nearby police station to report the incident. As I filed the report, an airport announcement urged passengers to be cautious due to an ongoing gang of bag thieves.

I couldn't help but think, why didn't this announcement come just fifteen minutes earlier? Inside my lost briefcase were my passport, tickets, credit cards, ID, and a huge lump of cash. With no option to fly to Delhi, I returned to my apartment and shared the story with my friend who was pursuing her master's degree in Paris. Together we cried for a long time. I started to believe that fate itself had conspired against me. That day felt like a dark mark in my life, stemming from a severe mishap that took away my huge amount of money and essential documents. The impact lingered for days in Paris, as well as weeks after I came back to Nepal, affecting my heart, mind, and soul.

Surprise Encounter With Mr. Eric Valli

The following day, I headed to the Nepali Embassy to secure a new passport. At the embassy, the Ambassador Mr. Keshav Raj Jha was already in the office. Mr. Eric Valli, the well-known French movie maker and photographer, whom I knew very well from Kathmandu, was also there for some work. I explained to everyone what had happened at Charles de Gaulle airport the previous day. While the Ambassador assured me of a quick issuance of a new passport, Eric Valli advised me to buy a belt to put my passport, money, credit cards, and air tickets in, and to wear it around my waist all the time, especially at the airport. Suddenly, I had a flashback of my fellow citizens, the Mananges, who always wore them during their business trips to Hong Kong and Singapore.

From this setback, I chose to stay in Paris a few more days, finding solace in its tranquil environment. Upon my return to Nepal, the incident continued to trouble me, causing pain and distress. It might sound superstitious, but I genuinely felt that this situation was a form of divine retribution for something I had done. It felt God had orchestrated my encounter with the thieves, allowing them to benefit from me.

Arrived in Calcutta Instead Of Delhi

During the middle of the year, 1969, I boarded a bus from Kathmandu to Birgunj. I had planned to find a route by train from Raxaul, which was a border city with Delhi. For this trip, I reached Raxaul in the evening, and as I was asking around to find my way to Delhi, I bumped into a Nepali guy at the station. We found out about one other destination, which happened to be Delhi and Calcutta. These were two cities located in opposite directions from one another, one thousand two hundred kilometers apart. His name was Upendra Dhital. He was a jolly fellow and spoke a bit of my native language, Newari. Somehow, he talked me into going to Calcutta, first to spend time with him, as well as time to spend a few days there. After my visit in Calcutta, I would then find a direct train, the Rajdhani Express, to New Delhi.

I was a person who could easily change plans, so I agreed and followed him to Calcutta, forgetting that I had a job at Casino Nepal which I had to return to and attend to at a certain time. In the process of rushing to catch the train, I forgot to buy food at the station, so I had very little food to eat with during my travel from Kathmandu to Raxaul.

I hurriedly boarded the train. By midnight, I was suffering a great deal because of hunger and was worried about how to spend the whole night in this way. The farther the train traveled, the hungrier I felt. It must have been around midnight when I felt a gust of air moving like a piece of marble from my lower stomach towards my heart. I felt a pushing sensation. In the beginning, I tried very hard to stop the pushing from reaching the heart, but slowly it was getting more and more unbearable. Then again, when the gust of air tried to move up to the chest, I tried to stop it by pressing my stomach with my fist. This pain continued until morning. Fortunately, I didn't die on the way. We reached the railway station in the morning. I hurriedly got out and grabbed some puri, deep-fried chapati, and curry. I felt like this food had given me a new life.

On a barge, we crossed the Ganga River and reached Patna rail station on the other side of the bank. We boarded the late-night train and finally reached Calcutta, half-dead from exhaustion. My whole face, including the nose, had become black because of the coal-burning smoke. That day we went to my friend's room and spent the night there. The next day he gave me a tour around the city, but I kept on thinking about Delhi and was in a hurry to leave Calcutta.

With the intention of getting to Delhi very soon, I went to the train station and tried to reserve a ticket for the next day. The station looked like a war zone and was crowded with thousands of people and their noise. I had no idea where to go and what to do. Finally, I found the ticket counter where they told me that there was no ticket for the next two to three weeks. For a while, my mouth went dry and I felt desperate; I couldn't muster up the idea concerning my next move. After a while, I thought that I should go by bus, but it would be even more impractical. The bus could take at least a week. In the evening, I discussed the issue with Upendra, and we came up with the idea to get a flight. The next day I went to the Indian Airlines office to buy my ticket, which was more than I could afford, but as I had no other options, I bought the ticket and returned to Upendra's apartment. Somehow, I felt relieved that I would reach Delhi the following day and wouldn't have to wait forever to get there. The next day I left for the airport to take my flight. When I was getting on the bus to travel from the terminal to the plane, a little accident happened. Going up the steps to the bus, I didn't see that there was a piece of pointed metal on the side of the steps. This tore my pants on the left side; however, I managed to get to my seat without other passengers and the air hostesses noticing the rip!

After the plane took off from the airport, I had two or three things heavy on my mind. The first thing that concerned me was how to hide my torn pants from other passengers. If I could just manage to get a needle and thread, I could take a few stitches. Another thing that concerned me was that half of the money I had with me for my Delhi visit had been spent on the airplane ticket. How many days am I going to stay in Delhi now? How much do I spend? As I was dealing with all these mental pressures the plane finally landed in Delhi airport two hours later. Once again, I tried my best to hide my torn pants on the flight and later in the Indian Airlines bus; I also managed to reach central Delhi and check into a hotel. After resting for a while, I called a Nepali student I knew, Geeta Chand, who was studying in a girl's college. Geeta and her friends visited me at my hotel the same evening and we went out for dinner and dancing at a discotheque. I had never experienced in all my life that much fun, even though I was the only boy surrounded by five other girls. The next day, I couldn't connect with Geeta and her friends, because of her college schedule so I went to see some Indian youth that I had befriended in the casino while in Nepal. I returned to Nepal fully content despite all the crazy things that had happened in just one week! Twenty years later, I met Mr. Upendra in the Department of Civil Aviation. He had already become Deputy Director-General. He asked me again, in my native language, Chhu kha Paasaa? meaning: "What's happening my friend?" Looking at him, suddenly all my crazy travels that had happened twenty years before came flashing into my mind!

Surprise Encounter with Denzel Washington and Family

After summer holidays in the mid-1980s, I was returning home from the US with my family, flying from New York to Paris. We boarded the plane and had been assigned the front row of business class. Directly in front of our row was the first-class section of the plane, where a row of four seats remained unoccupied. Just before the plane door closed, a family of four—a mother, father, and two kids—boarded, escorted by a flight attendant.

As they approached their first-class seats, I realized the man was none other than Mr. Denzel Washington, an American actor whom I'm very fond of. I had the opportunity to nod at him, and he smiled back. I felt really elated.

I observed them stowing their bags and getting settled into their seats; they were very reserved, speaking only to each other in hushed tones.

After takeoff, they closed the partition between business and first class, but I could still hear them talking quietly.

I was very impressed by what a gentleman Mr. Washington was, which made me respect him even more. This is where I learned that a gentleman should speak with a mannerly tone in public.

First The Daughter, Then The Mother Proposed To Take Me To A Discotheque

On the thirty-first of July, nineteen ninety-eight, I flew from Paris to Nice, which is a very beautiful city on the French Riviera bordering the Mediterranean Sea. This is one of the most beautiful and touristic cities in all of France. From there, my next destination was to reach the house of my business associate, Roland Etroy. He was in a small village on the hills very near to another major tourist city called Saint Raphael. Our plan was that I would take a train from Nice and reach his small town. On arrival, I would make a call to him, and he would come and pick me up. This was also a dream of mine as it was a beautiful Mediterranean belt called the Riviera which stretched from Italy to France and all the way to Spain. It was more than three hundred kilometers long. Similarly, long were the fifteen hundred feet high cliffs that stretched out just like the seacoast. These hills housed tens of thousands of villas with large gardens and swimming pools that were used by the owners and vacationers.

Due to my impatient nature, I boarded the wrong train which traveled at about five kilometers per hour and stopped every three minutes! I was nervously jumping up and down on the train, complaining about the stops and the speed the train was traveling! At one point, it finally stopped, which I found out was only halfway through to my real destination! All the passengers got off the train within two minutes and they disappeared. What was left? It was me, the train, and the marketplace across from the station. It was completely closed with no one around the area. I felt as though I had arrived in a ghost town. I felt chills in my body as the ghost town was getting darker. Finally, I saw a telephone booth where a taxi number was written. I called for a taxi, and I was also able to call my friend Roland with an update. The taxi arrived ten minutes after I called him, then he headed toward my friend's house. The meter was clicking at the most expensive tariff called 'C'. It was one of the costliest taxi rides in my life! Finally, I reached Roland's house, and it was only after that I breathed a heavy sigh of relief.

I was so delighted to see the infrastructure, architecture, and the grandeur of the place. There were rock walls nicely built into the layers of a large garden. The garden was also full of trees and there was a turquoise-colored swimming pool. In this mountainous surrounding was a beautifully constructed two-story house from where you could view the boundless sea. At first, they served a welcome drink and then some snacks. In the meantime, his daughter Catherine proposed that I go for a swim. As she got into her swimsuit, she came to me and asked for company. I told her that I didn't know how to swim well, but she was just interested in having me as company. I agreed. I went along with her and watched her swim. Roland's wife had been preparing a grand dinner along with appetizers and drinks which was also equally appealing. After a whole day of travel, filled with frustration, the welcome experience made me feel like I was in heaven. I tasted a lot of the delicious red wines. In the meantime, Roland's wife was continuously moving in and out of the house. Catherine said to me: "Shyam, tonight I'm going to take you for a dance at a discotheque in St. Raphael." Unfortunately, that night I was absolutely exhausted because of my travel troubles during the day but I still said OK, however, I was in no shape for a dance. After dinner, I was having an interesting conversation with Roland's wife on one side of the kitchen. She said to me: "Shyam, tomorrow night I'm going to take you to a discotheque in Saint Raphael." I also said, "OK!"

I got up late the next day and upon waking up I saw that a grand breakfast had already been prepared. I sat down at the table for breakfast when suddenly Roland said to me: my friend, my daughter seems to have liked you. Catherine was swimming alone before breakfast. Then Roland's wife said: my daughter is a special one, a lot of guys try to attract her by boasting about their wealth, but my daughter doesn't care, these fools do not know how wealthy her father is. In my mind, I was realizing that I had a friend who was very rich. I was now secretly fearing inside my heart whether Roland would say that his wife also liked me. I hurriedly started talking about business to change the topic.

It was a place of heavenly beauty with serenity all around, deep blue sky, bright warm sun and the view of the deep blue Mediterranean sea. It was a healthy environment with expert culinary expression, complemented with French branded delicious wines. Along with the warmth of the mother-daughter relationship and a grand welcome from a friend, I spent three of the most wonderful days in complete happiness and pleasure before finally returning to Paris. I thoroughly enjoyed those three days which remain a sweet memory even today.

3.3 OTHER ACTIVITIES AND EVENTS

Concorde in Kathmandu, And my Opportunity to get on Board.

The eleventh of October, nineteen eighty-seven, has remained a very special day in the history of Nepali aviation. That day, an aircraft with a nose resembling a needle and with wings spread out like that of an eagle was seen flying in the Nepali sky. It touched down on the runway at Tribhuvan International Airport with a deafening sound that had never been heard before; it broke many windows panes in the area. This was an extraordinary achievement for airplane manufacturers around the world. To fly in the Concorde was very expensive. It cost more than a first-class ticket on a conventional airline. The whole team of Air France had come from Delhi for ground handling of this plane. It was carrying one hundred passengers on a round-the-world trip.

That evening, I hosted a reception at my house, "Miraval," in Budhanilkantha. I managed to talk to the captain of the Concorde and asked for a ride to Paris from Kathmandu in that airplane. I managed to get a ride the following day. My boss, however, said that there was a meeting the same day in Delhi, so I had to stop there. I was such a lucky person to be able to fly in a Concorde whereas my bosses had to take a regular Boeing 727 back to Delhi.

In Rescue of a French Company in 1992

As part of the economic collaboration between France and Nepal, it was agreed that France would rebuild the forty-two-kilometer-long ropeway from Hetauda to Teku in Kathmandu. This length of ropeway has not been in use for a long while. There was a tender announced by the Nepali government for French companies to bid. GIMAR and POMA were in the final competition for this contract. Between the two, GIMAR was a small company and was unfit for the job.

Due to their political reach, representatives of GIMAR had built up rumors that POMA was considered unfit for the job instead. The final contract had reached the minister's table for approval. After calling the contemporary minister, the late Khum Bahadur Khadka, and explaining everything, the Minister recalled, and the rightful French company Poma finally got the tender. I was able to provide justice to a French company.

When Prime Minister Koirala Lost His Temper

This is an unforgettable incident that took place with the late Prime Minister Girija Prasad Koirala in the late nineties. On occasion, I would visit him for a special purpose. One day during nineteen ninety-eight, I went to visit him at his office in Singha Durbar.

I was served tea, then we chatted for a short while. He then asked me directly for some service in favor of some of his party people. At that time, I was also in a troubled period myself. I told him that I couldn't possibly fulfill his request but would try to do something else.

As the Prime Minister was known to be short-tempered, he said in a rather high-pitched voice, "Get out, get out, do you deal with a Prime Minister in such a way?" I decided not to explain anymore and quietly got up and walked to the door. His private assistant Gokarna Poudel was waiting for me. He asked me what had happened, and I told him the entire story. He assured me that I wasn't to worry, and that he would pacify him.

Two days after the incident, I met with the Prime Minister's daughter, Ms. Sujata Koirala. I told her about the incident. She burst into laughter. Two to three months after the incident, I went to meet the Prime Minister at his residence. Mr. Gokarna took me into a large meeting room. As soon as I entered through the door, the Prime Minister saw me and said, "Aaiye aaiye, come, come." I was thinking inside my head, is this the compensation for the scolding that I received the last time!

During my conversations with him, I told him about my upcoming hotel and requested that he kindly inaugurate it. On the eighteenth of September, nineteen ninety-eight, Prime Minister Girija Prasad Koirala inaugurated Mirabel Resort Hotel, my dream came true. That day I thought, everything has its time.

Papier Du Riz Du Nepal!!! Papier Du Riz Du Nepal!!! (Rice Paper From Nepal)

After becoming employed with Air France in the beginning of 1972, I regularly went to Paris for training, as well as a few times in London. The company arranged for my stay there. I was also given a daily allowance of one hundred francs which was a minimal amount. It had to be managed on a personal level.

I always felt the lack of money to fully enjoy Paris. I was constantly frustrated because I was always the poorest one when I went out with friends. One day a friend called Gerard Dolain said to me, "Hey Shyam, whenever you come from Nepal, bring some items with you, sell them here in Paris for a profit and you will have some money to spend for yourself." I began to think about what the most convenient item would be to bring from Nepal and then sell it.

There were many greeting cards and postcards available using Nepali handmade paper. There were pictures of various gods and goddesses being sold in the tourist shops of Thamel, Boudha, and Swayambhunath. The cost of each painting was two Franc (0.30 Euros). On another visit to Paris, I bought a bundle of rice paper-colored prints. I called Gerard and showed him the products. He liked them and proposed that we go to the banks of the Seine River in central Paris.

Gerard placed them on the footpath and tried to attract the attention of the passersby by saying, "Papier du riz, Papier du riz du Népal" Rice Rice paper prints from Nepal. Some people, passersby looked at them, some started to buy them and some just ignored the call. While Gerard was trying to call the attention of the passersby, I felt shy and stayed a bit far away from him.

Each piece of print was priced at 10 francs, about 2$. We were situated just to the lines of the bookshops which sold old books, old paintings and block prints on the banks and sidewalks of the Seine River.

One of those shopkeepers called Madame Moziere, who always had a cigarette in her mouth (was probably fed up with us) bought everything for half the price. I was happy with it. It cost me in Nepal only 1 franc.

On my next trip to Paris a couple of months later I brought more rice paper prints to Paris. This time my friend Gerard was not in Paris but my friend Bernard Chiku was there. He went to Madame Moziere with the bundle to sell them. As soon as Madame Moziere saw Bernard, she suddenly put her two hands on her head and said loudly, "Oh La la … These rice paper prints again. I have not even sold half of what I bought two months ago." Bernard came back and explained the situation and we both enjoyed a great laugh. I do not remember what we did then but may have sold for one quarter of the price to her again.

When Shyam Shrestha Became Hari Shrestha in Washington D.C.

It was in the month of June, 1973. After the completion of my first year of employment at Air France, I was entitled to my first one-month long leave. Upon thinking hard about where I was going to go, I finally decided to go to the U.S.A., where I had been in contact with my friend Gorkhali. I flew from Kathmandu to Bangkok with my connection to board the Air France flight to Paris, and then on to the U.S. My first effort to go to the USA in 1970 had failed, so this was a new attempt.

On the first day of my holiday, I arrived in Bangkok. In the evening, I checked into a two-star hotel. I went to have a beer at the restaurant of the hotel. A Thai girl came to join me without even asking my permission. We spent some time laughing, chatting, and drinking. The situation progressed into greater intimacy in which she followed me to my room. As it had been very late that night, I didn't know how fast I had fallen asleep. I woke up at five am the next morning to go to the toilet. I didn't see the girl in the room and immediately rushed to open my suitcase. I looked for the cash in my purse but there was none. I panicked. Fortunately, I still had the American Express traveler's check with me. Later when I went down to the reception to talk to the staff about the incident, I was informed that they do not take responsibility for such thefts. They went on to say that I needed to keep all my money in their safe boxes for proper safety and security.

I didn't want to stay in Bangkok any longer. Luckily, I had bought a traveler's check in Kathmandu worth three hundred dollars. I got a refund from American Express early in the morning. With a bitter experience and a gloomy face, I boarded the flight to Paris, then on to Washington D.C. to meet my friend Bhagat Lal Gorkhali. I spent a few comfortable days in Washington D.C. chatting and drinking beer with my friend Gorkhali. Slowly the stolen money in Bangkok started to worry me because that money was given to me by some travel agencies and my airline colleagues. They had ordered Seiko watches, gold chains and suit material from Hong Kong and Bangkok. I was going to be in real trouble. I had no money of mine to buy any of the gifts that my colleagues had ordered. They may not really believe my story about what had happened to the money and my story was true. They might assume that I had made all of this up to gobble all their money. I talked to my friend in the U.S. and came up with this idea. If I could find work for a month in Washington, D.C., I would have enough cash to buy what they had requested before heading back home.

A few days after arrived in Washington, D.C., I went to The L'Enfant Plaza Hotel upon hearing that there were vacancies for busboys and waiters in the restaurant. Luckily, there were vacancies. The salary was three hundred dollars per month. My interviewer was a lady from Panama. She said to me, if you want to join then fill up this form immediately. Tomorrow, you may not get it. At first, I was confused but then I thought about what my friends would say about me if I returned empty-handed to Kathmandu. Some of them were waiting for their Seiko5 watches, some for their suit pieces and some for their gold chains. Remembering all these demands from my friends, I immediately went ahead to fill out the form. Upon seeing my clumsy and hurried attempt to apply, the woman from Panama proposed to fill out the form herself. At first, she asked me my full name. I hesitated a bit, thinking, if I give my real name here, I could get into trouble in the future? Moreover, I am a staff member with Air France. What happens if all this incident goes public, I then said that my name was Hari Shrestha. She also asked for the spelling. On the one hand, I had lied about my first name; I cursed myself for getting into such a messy situation. On the other hand, I was worried about what would happen to my Air France job if I got entangled in some tax-related issues here. I found it hard to get words out of my mouth. Noticing my confusion, she exhibited even more hurriedness and asked me again, what is your name? Slowly and with a very somber tone, I said, Hari Shrestha, and then spelled it. She repeated by saying, I couldn't understand a single letter you said! In those days my English language pronunciation wasn't that good and because of the stress and tension, the pitch of my voice had gone low. She then shouted out each letter of my name and filled up the form as H.a.r.i S.h.r.e.s.t.h. a, teasing me as if I were a child. After everything was done, she asked me to come again at five am the next morning. I was relieved because she didn't ask for my passport or any other type of ID card. For the country of citizenship, she wrote the name Nepal and recorded my friend's Washington, D.C. address. Leaving the office after everything was done, I took a long deep breath mixed with both fear and happiness.

Upon returning to the apartment, I explained everything that had happened during the day to my friend. He then said, if you're going to reach there at five am then you need to wake up at three-thirty am. After taking a shower and getting ready you must walk for forty-five minutes. I had a beer before going to bed that night and my eyes were still tightly closed when I woke up at three-thirty the next morning. I tried to open my eyes again but was unable, I had no strength to even sit up on the bed. It was so difficult that I thought to myself, to hell with this job! I cannot do it! I went back to sleep. I woke up again and felt the threats that I would have to face once I got back to Nepal. I slowly moved my feet towards L'Enfant Plaza! It was really tiring for me to reach there, and I was feeling sleepy all the time. I barely managed to reach the place in forty-five minutes. They served breakfast to the staff first. You could have as much egg, bacon, butter, toast, beans, coffee and milk as you wanted. While enjoying the delicious breakfast, I noticed that the waitresses were serving the same food to the customers upstairs as we were eating. This was a new experience for me to observe.

After the busy hours were over in the morning, the Panamanian woman introduced all the waiters and waitresses to Ms. Lee, an African American woman, who was the manager of the restaurant. When my turn arrived, I nodded my head to greet everyone but inside I was feeling very awkward and inhibited. In the next few days that followed, Bhagat Lal Gorkhali was invited for dinner by his friend Shambhu Acharya, who was an officer of Nepal Rastra Bank. He was working on a mission with the World Bank in Washington, D.C., and I was also asked to come along. There were other Nepali personalities invited as well. The drinks were served, and we were all having fun. I drank two to three bottles of beer and some whiskey. The dinner was still a long way off. Since I had gotten up very early that morning, and had worked all day, and had walked several kilometers to and from work, the drinks that evening hit me hard. Unable to control myself, I began to fall asleep at seven pm right on the sofa! Even though I was asleep, my ears could still hear a little. Some of the guests were asking, why had Shyam ji fallen asleep so early in the evening? I kept on lying there and couldn't gather up the strength to get up, my friend said nothing to me. It was only at around ten pm that I finally woke up and had dinner. We then returned home; I was asleep in the car the entire way. The next day I woke up at three-thirty am and went to work. Like the previous day I was constantly falling asleep as I walked. I became more awake once I reached my workplace. That morning, Ms. Lee was calling out a name, "Harry." After some time, she called again, "Harry, Harry!" I stayed quietly at my place as I thought she was calling someone else. When she shouted "Harry" again, I suddenly realized, "Oh no, my name is Harry! I ran towards Ms. Lee. She then questioned me by asking, "Don't your ears work? Didn't you hear me calling?" I replied that I was sorry, while bowing my head. I reminded myself that I needed to be more aware of my name Harry, in this workplace. The next day, Ms. Lee made another complaint by saying, ''Harry, you have an odor. Don't you use any deodorant?" I just kept quiet and hung my head in shame. Earlier, the Panamanian woman had also questioned me about my armpit odor. The next day, before leaving for work I sprayed Eau-de-Cologne all over my body which I had found in my friend's bathroom. That day Ms. Lee, as well as the Panama girl complimented me by saying, ''Oh, you smell so nice today" and then they gave me a smile. And from that day onwards I regularly used the same Cologne before going to work. I also bought my own deodorant which was the first one I have ever used in my life. After a week or so my relationship with everyone at work was friendly and strong.

My friend Bhagat Lal was often invited by his other Nepali friends, and I regularly joined him. At around seven pm, after one or two drinks I could hardly keep myself awake and then searched for a sofa in some corner to take a nap. This made all the friends and guests wonder why I would fall asleep so early at every party.

I didn't tell anybody that I went to work at three thirty in the morning every day. In another few days, the old friends invited us again. It was still the same old routine for me, after a beer or two I would always fall asleep. The friends started complaining by saying, Shyam ji, what is this? You are always very sleepy and it's always very early every time. I would simply smile.

In this manner, my nights were difficult in Washington, D.C. Forty-eight years later, I met Mr. Shambhu Acharya at his home and handed him over the book I had written on land route travel to France. I finally revealed to him why I was always asleep during those parties in Washington, D.C.

I had been in Washington, D.C. for a month. It was already late for me to be back at my work in Nepal, however, my work in L'Enfant Plaza had only been for three weeks. I still needed to work for one more week. So, I stayed one extra week waking up at three-thirty, walking to work with a half-dead body.

The day I completed one month of work, I went to see Ms. Lee and told her that I had an emergency and that I needed to leave the following day. I requested that she kindly give me my salary for the month that I had worked. Ms. Lee was really surprised and said that it would not be possible to get my salary in a single day. The hotel has a process that must be followed to grant a leave and then receive the salary earned.

My face turned red and then blue upon hearing this. My lips and my forehead went dry, and a tornado whirled inside my mind. I thought, oh no, what am I going to do next? It doesn't seem like I'm going to get my pay despite such hard work. I became dumbfounded and stayed quiet gazing down at the floor. Miss Lee must have realized the gravity of the situation and after a while slowly said, ''There is a way if it's such an emergency. I need to fire you from work citing the reason for my incompetence at work!''

In this way and by the evening you can get the payment for all your work. Hearing this I was suddenly elated and therefore I requested that she follow the necessary procedure. After the quick dismissal process, I left the restaurant in a hurry.

Though I had been "fired" it was a joyous moment with three hundred dollars of cash in my hand. At his home, I told my friend Gorkhali the whole story and flew to Paris the very next day. After staying in Paris for a day I then flew to Bangkok. There I bought as many items as I could manage with the money I had earned. There was not enough money for the suit piece my friend BB Shrestha of Yeti Travels had ordered. He was not happy with me for a long time and didn't speak to me for quite a while.

When I finally landed in Kathmandu two weeks later, I joined my office the very next day. Mr. Reiffel, my boss, had been angrily waiting for my return, but he was also very happy to see me back. His secretary Anne Marie Ro Landeau kept giggling while watching us, the more the old man got angry, the more she giggled.

After becoming diligently involved in my job once again Mr. Reiffel let go of his anger towards me and behaved with love and care.

Returning The American Green Card To The Embassy In Kathmandu

After Kathy and I were married in March, 1976, we went to visit my father-in-law and other family members in America. I would always apply for a tourist visa for the United States. This required time, money and hassles at the American Embassy. So, I applied for a green card, and I was given one immediately. One of the reasons I applied for a green card was because the Immigration Officer at the entry point would always ask me why I had come to the United States. He would also ask how much money I had and other irritating questions.

The summer of 1978, when I had received a green card, I arrived at JFK airport in New York and went to the queue of American citizens and green card holders' line.

The plane I flew in had brought in five hundred passengers. There were also other flights that had brought in many more passengers. In my line, even though it was a queue for American citizens and green card holders, there was a huge crowd. I was in the middle of it with these tall Americans. Being a short man, I felt like I was inside a jail and these tall black and white Americans were like the walls of the jail.

When I arrived at the immigration counter, the officer didn't ask me the regular questions, instead he asked me other questions: when did you go to Nepal from the US? How long did you stay there, and did you fill up the American tax form last year?

It was a long list of questions. These questions really irritated me, and I said, "I got this green card last year. I live in Nepal, and I work there. It's because my wife is an American citizen, and it is too much of a hassle for me to get a tourist visa every time. This is the reason I applied for and got the American green card. I have not filed any American tax form because my income and expenses all take place in Nepal."

Hearing this, the officer asked, "Why did you get the green card if you were going to stay in Nepal? You can return this card to the American Embassy after you return to Nepal".

And then I said, "Alright, I'll do that!" Upon my return to Kathmandu after a month-long vacation, I went directly to the American Embassy and returned my green card. The officer receiving back my green card seemed to be asking himself inside," What the heck. is happening?" "The American Green card is one of the most sought-after documents in the world and this guy is giving it back." The story of the green card in my life ended in this manner.

He Is The Smartest Of All Of Us Here In The Party

In December, nineteen eighty-nine, the tenure of Mr. Le Borgne as general manager of Air France for the subcontinent was coming to an end. During that year, in the winter, a two-day seminar program was organized at Mumbai's Oberoi Hotel, and I was there representing Nepal. All the delegates from the Asia Pacific region were busy throughout the day because of the conference, lunch, and tea breaks. In the evening, a cocktail dinner was arranged on the open roof garden of the hotel which was on the thirty-second floor. The program was attended by managers from all the countries in the region.

By nature, I am not the kind of person who likes to mix with many people. At this gathering, I talked to a few Indian friends who I was fond of and sometimes I stayed alone. After the cocktail was over the dinner queue started and I joined in. The dinner was inaugurated by Mr. Gerard who was the Vice President of the Asia Pacific region. Following him was Mr. Le Borgne, the general manager in India. After that, the buffet was followed by all the other participants without hierarchy. All the important people were on one table and the other delegates were spread throughout the room.

After getting my food, I was slowly sneaking by the VIP table, suddenly I heard someone calling me loudly. It was Mr. Le Borgne, ''Srestraa! Srestraa!''. This is because the French always called me Srestraa instead of Shrestha. When I slowly turned my head towards the table, I was asked to join them. I wondered what was happening and why I was being called? Hesitatingly and slowly, I moved towards that table and then he pointed at me and exclaimed to the Vice President,''il est le plus malin parmi nous ce soir'' ''This Shrestraa is Nepal's manager. He's the sharpest man among all of us at the party tonight''. At that very moment everybody at the other tables looked at me and smiled. I became a little shy. Seeing this, the general manager, Le Borgne said, "Of course after me!" I smiled and slowly went my way because if I had stayed there, I would have had to communicate with all of them in French which I did not want to do at that time, I just didn't feel comfortable.

The Heritage Ball Surprise At Soaltee Hotel Kathmandu

At the end of 1984, as they did every year, some of the big Rana families organized a gala dinner program with entertainment and lucky draws, with a view to raise funds that would be used in renovation of historical World Heritage sites in the city of Kathmandu. This program was generally attended by two hundred well-off people from the city.

At the end of the dinner program, there was a raffle prize distribution. The lottery was announced sometimes at midnight. After all the other winners had been announced, the second and the first prize winners from the raffle draw remained to be drawn. The second place was drawn, and it was announced that it went to Kathleen Shrestha; everybody shouted hurray.

Finally, it was time to draw for the first prize winner, and while looking at the ticket, the person who drew, announced that the number one winner was Shyam Shrestha. When this was announced, there was a chaotic situation with happy hurray's and boisterous bravos. What a coincidence……husband and wife, number one and number two! One of the mathematicians presents was heard to be saying, this kind of coincidence can happen only once in one hundred thousand times!

All Night Staggering On The Streets Of Prague, Czechoslovakia As A Half Dead Man.

In 1984, I flew to Prague having had a two-hour delay of my flight from Paris. I arrived in Prague around 11 pm. At that time, It was still under Communist regime. At the airport, the immigration people took me off the arriving passenger line for more interrogation, even though I was holding a visitor's visa issued by the Czech Embassy in Paris.

The process of their inquiries delayed me even further in reaching my hotel, The Intercontinental. It was in downtown Prague and had been booked by a friend of mine who lived in Prague. By the time I reached the hotel in a taxi, I was exhausted and almost half dead due to my delay in Paris. Waiting in the Paris airport, the two-hour travel in a crowded plane, lack of a proper dinner, the integration process and the time lapse, along with the taxi ride to the city, as I remember, I was dozing all the way from the airport to the hotel.

Upon arrival, I gave my passport to the reception for check in. The man looked for my name on the computer and took a long time to say that I had no reservations. I panicked and almost fell on the floor because I was dead tired. I gave the name of the person who booked but the man continued to say, "No reservations" and no room available…I could not reach my friend despite my effort with landline, there was no mobile phone in those days.

In my previous visit to this city in 1982, I had seen that it was a very backward city as compared with other western European cities. The entire city was a dark city, and all the nice buildings were dark, due to the lack of cleaning, washing and painting. The shop windows were very small and had not much on display. Inside there was a lot of dust on which the display objects were placed. Basically, Prague was in a very sad condition.

Despite that, I thought I would spend the night on the hotel sofas, so I moved quietly towards them. No sooner had I sat on the sofa, the receptionist at the counter came and said," No you CANNOT stay here . Please leave the hotel with your suitcase"

Dumbfounded, I quietly left the hotel and went to the street hoping that I would see another hotel on the corner. I dragged myself and the suitcase along the street. Alas, there was nothing on the street, I dragged on to another street without any knowledge of anything, any address or any of the geography of the city. Within an hour, I melted on the sidewalk. I sat on the sidewalk with my head on my suitcase. But it did not bring any relief to me. My body demanded that I lie down on a bed or on the ground. The street was dark and scary. One or two cars raced every half hour or so. I found it dangerous and was ashamed to be sitting on the sidewalk like that. Moreover, it was getting cold.

I knew I was near the river, so I thought it would be better to spend the night under the bridge and on the pavement rather than stay on the sidewalk. It must have been about 3 am by then. Once again, I gathered all my remaining strength and got up and began to drag myself and the bloody suitcase. Finally, I reached my resting place under the King's bridge around 4 am! I sat on the pavement with my suitcase as a cushion. Due to fatigue, I dozed off for a couple hours and by about 6 am I woke up less tired and ready to go on.

I walked back to the Intercontinental Hotel thinking that my friend would come to see me there, as I was booked there but without a room. I was able to get fresh coffee and something to eat on the way to the Intercontinental Hotel. When I arrived at the hotel, the staff at the counter from the previous night were gone and a new receptionist, who was much kinder, was in place. In the meantime, my friend called me, and I was then registered at the hotel. (It appeared , the night before , the receptionist might have sold my room as a price advantageous for him.)

My friend came along with another friend of hers and when we sat for breakfast, my head fell on the table continuously from the fatigue of the night before. As a consequence, I had to go straight to my bed instead of devouring the breakfast. I slept the entire day!

Opening A Champagne Bottle With A Sword

Sometime in the winter of 1988, I went to Colmar, France to see my friend Christine and her then husband Maurice. They picked me up from the Mulhouse Airport, and we drove about two hours to reach their home, just in time for an aperitif.

I rested in the living room after I dropped off my luggage in my guest room. I saw Maurice coming to the living room with a scary sword in his right hand and a bottle of chilled champagne in his left hand, while Christine carried a platter of cheeses, olives, and saucisson.

Maurice said to me, "Hey Shyam… do you want to try to open the bottle of champagne in a historic old manner?" He went on to explain that in old times, one way of opening champagne was to chop off the neck with a sword.

I began to worry about what to do or say. On one hand, this situation was entirely unfamiliar to me, and on the other hand, wielding a sword like a warrior to chop off the neck of the bottle seemed equally frightening. If I did not cut it fully and the glass neck shattered into pieces, I was afraid it would mean the loss of a Moet Chandon and a messy floor with pieces of glass and spilled champagne.

Without thinking much further, I took the heavy sword and chopped off the neck without spilling a drop of champagne! Maurice and Christine were in awe! Perhaps due to my Nepali height and stature, they might have thought that I was unable.

This, for me, has remained a landmark memory. In a world of 8 billion people, how many people would have the opportunity to experience such a historic French ritual?

Very Angry With Air France

In the decade of the 1980s, John Louis Rattier was the Deputy Managing Director at Air France in Paris. He was a Nepal lover and came to Nepal quite often. This is how I was able to build a strong friendship with him. One day during a dinner at a common friend's house in Paris, he was telling some of his funniest stories that had happened in Air France. Jean Louis, at the time, was also in charge of passengers' complaints.

One day, an older passenger came to make a complaint to him and said, "I am very upset with Air France. It has very much looked down upon me." Jean Louis asked the gentleman what had happened. Then the elderly passenger said, "Two days ago I was on an Air France plane traveling from Rome to Paris. I had gone to the toilet, there was some turbulence, and I was trying to get up and out of the toilet. I heard an announcement from the captain telling us to return to our seats. So, I did and sat back down on the toilet again. I waited for another announcement, half an hour later I still hadn't heard an announcement. Half an hour later when I finally opened the toilet, I saw that there was no one inside the plane, and everyone had left. The Air France crew were closing the plane door, leaving me alone in the aircraft." Jean Louis had a great deal of difficulty trying to explain the situation to him to pacify his complaint.

Your Appointment Is At 11 At Night

Mr. Rattier also told me of another incident. At one time the chairman of Air France was Mr. Henry Ziegler. He was a very effective chairman and was always extremely busy because Air France fully belonged to the French government. At the time Mr. Rattier was the Marketing Director, he had requested an appointment with the chairman. The secretary said, "Eleven o'clock in one week."

Mr. Rattier appeared at eleven am at the chairman's office; there was a different secretary there who told Mr. Rattier that his appointment was not listed. He repeated to the secretary that it had been noted down on the schedule. While scrolling down Mr. Ziegler's schedule for all his appointments, she said, "Mr. Rattier, your appointment is at eleven pm tonight!"

Fed Up With My Boss

The French ambassador to Nepal, Mr. Michel Jolivet, was in Nepal in the year twenty ten. One day while having lunch at my place he narrated some funny incidents. Some years before that he was the First Secretary at the French Embassy in one of the African countries.

There was no Air France flight in that country, only KLM. So, he had to use this airline to go to France. One day, the KLM airport manager shared an incident which had happened to him: the airport manager's boss, who was the general manager of the company, worked in the city's head office. He was a vicious and a hard person who made the airport managers' life miserable because he always criticized him. Coming home from the airport, the airport manager always exclaimed to his wife the same phrase, "I am fed up with my boss, I am fed up with bloody KLM."

The airport manager had also raised a parrot at his house. At one point, the airport manager had invited his boss along with his wife for dinner to his home. As soon as his boss and his wife entered the house, the parrot said, "I'm fed up with my boss, I'm fed up with KLM". The airport manager told the French Ambassador, Mr. Jolivet, this story and that he didn't know how to handle the situation, and he didn't know what to say!

Another incident the French ambassador, Mr. Michel Jolivet, told was when he was traveling from an African country to Paris in Air France's economy class: He was well settled when an air hostess came and proposed to take him to the front of the plane. He followed her to the first-class cabin and was assigned a seat. After the plane took off, the air hostess began to serve him in a five-star way with a smile on her face all the time. He was served the first-class meal with the best champagne and wine. The passenger next to him was also a Frenchman who didn't speak very much. Mr Jolivet couldn't understand what was happening and why he was being treated so well. When the plane landed, he found out that his neighbor was an inspector of Air France, secretly watching the quality of service of the air hostesses in first class. Then Mr. Jolivet understood and smiled within.

3.4 SHYAM SHRESTHA REBORN

The Crash Of Thai Airbus 300

On the thirty-first of July, nineteen ninety-two, the Thai Airways flight TG 311 entered Kathmandu Valley and crashed on the slopes of Ghopte Bhir Mountain in Nuwakot. Most of the deceased passengers were Nepali nationals, along with some foreigners. Among the list of passenger names was 'Shyam Shrestha'. One newspaper later confirmed that it was Shyam Shrestha of Air France. This situation created havoc among my near and dear ones.

The following morning, a high-level government secretary, Mr. Bishnu Pratap Shah, suddenly appeared at my door at six a.m. I went downstairs to open the door. He looked at me with a stunned expression and then said, "Okay, Okay, it's enough."

Then he quickly turned away. I ran after him to call him back to my house for a cup of tea, but he repeated, "It's okay, it's okay," and didn't return. It seemed that he was assured that I was alive. That morning's scene flashes at me even today, along with a sense of gratitude.

Nearly On The Way To Heaven From An Allergy

Sometime during 1986, I visited a restaurant for dinner with a friend from Paris. She was, in fact, a British friend of Kathy who was living there. She ordered mussels, which is seafood. I don't generally eat seafood. Therefore, I ordered something else.

But when her dish was served, I was tempted to try one, and so I did. Unfortunately, I felt my ear start to turn red and hot. My body began to swell up along with skin rashes, and I suddenly felt like I was going to throw up, so I hurriedly ran towards the toilet. There, I vomited heavily, and I also got diarrhea.

I immediately felt feverish and was becoming incapable of physical movements. After that, I returned to my seat and described the incident to my friend. After paying the bill, I went directly back to my hotel, Le Méridien. By the time I reached there, my body was completely itchy and red, with rashes appearing all over.

At that time, Hotel Le Méridien was under the direct ownership of Air France. After my condition became unbearable, I reported my situation to the reception at 1 am. The doctor arrived immediately, and after the checkup, gave me an injection, after which my condition started to improve slowly. I spent the whole next day in my room.

Second Allergy In Paris

In the year 1992, I was staying in my own apartment at 22 Rue Emeriau in Paris fifteen. One day, I returned home after having lunch with my friend Corneille and Simone Jest. After lunch, I found out that the meat sauce contained mussels. That night, the allergy returned, and my face along with my whole body developed red rashes, and the condition became unbearable.

I called the doctor at midnight. He gave me an injection, and to my surprise, within a minute, I fell from the sofa like a molten candle. The doctor immediately checked my blood pressure. It had lowered down to 60/40. The doctor himself panicked upon seeing this and immediately called for an ambulance.

Around 1:00 am, three to four health workers arrived at my fifteen-story high apartment with a stretcher. I paid for the doctor's fee in limited consciousness, and he went his way. The ambulance took me to the hospital, blowing a siren all the way. It felt strange to be inside one of them, as I was already unconscious before reaching the hospital.

Fortunately, the doctor at the emergency had left a written note that I should not be prescribed a certain type of anti-allergen as it immediately reacted to my body. Therefore, I was treated with some other medicine at this hospital. I only woke up at 5 am.

The staff told me to kindly leave the hospital since I didn't have any insurance papers, otherwise, I would have to pay 5,500 francs a day exclusive of all other medical expenses. I told them I had credit cards with enough backing, and I could pay whatever it cost. They didn't agree because it was compulsory to have the insurance papers. Finally, they called a taxi for me, and I went home with it. They also wrote on a piece of paper the name of the hospital, which specialized in allergy cases.

I spent the whole next day in that hospital called Hospitals Bichat. The discovery at the end of the day was that I was allergic, not to the mussels, but to 'Metabisulphite' declared by Dr. Sicard. He said, "Be careful, next time it can be life-threatening!"

During my recovery in Paris, Kathy arrived from Cairo on her way back to Kathmandu after attending a teacher's conference. She took care of me for two days and then went back to Kathmandu. I had to remain several extra days to recuperate.

Almost Bye Bye In The Swimming Pool At Meridian Hotel In Singapore

During the month of January 1989, when Robert and Cecile were still very young, we visited Singapore for a vacation. Enjoying the five-star hospitality and facilities, we were happily spending our holidays. Robert and Cecile were always interested in going to the swimming pool. They spent most of their happy times there. One day, I escorted them to the pool and returned to the room to get some rest.

While lying down, my eyes fell upon a bottle of whiskey, and I poured two shots to enjoy. After an hour, I went to the swimming pool to see what the children were up to. Seeing them happily jumping and playing in the water, I had the desire to join in myself and unknowingly jumped into the deeper side. I knew very little about swimming. I could float and swim around. But as I jumped into the water, I unknowingly jumped into the deep end of the pool and then couldn't manage to swim up to the surface.

I was stuck under the water and tried to move my hands and feet, but to no avail. Even though I tried hard to come up to the surface, I couldn't manage it. I had already gobbled up a few ounces of water. In the meantime, I could also see the horror in my children's eyes who were watching me from outside the pool and screaming, "Dad! Dad! Are you alright?" It must have given me a boost; I pushed both my hands down towards the bottom of the pool and tried to resurface. This time I was a little successful.

I repeated the process again and finally, my head was out of the water. Now the problem was that I still had to reach the edge of the pool which itself required energy. I had very little of it left in my body. The children had been shouting continuously, "Dad! Are you all right?" I felt my heart pounding but still replied, "yes, yes," and slowly swam to the edge of the pool and hung there. Robert reached into the pool and helped me get out.

That day, I learned a lesson that one should never go swimming under the influence of alcohol. Sure enough, I learned that it is a universally understood fact!

While all long-haired passengers had to shorten their hair at Singapore Airport.

In 1975, I visited Singapore for the first time. During those days, the popular fashion for young men was bell-bottom pants and long hair. The plane I landed in Singapore carried many Westerners, Thais, as well as Singaporeans. Most passengers from Thailand and Singapore easily passed through the immigration counters, but when I reached the immigration officers, they made me stand in the same line as the Americans and Europeans.

Later, the immigration officer told passengers with long hair that they must get a haircut before immigration or else they should return to where they came from. There was a huge outcry, with some exclaiming: "What is this bloody rule?" The immigration officer also warned the passengers that they must not make any noise.

In the end, everybody got their hair chopped very short. I had to do the same thing even though my hair wasn't that long.

Kathy Leaves Kathmandu (Leaving a warning) Au revoir the beautiful MIRAVAL

In early 2017, Kathy told me during a casual family talk that she had lived in Nepal for forty-one years and had worked at the American School for forty years before retirement. She explained that our son and daughter both live in the US, as well as her brother, sister, and other family members. "I have decided to go and live in the U.S. You can visit us once or twice a year," she added.

I was shocked to hear this. It took a little while to understand, but then I found that it made sense. I said, "Alright, in any case I visit France three to four times a year. Flying from there to the US is not an issue. That's why I think your plan is alright."

After that, she said, "We can sell the house and split the money. You already have a house in town." The idea of selling Miraval saddened me deeply. My second thought was this: I planned to sell my house in Italitaar and then add sufficient money to pay Kathy off.

When I disclosed my plans to her, she suddenly exploded, "If you do that, I will come in a helicopter with a Khukuri (a large knife, similar to the machete), along with Robert and Cecile, and shoot you from above!" Her intense reaction made me reconsider my initial thoughts.

Eventually, in 2017, she moved to the US as planned. Since then, I have been visiting the family on a regular basis. After having lived for nearly thirty-five years in that beautiful house, we sold it in 2018. This made me realize that nothing lasts forever.

I DECIDED TO ADMIT

It wouldn't be fair to my life story if these events were left out.

Before finishing the last page of my book, I reflected deeply on some painful memories from my past. The idea of omitting them made me uncomfortable because they are an important part of who I am and who I have been.

1. Chandragiri Cable Car

From 2010 to 2013, I worked hard on a project to build a cable car system to the top of Chandragiri Hills for tourism development and pilgrimage. The technology and installations were sourced from the French company POMA, for whom I was a consultant in Nepal. The developers were IME Group, led by a business tycoon. After years of intense negotiations, we reached an exclusive agreement for the project, based on trust and ethics. But to my utter disbelief, I soon realized that such agreements mean little to dishonest people. Nine days before we were to sign the final agreement in France, the developer secretly signed the deal with a competitor without giving us a clue. This became a valuable life lesson I will never forget.

2. A thunderbolt

In the late 1990, a thunderbolt struck me out of nowhere. I lost my balance and became infatuated with a young woman in Paris. That infatuation quickly turned into a love so deep that I lost sight of everything else. For six years, I experienced a whirlwind of extreme joy, pain, and confusion. These memories will likely stay with me for the rest of my life.

3. A cheating unimagined

There's a saying: "Don't share your plans with others, or they might take advantage." I didn't know that at the time. After I built and began running my hotel in Dhulikhel, one fine day, I invited one of my brothers (out of my mind), a very ungrateful businessman, to visit the hotel. After touring the entire property, which spans nearly four acres, we arrived at the large terrace on the 4th floor, with a panoramic view of the Himalayas to the north. Across from the hotel, down the hill, there was a large piece of land, about five acres in size. I mentioned to him that I was in the process of negotiating to purchase it at a particular price.

Soon after, I traveled to France for a week or two. When I returned, I discovered that he had bought the land for himself. Now, he reaps the rewards with no shame.

MY DEDUCTIONS

I remember now, back in those days, I was a youngster who lacked wisdom and long-term vision. I just kept on traveling around without any assessment of the situation and its limited possibilities. To fulfill my desire of visiting France, I hadn't done any proper thinking and assessment. It was only because one of my friends who was heading for the US on an immigrant visa, while strolling one evening on New Road in Kathmandu, had said to me, "Shyam, what can you do here in Nepal? Come to the U.S." Without properly analyzing the situation, as well as asking my friends and family about my plans, I decided to follow my friend's suggestion and travel to the US.

Based upon the decision from my own thoughts, I was delving into a whirlpool of uncertainties. This is why I had to come face to face with various obstacles. Looking on the positive side, the experience of various types of achievement because of my own decisions was very important as well.

The kind of entertainment and self-satisfaction that land-based travel provides cannot be achieved through flight. Traveling by land, you get to step into many countries one at a time, see many cities, experience various lifestyles and customs, and meet all kinds of people during the journey. These things make traveling by land highly memorable.

I returned to Nepal after spending more than seven months in France and other parts of Europe. I had planned to write a memoir about the land route travel, but I couldn't manage to write more than a half page. It feels unbelievable to myself that I have been able to do this fifty years later. This has given me immense pleasure.

My View on Discipline

Coming up to this stage in my life, from my school days and beyond, I believe that discipline and self-education are always the most important factors in a person's life, whether it be in school, with friends and family, politics, organizations, or even the government.

Among the various developed, developing, and underdeveloped countries that I have visited, I feel that the experiences I have learned have been applied. Developed countries normally have a very good reputation in terms of discipline. Moderately developed countries will have a moderate level of discipline, and the least developed countries are often the least disciplined. You can observe these differences when you visit the city, the market area, and the society of a particular country.

From what I've seen, if the parents are well-disciplined, then the children also tend to follow the pattern of their parents to a great extent.

When the Prime Minister of a country remains fully disciplined, his cabinet of ministers, as well as other subordinates, are bound to follow the same path. If a minister is fully determined to maintain his discipline, then the secretary, as well as the deputy secretaries, will have to work accordingly. When the secretaries and deputy secretaries are diligent and disciplined, the staff under them have no other choice but to work within the boundaries of discipline. This can have a direct impact on the overall operation of the government. If this trend continues for a whole year, then it will have a very positive impact on the country's development and progress.

Irrespective of the field, the government, guardians, teachers, and political leaders must learn and practice discipline themselves. They must also help their near and dear ones practice discipline. Considering this as an utmost priority is in high demand today. I also have yet to fully practice discipline.

Patience

In this topic, I consider myself a student. It's not that anybody needs a lesson on the importance of patience these days, but still, the human species cannot easily and swiftly apply patience in their everyday life. My high blood pressure for the last three decades could also be a reason; time and again because of my impatience and hurriedness, I become panicked. This has impacted my professional life as well as my personal development.

When we make hasty decisions based on anger, this may lead to regret for the remainder of one's life. I learned this lesson later in life and became a victim of impatience many times myself. The lessons of patience should flow in everyone's veins.

The people in our society and country have grown up following ancient rites and rituals, as well as the history of our civilization. Due to my long experience and companionship with people, I think most of us are still very immature on these topics. Why is this so? Is it because of illiteracy, lack of wisdom, or is it purely selfishness?

Coming up to this moment, we have made a lot of progress, but I still feel it is not enough yet. For me, civilization means a minimum level of decency, harmony, love, and goodwill that one person can give to another. We are always ready to jump the queue anywhere, be it at a bank, a post office, or a ticket counter. We can find breaches of basic human norms in many places and areas. Therefore, the government, families, as well as schools should give equal coverage toward decency, harmony, love, and goodwill. In my opinion, these six skills should be taught and developed in all sectors so that we can contribute to the development of society and the entire nation.

On Positive Thinking

The slogan "positive thinking," which has been fast spreading around the world, has to be carried meaningfully in life. As a result of this, we can make a positive impact on ourselves, as well as on the development of society. It won't be an exaggeration if I claim to have taken fifty years in preparation for this book. I have mentioned this once or twice in the background as well. More importantly, I couldn't manage enough time in the past because of a very hectic schedule and workload in my life.

I had promised myself and some of my friends to write a book about my life between 1970 and 2020 as a recollection of a fifty-year-long career within Nepal and my land route travel to France. In a rush to fulfill that promise, there are obviously some linguistic errors. Along with this, these are incidents that happened half a century ago and there may be a few friends from Paris and Marseille that I have forgotten. There may be some incidents also that may not have the exact depiction here as they originally happened. Considering the constraint of time and other factors, I will work on correcting those errors in future editions. For this time though, I ask for your apology.

Shyam Mohan Shrestha

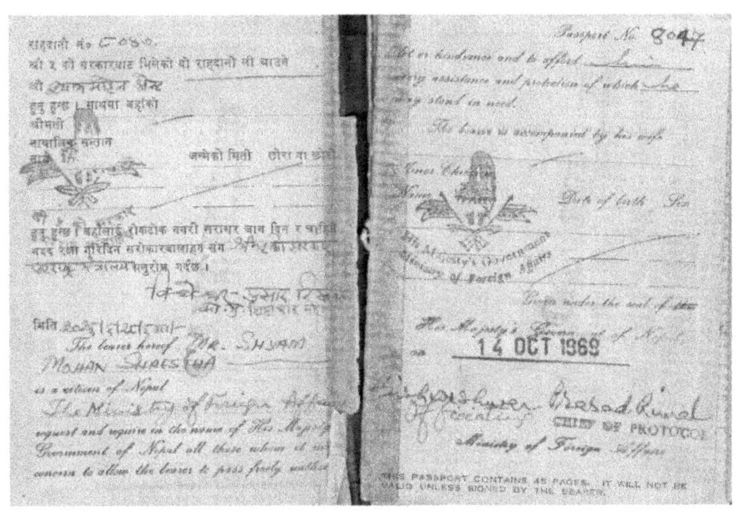

My first passport for overland travel was issued on 14 October,1969

Father Chandra &
Mother Sakuntala Shrestha

Mother at 100

Starting job as croupier
in Casino 1968

Marseille
France,
April 1970

Casino Fashion in 1969

With Jean Michel, Liliane &
baby Leanore April 1970

Arc de Triomphe Paris,
June 1970

With Le Petit Cluny café Paris
Brigitte and Daniel, June 1970

Sophie, Zurich,
September 1970

Venice, Italy, September 1970

Afghanistan custom from Iran, October 1970

Istanbul, Turkey, October 1970

Mt. Ararat, Turkey, October 1970

Courting with Kathy before
marriage early 1976

Marriage day March 8, 1976
at Surya Binayak, Bhakatapur

After Marriage 1977

With Family son Robert, Daughter Cecile and Wife Kathy
at Miraval 1998

Kathy's father Horton Amsden and mother Margaret Amsden

With sister in law, Sally Amsden

Kathy, Sally (far right) and family members

With granddaughter, Siena, and family in New York City 2018

Karchungma Lama
Diki's Mother

Kalsang Lama Diki's Father,
head prist of Sermathan

Toljang
(Life Partner)2009

Diki's sisters Tashi, Sarkini, Nima and Fathers Mother

With Diki in London, July 1983

Shyam in Athens, Jan 1970

Shyam 50 years later in Athens 2020

With Diki and Angela, Athens, Jan 2020

Miraval Under Construction, Budhanilkantha 1981

Budhanilkantha 2021

Chapali, Way to
Budhanilkantha 1981

Chapali, Way to
Budhanilkantha, 2023

From Mirval view of Budhanilkantha 1982

From Mirval view of Budhanilkantha 2017

Miraval Budhanilkantha 2017

Welcoming French President
Fr. Mitterand, 1983

With Mr. Rieffel, My God Father in
Miraval, October 1974

Childhood
friend
Neer Shanker
Shrestha

Welcoming AF Supersonic Concorde crew in October 1967

Boarding Concorde 2 October, 1987

Michael Hoffman, 1971

First USA trip Washington D.C., 1973

Assuming presidency of Nepal France chamber of commrace and industry from H.E Daniel Dupont, in 1996

Reception of NFCCI at Shyam's residence Miraval 29 Dec 1996

Great friend Pierre Ract from POMA

Former Minister of France Mr. Maurice Herzog addressing NFCCI reception at Miraval

Tara and Al mattocks Kathmandu

Family with mother in Italitar house

With H.E.Ambassador Claude and Madam Liliane Ambrosini, 2003

My friends of six decades Jean Mischel,
Late lillian Binoist

My Great Friends of 54 years Christine
& Anette

Late Yvon Comoli Vice President of CCIP
& Late DB Pandey Director of RNAC

My funniest French businessman
friend Roland Etrois, daughter
Catherine and son Jean, 1998,
Reviera, France.

My great friends
Mark & Francoise
Benedetti
from France

Inauguration of Mirabel Resort by Late Prime Minister Girija P. Koirala
19 September 1998

Aerial View of Mirabel resort, Designed by the Author

Welcoming Late Prime Minister Krishna P. Bhattarai and Dr. Narayan Khadka
Congress Party leader first on the right in 2000.

Welcoming Prime Minister Puspa Kamal Dahal
(Prachanda), 2007

Former Prime Minister Sher Bahadur Deuba, 2003

Prime Miniser
Lokendra Bahadur Chand 2002

Welcoming Late Prabhakar Rana
and his family im Paris 1993,

Welcoming former Prim Minister
Mr. Madav Kumar Nepal, 2008

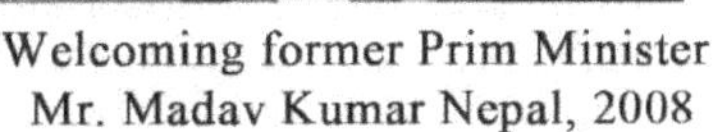

Bhagat Lal Gorkhali , Ram Lama
Washington DV, 1973

Welcoming Actress Mnisha and
mother Susila Koirala in Paris,1993

Receiving French high-level Medal "Chevalier dans l'Ordre National de la Légion d'Honneur" 2019.

AMBASSADE
DE FRANCE
AU NÉPAL

Liberté
Égalité
Fraternité

L'Ambassadeur

Kathmandu, 7 February 2020

Dear colleagues & friends,

Dear Shyam Mohan Shrestha,

Bonsoir and Namaskar

My name is François-Xavier Léger and I am the French Ambassador to Nepal.

Today, we will celebrate the conferring upon Mr. Shrestha of one of the highest decorations of France, Knight of the National Order of the Legion of Honour, which was created in 1802 by Napoleon 1st.

Let me tell you a few interesting things about Shyam: Shyam's first visit to France was in 1970 and it has now matured to 50 years of history and his close association with France has been a remarkable milestone. He must have traveled to France possibly more than 400 times and has continued to put in efforts for the enhancement of bilateral relations both in the social sector and in the bilateral trade sector.

In 1983, Shyam was among those who welcomed French President François Mitterrand at the airport when he paid an official visit to Nepal.

It is with great pleasure to say that Shyam has been a great friend of France and of the French people who will always play a role of a strong bridge of friendship and co-operation between Nepal and France.

Now, in order to confer upon Shyam Shrestha, the Légion d'Honneur, let's move on to the formal part of the ceremony, which I have to do in French:

Shyam Mohan Shrestha, au nom du Président de la République et en vertu des pouvoirs qui me sont conférés, je vous fais Chevalier dans l'Ordre National de la Légion d'Honneur.

I thank you for your attention and wish you all a very pleasant evening.

Good evening and namaskar,

François-Xavier Léger

Toasting My Medal, Chevalier dans l'Ordre National de la Légion d'Honneur."

REVIEWS

"A story of life led by courage and enthusiasm

-Ratna Prajapati, Sahitya Post(Literature Post)

It is a model of honesty that any writer can write about the light and dark as well as positive and negative aspects of her/his life without hiding or masking it. This book is free from the influence and pressure of self-praise. The new generation can get enough inspiration from this travelog and autobiography of Shyam Mohan Shrestha.

Devendra Pratap Shah

Banker and writer

This book is mesmerizing going through the first pages and irresistible to go through to the end. The book, presented in a very simple and lucid way, contains innumerable events. The book reflects the ebb and flow of Shyam's life. He had and still has a distinct lifestyle which is very alluring to people from all over the world. While reading his book, one can sense the immense effort he has put on writing his vivid life stories.

A life led by courage and courage

-Nir Shah

Renowned Nepali Actor and writer

I have also seen bad writing by the authors but got the opportunity to read the good writing by the draftsman. From Shyamji's book, I came to know that a struggling, courageous and fearless personality was also deeply established within that personality. That's why I find this book extremely interesting, and I have no hesitation in saying that everyone who believes in karma should read it once.

For a good and readable book, my first priority is human sensitivity. In this book, human sensibility is scattered everywhere in a very subtle manner.

Kedar Bhakta Mathema

Former V.C. Tribhuvan University and former Nepalese Ambassador to Japan

The book, "Kathmandu Paris Kathmandu "is the story of Shyam ji's life, candidly told, his life of humble beginning ,struggle and constantly pushing ahead and never giving in –in short, a life of success. Steeped in honesty, this book should be an inspirational read for young ones who are struggling to find a place of their own in their societies. I find the book enthralling, particularly because it is a tale of our own generation.

Mohan Krishna Shrestha

An author, and former Ambassador of Nepal to France

I read the manuscript of his book so carefully in which the author has narrated his life of seven decades. In a nutshell, this book of Shyam Mohan Shrestha can be taken as a life story of a man who is courageous, struggling, active and undaunting despite failures. This book is full of inspiration. I read the book not only once, I read it twice thoroughly. His honest writing has made the book free from any narcissism and worth reading. I wish great success for the book.

Kashiraj Pandey, PhD

Associate Professor of English (Kathmandu University, Nepal)

Kathmandu-Paris-Kathmandu, a delightful travelog has so well captured the hilarious life of a young Nepali boy and his dreams come to a reality.

Like Paulo Coelho's *The Alchemist*, Kathmandu-Paris-Kathmandu weaves around the fairy tales of the roots and wings of a young boy. The book is an easy read for both young and elderly people; they can feel a kind of close association with the events and characters they meet along the reading. The book has much more insights to offer to the young entrepreneurs, adventure lovers, enthusiastic explorers, and those who have interest in people and culture.

Dileep K Adhikary PhD.

Economist, and a writer

'An Overland Adventure: Kathmandu to Paris in 1970'

Shyam Mohan Shrestha has put in writing his adventurous life so eloquently one would not only enjoy reading it, but would also get thrilled by his daringness to face the course of events being humble and decisive at the same time. His adventurism is worthy of a film script for a thriller movie on the one hand and is exemplary for leading a life determined and focused in the challenging trails of one's own living on the other. His eventful life provides an illustrative learning that one should not deter in making an objective move that makes this book worth reading.

Sushil Ram Mathema

Columnist, Former Executive Director, Central Bank, Nepal.

The book is just like an attractive novel, the more you read the more you feel like a clean stream of water flowing in its course! He is so bold and frank enough to play back all the events in words ignoring the reaction of conservative society of our materialistic world. Another astonishing attribute of Shyam is how he could recall each minor incident that he went through 50 years ago!

BN Joshi,

Author,

An Eye opening Travelog

The book is an adventurous romantic travelog of the Hippie era.

Shyam Mohan Shrestha's book 'Kathmandu-Paris-Kathmandu 1970' tells the reader the story of the 1970s society and the young people of that time. It is an exciting journey of a Nepalese boy's adventure in the hippie era.

Some notable extracts:

"An older German he met in the Afghan Embassy in Delhi tricked him into buying a ticket to Afghanistan and offered him $10 in exchange for sleeping in the same bed in a hotel in Kabul. Awed by his proposal, he refused to bow down and he stayed awake all night at the hotel."

"Shyam Mohan's relationship with a mother and daughter he met in Istanbul took a dramatic turn. The mother proposed to the author, traveler Shyam, to marry her daughter Emil and take her with him on the trip. The topic of the Turkish mother and daughter not wanting to let him separate at the end is emotional."

There are so many events and anecdotes alike in the book! There are hundreds of photographs, which bring to life the surroundings of the time.

Gyanendra Bahadur Karki

MP (Former Minister)

After sitting down to read the adventure story of a Nepalese boy full of courage and courage, written by Shyam Mohan Shrestha, it is impossible not to finish the book.

This book is a good example of how a young person should resolve to realize his dreams. Writer Shyam Mohanji has given a positive illustration that determination towards action makes a person stick to the goal.

Jagadish Chandra Pokherel

Former Lt. Gen. Nepal Army.

This book is a true story of a young Nepali boy, who comes from a lower middle class Newar family in Kathmandu, Mr. Shyam Mohan Shrestha where he explains the situation and events of 1970's. The author is lucid in his writing and has been successful in explaining the events which took place 50 years ago but the readers will feel that as if it happened not more than a week ago.

Starting with a keen interest in French language and culture, later, he became "The Knight of the Legion of Honor" (Chevalier dans l'ordre *de la Légion d'honneur)*. On the whole, the book is a fairy tale like the true story of "The Alchemist" by Paulo Coelho.

"Shyam Sir, I really enjoyed reading your book. It's an amazing book of yours and many of us can learn various lessons from your experience.

Hearty congratulations to you for such an excellent gift to the generations to come."

Prakash Shrestha

Hotelier and Banker

Great story with a masterful narrative of exciting adventures! Shyam has penned this gripping book from his heart. His ability to observe the situation and put it in simple words is amazing. He has been sincere and honest all through the pages. He proves to be a master in painting the landscape, romance and expressing the human relationships in this book. A book definitely worth reading!

Karna Shakya

Hotel Industrialist, Environmentalist, and author of the 7 best seller books,

"Shyam, I found your book a timeless reading."

I read your book in two days' time; very interesting, full of humor.

While I was reading your picture and actions, it brought a flashback in my head. I truly enjoyed your book. Congratulations, my friend.

Dr. Swoyambhu Man Amatya

Former Secretary Government of Nepal,

I went through the book without rest. I could not help myself reading the book line by line. I found it very interesting and very encouraging as well. Actually, I was carried away with the book especially on the first journey (Kathmandu-Paris) you had. And the struggle you had to get a job. I have enjoyed reading your unique personal life experience. It is very touchy

Dr. Josie Baral

Professor

I had read the book thoroughly without missing one page. It was really well written, your life yatra was unique, challenging and a breathtaking mission. We never know where a blessing can come from.